※ VOLUME 1 ※

HOW DO WE KNOW THE BIBLE IS TRUE?

KEN HAM & BODIE HODGE

GENERAL EDITORS

First printing: July 2011

Master Books®, P.O. Box 726, Green Forest, AR 72638
Master Books® is a division of the New Leaf Publishing Group, Inc.

ISBN: 978-0-89051-633-1
Library of Congress Number: 2011932373

Cover by John Lucas

Unless otherwise noted, Scripture quotations are from the New King James Version of the Bible.

Please consider requesting that a copy of this volume be purchased by your local library system.

Printed in the United States of America

Please visit our website for other great titles:
www.masterbooks.net

For information regarding author interviews,
please contact the publicity department at (870) 438-5288

Master
Books®
A Division of New Leaf Publishing Group
www.masterbooks.net

Acknowledgments and special thanks for reviewing chapters in this book:

Tim Chaffey (executive editing), Roger Patterson, Bodie Hodge, Dr. Terry Mortenson, Dr. Bob McCabe, Steve Fazekas, Dr. Jason Lisle, Ken Ham, Mark Looy, Dr. Alan White, Dr. Steve Falling, Dr. Steve Carter, Dr. Tommy Mitchell, and Steve Ham

Acknowledgments and special thanks for editing chapters in this book:

Jeremy Ham, Karin Viet, Doug Rumminger, Tim Chaffey, Becky Stelzer, Mike Matthews, Anneliese Rumminger, and Bodie Hodge

Illustration and photo credits:

Dan Lietha, Chuck McKnight, Laura Strobl, Bodie Hodge, and Tim Chaffey

Contents

Introduction

What Does Biblical Authority Have to Do with Today's Church and Culture?

Ken Ham

❧❧❧❧❧❧❧❧❧❧❧❧❧❧❧❧❧❧❧

Change the Culture?

What is your real motivation at AiG? Are you political activists? Are you trying to get creation taught in the public school classroom? Does your ministry aim to change the culture? Isn't the Church irrelevant in today's world?

These are just a few of the many questions I have been asked by the secular media over the years, particularly during the media blitz surrounding the opening of the Creation Museum in 2007. In these interviews, I made it clear that the thrust of Answers in Genesis (AiG) is to uphold the authority of God's Word as we not only provide answers to the questions of skeptics but also preach the gospel of Jesus Christ and see people won to the Lord.

At AiG, we understand that the Christian culture we once had in America (and the once-Christianized culture of the West in general) has become increasingly secularized over the past few years. AiG helps the Church understand that this societal change occurred from the foundation up — that is, instead of the culture generally being founded on the teachings in God's Word, generations were eventually taught to exalt autonomous human reason instead and build their worldview on that foundation.

And what has been the basic and most successful mechanism for this secularization of the culture? Over the decades, millions upon millions of Americans, one person at a time, have been indoctrinated to believe in the idea of evolutionary naturalism and millions (billions!) of years and thus to doubt and ultimately disbelieve the Bible as true history.

As generations began to reject God's Word as reliable and authoritative, they began to consistently build a secular worldview based on moral relativism. As this change occurred, many such secular humanists moved into positions in education, the government, legal systems, etc. The worldview they had adopted determined how they would vote in passing laws, establishing curricula, making moral choices, and so on. The Western culture changed from a predominantly Christian worldview to an increasingly secular worldview. To understand how important a person's worldview truly is, consider what the Bible teaches about how a person's actions are governed by their thoughts.

> For as he thinks in his heart, so is he (Proverbs 23:7).
> For out of the abundance of the heart the mouth speaks (Matthew 12:34).

As people repent, are converted to Christ, and are then taught to build their thinking consistently on God's Word (and as Christians are challenged to de-secularize their own thinking and build a proper worldview), then they can make an impact on the culture. After all, God's people are told to be "salt" and "light" (Matthew 5:13–14) — and thus affect the world for good. Jesus said, "Let your light so shine before men, that they may see your good works and glorify your Father in heaven" (Matthew 5:16). That's why I often explain to the secular media that the ministry of AiG and the Creation Museum is to preach the gospel and hope to see people converted to Christ and thus be "salt" and "light" in their daily living. As these people find themselves on school boards, are elected to local government, or obtain influential positions in the media, their worldview will govern the way they vote and effect changes.

The AiG ministry is providing answers to the skeptical questions of our day that cause people to doubt the Bible's historicity and truthfulness.

And in this era of history, the most attacked part of the Bible's history is Genesis 1–11. When people understand they can trust the history in the early chapters of Genesis, they can better understand and be more responsive to the gospel — the gospel that is based on that history. Of course, countering the skeptics brings up other apologetics questions that need to be answered.

AiG's aim is not to change the culture. Changing the culture is a byproduct of a much bigger and more eternally significant goal. As one life at a time is changed, each of those Christians can have an impact on the culture for the glory of Christ.

So this is what AiG and the Creation Museum are "about" — and what we believe every Christian should be doing: presenting and defending the life-changing gospel message to see lives changed for the glory of God and to see the Church return to the rock-solid foundation on which it was built (Matthew 16:18; Ephesians 2:20).

Is the Church a Relic?

The Grand Canyon is a form of relic. What do I mean? Well, the present processes operating at the Grand Canyon in northern Arizona, such as the minimal erosion by the Colorado River, cannot explain how the canyon was really carved. In addition, no processes operating today at the canyon can explain the laying down of the massive sedimentary strata that I have seen there (e.g., Coconino Sandstone), nor the massive sheet erosion that resulted in the Kaibab Plateau.

In order to produce this "relic" of a deep canyon and layers we see today, something very different than what is happening in the present occurred in the past. It was the result of the aftereffects of the global Flood of Noah's time.

To me, this is analogous to something happening with the Christian Church in our Western world. For example, I have traveled to the United Kingdom many times over the past 25 years. Several years ago, I began taking photos of British churches that have been turned into bars, nightclubs, Sikh temples, theaters, shopping centers — the list is a long one.

The U.K. was once predominantly Christian. Today, most of the U.K. has become extremely pagan; just a remnant of Christianity remains in England and the other U.K. nations. Even though there are some new churches (thank God!), "relic" churches exist all across the U.K. The Christian influence is largely gone.

You see, just like the Grand Canyon, something was different in the past. The current state of England and the rest of the U.K. does not explain why there were so many churches in the past and why they had considerable Christian influence on society.

I want to suggest to you that where the U.K. is today, America will be "tomorrow" — and for the same reasons if we continue on this trend. The Church could very well become a "relic" in America if God's people don't deal with the foundational nature of the problem that has produced the sad situation in the U.K. today. Imagine how this must grieve the heart of God!

Here is one thing that particularly alarms me: research by George Barna has shown that of those students from Christian homes in America who go to public schools (about 95 percent of all students), at least 70 percent of them will walk away from the Church and the faith of their parents once they leave home.[1]

A fairly recent report states: "A new study by The Barna Group conducted among 16- to 29-year-olds shows that a new generation is more skeptical of and resistant to Christianity than were people of the same age just a decade ago."[2]

These statistics were confirmed in *Already Gone*, the book I co-authored with Britt Beemer from America's Research Group. In fact, our research revealed that many of these young people who walk away from the Church once they leave home have actually "checked out" long before leaving home. These young people have serious doubts about biblical authority, particularly in the first 11 chapters of Genesis.

AiG has been continually bringing to the Church's attention a major challenge of the day: our culture is filled with increasing numbers of people who do not believe the Bible is a credible book. As a result, the culture has lost faith in biblical authority.

1. Barna Research Online, "Teenagers Embrace Religion but Are Not Excited About Christianity," January 10, 2000: www.barna.org/...teensnext.../147-most-twentysomethings-put-christianity-on-the-shelf-following-spiritually-active-teen-years.
2. Barna Research Online, "A New Generation Expresses Its Skepticism and Frustration with Christianity," September 24, 2007: http://www.barna.org/barna-update/article/16-teensnext-gen/94-a-new-generation-expresses-its-skepticism-and-frustration-with-christianity.

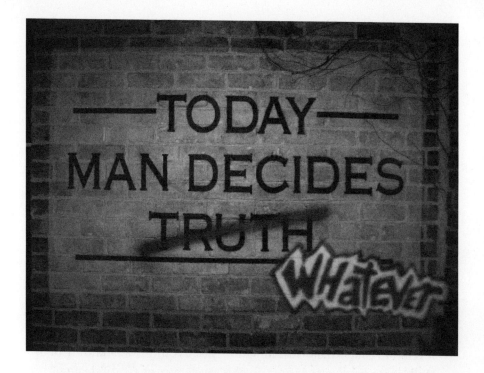

And why has this happened? It did not occur overnight. Generation after generation, there has been a slow erosion of biblical authority in America. In fact, ever since the early 19th century the idea of a millions- or billions-of-years-old age for the earth/universe was beginning to become popular in the U.K. and the United States. Much of the Church quickly adopted the old-age view. And they reinterpreted the days of creation and Noah's Flood in Genesis.

Soon, much of the Church also adopted many of Darwin's blatant evolutionary beliefs (and just added God to this). Generation after generation, the Church has reinterpreted God's Word in Genesis in response to secular ideas. Each subsequent generation has become more firm in the belief that if the first part of the Bible (which is the foundational history for all Christian doctrine, including the gospel) is not true, how can the rest be? Biblical authority is undermined, the Bible's credibility is destroyed, and the Christian influence in the culture is eroded.

AiG has been raised up by God for this era of history to help challenge the Church concerning biblical authority, which could (as God blesses) ultimately change the culture. Remember: "If the foundations are destroyed, what can the righteous do?" (Psalm 11:3).

Calling for Reformation

Here is an example of how the foundation has shifted for one particular group. In 1977, the Assemblies of God denomination adopted a "Doctrine of Creation" report, which stated the following:

> This Bible record of creation thus rules out the evolutionary philosophy which states that all forms of life have come into being by gradual, progressive evolution carried on by resident forces. It also rules out any evolutionary origin for the human race, since no theory of evolution, including theistic evolution, can explain the origin of the male before the female, nor can it explain how a man could evolve into a woman. . . .
>
> The account of creation is intended to be taken as factual and historical. Our understanding of God as Creator is rooted in a revelation that is historical in nature, just as our understanding of God as Redeemer is rooted in the revelation of God's dealings with Israel in history and in the historical events of the life, death, and resurrection of His Son.[3]

But fast forward to 2010 and see what has changed. A new "Doctrine of Creation" was adopted by the "General Presbytery," the governing body of the Assembly of God churches. Here is the denomination's official view today:

> The advance of scientific research, particularly in the last few centuries, has raised many questions about the interpretation of the Genesis accounts of creation. In attempting to reconcile the Bible and the theories and conclusions of contemporary scientists, it should be remembered that the creation accounts do not give precise details as to how God went about His creative activity. Nor do these accounts provide us with complete chronologies that enable us to date with precision the time of the various stages of creation. Similarly, the findings of science are constantly

---

3 "The Doctrine of Creation," copyrighted by the General Council of the Assemblies of God; adopted by the Assemblies of God General Presbytery, August 15–17, 1977.

expanding; the accepted theories of one generation are often revised in the next.

As a result, equally devout Christian believers have formed very different opinions about the age of the earth, the age of humankind, and the ways in which God went about the creative processes. Given the limited information available in Scripture, it does not seem wise to be overly dogmatic about any particular creation theory. . . . We urge all sincere and conscientious believers to adhere to what the Bible plainly teaches and to avoid divisiveness over debatable theories of creation.[4]

My heart was heavy as I read the statement "the findings of science are constantly expanding; the accepted theories of one generation are often revised in the next." Well, at least the Bible hasn't changed in the past 33 years. But man's ideas certainly have!

The message here from this denomination is essentially this: because of "the theories and conclusions of contemporary scientists" regarding origins, Christians must change their interpretation of the Bible in Genesis! This low view of Scripture and esteeming man's ideas is a major problem within many denominations. In fact, the tragedy of reinterpreting God's clear words to fit in man's beliefs has always existed with God's people. The same problem is recorded in Genesis when the serpent tempted Eve by asking, "Did God really say . . . ?" (Genesis 3:1; NIV).

Creating doubt regarding God's Word has greatly undermined biblical authority in society as a whole, even its churches.

We live in an era of great scientific advancement. But remember: *science* means "knowledge." There is a big difference between knowledge gained by observation that builds our technology in the present ("operational science") and knowledge concerning the past ("historical science"), which cannot be observed directly. "Historical science" is being used as the authority over God's Word.

The Assembly of God denomination is insisting that fallible man's historical science (beliefs about the past concerning origins) must be used to reinterpret God's clear and infallible Word. (By the way, I thank God

4 "The Doctrine of Creation," copyrighted by the General Council of the Assemblies of God; adopted by the Assemblies of God General Presbytery, August 9–11, 2010.

for the many pastors in these churches who stand on the Word of God and cringe at their denomination's new position.)

AiG's mission statement declares that we are to be "a catalyst to bring reformation by reclaiming the foundations of our faith which are found in the Bible, from the very first verse."

What can the righteous do as the foundations of Christianity are being destroyed? We need a new reformation in our churches. Christians need to be figuratively nailing Genesis chapters 1–11 on the doors of churches and Christian colleges/seminaries, challenging God's people to return to the authority of the Bible.

We will continue to see a decline in our nation, churches, and families — unless God's people repent of compromise and return to His Word! We need to understand that the Bible is true and it is the authority when it comes to creation apologetics as well as general apologetics. This book is designed to show you how to answer many of the skeptical questions of our day while firmly standing upon the Word of God. It is time for a new reformation, a time to return to the 66 books of the Bible as the absolute standard in all areas.

Chapter 1

How Do We Know the Bible Is True?

Jason Lisle

❀❀❀❀❀❀❀❀❀❀❀❀❀❀❀❀❀❀

The Bible is an extraordinary work of literature, and it makes some astonishing claims. It records the details of the creation of the universe, the origin of life, the moral law of God, the history of man's rebellion against God, and the historical details of God's work of redemption for all who trust in His Son. Moreover, the Bible claims to be God's revelation to mankind. If true, this has implications for all aspects of life: how we should live, why we exist, what happens when we die, and what our meaning and purpose is. But how do we know if the claims of the Bible are *true*?

Some Typical Answers

A number of Christians have tried to answer this question. Unfortunately, not all of those answers have been as cogent as we might hope. Some answers make very little sense at all. Others have some merit but fall short of proving the truth of the Bible with certainty. Let's consider some of the arguments that have been put forth by Christians.

A Subjective Standard

Some Christians have argued for the truth of the Scriptures by pointing to the changes in their own lives that belief in the God who inspired the Bible has induced. Receiving Jesus as Lord is a life-changing experience that brings great joy. A believer is a "new creation" (2 Corinthians 5:17). However, this change does not in and of itself prove the Bible is true. People might experience positive feelings and changes by believing in a position that happens to be false.

At best, a changed life shows consistency with the Scriptures. We would expect a difference in attitudes and actions given that the Bible is true. Although giving a testimony is certainly acceptable, a changed life does not (by itself) demonstrate the truth of the Scriptures. Even an atheist might argue that his belief in atheism produces feelings of inner peace or satisfaction. This does not mean that his position is *true*.

By Faith

When asked how they know that the Bible is true, some Christians have answered, "We know the Bible is true *by faith.*" While that answer may sound pious, it is not very logical, nor is it a correct application of Scripture. Faith is the confident belief in something that you cannot perceive with your senses (Hebrews 11:1). So when I believe without observation that the earth's core is molten, I am acting on a type of faith. Likewise, when I believe in God whom I cannot directly see, I am acting on faith. Don't misunderstand. We should indeed have faith in God and His Word. But the "by faith" response does not actually answer the objection that has been posed — namely, *how we know* that the Bible is true.

Since faith is a belief in something unseen, the above response is not a good argument. "We know by faith" is the equivalent of saying, "We know by believing." But clearly, the act of believing in something doesn't necessarily make it true. A person doesn't really know something just by believing it. He simply believes it. So the response is essentially, "We believe because we believe." While it is true that we believe, this answer is totally irrelevant to the question being asked. It is a non-answer. Such a response is not acceptable for a person who is a follower of Christ. The Bible teaches that we are to be ready to give an *answer* to anyone who asks a reason of the hope that is within us (1 Peter 3:15). Saying that we have faith is not the same as giving a *reason* for that faith.

Begging the Question

Some have cited 2 Timothy 3:16 as proof that the Bible is the inerrant Word of God. This text indicates that all Scripture is inspired by God (or "God-breathed") and useful for teaching. That is, every writing in the Bible is a revelation from God that can be trusted as factually true. Clearly, if the Bible is given by revelation of the God of truth, then it can be trusted at every point as an accurate depiction. The problem with answering the question this way is that it presupposes that the verse itself is truthful — which is the very claim at issue.

In other words, how do we know that 2 Timothy 3:16 is true? "Well it's in the Bible," some might say. But how do we know the Bible is true? "Because 2 Timothy 3:16 assures us that it is." This is a vicious circular argument. It must first arbitrarily assume the very thing it is trying to prove. Circular reasoning of this type (while technically valid) is not useful in a debate because it does not prove anything beyond what it merely assumes. After all, this type of argument would be equally valid for any other book that claims to be inspired by God. How do we know that book X is inspired by God? "Because it says it is." But how do we know that what it's saying is true? "Well, God wouldn't lie!"

On the other hand, some Christians might go too far the other way — thinking that what the Bible says about itself is utterly irrelevant to the question of its truthfulness or its inspiration from God. This, too, is a mistake. After all, how would we know that a book is inspired by God unless it claimed to be? Think about it: how do you know who wrote a particular book? The book itself usually states who the author is. Most people are willing to accept what a book says about itself unless they have good evidence to the contrary.

So it is quite relevant that the Bible itself claims to be inspired by God. It does claim that all of its assertions are true and useful for teaching. Such statements do prove *at least* that the writers of the Bible considered it to be not merely their own opinion, but in fact the inerrant Word of God. However, arguing that the Bible must be true *solely* on the basis that it says so is not a powerful argument. Yes, it is a relevant claim. But we need some additional information if we are to escape a vicious circle.

Textual Consistency and Uniqueness

Another argument for the truthfulness of the Bible concerns its uniqueness and internal consistency. The Bible is remarkably self-consistent, despite having been written by more than 40 different writers over a time span of about 2,000 years. God's moral law, man's rebellion against God's law, and God's plan of salvation are the continuing themes throughout the pages of Scripture. This internal consistency is what we would expect if the Bible really is what it claims to be — God's revelation.

Moreover, the Bible is uniquely authentic among ancient literary works in terms of the number of ancient manuscripts found and the smallness of the time scale between when the work was first written and the oldest extant manuscript (thereby minimizing any possibility of alteration from the original).[1] This indicates that the Bible has been accurately transmitted throughout the ages, far more so than other ancient documents. Few people would doubt that Plato really wrote the works ascribed to him, and yet the Bible is *far* more authenticated. Such textual criticism shows at least that the Bible (1) is unique in ancient literature and (2) has been accurately transmitted throughout the ages. What we have today is a good representation of the original. No one could consistently argue that the Bible's authenticity is in doubt unless he is willing to doubt all other works of antiquity (because they are far less substantiated).[2]

To be sure, this is what we would expect, given the premise that the Bible is true. And yet, uniqueness and authenticity to the original do not necessarily prove that the source is *true*. They simply mean that the Bible is unique and has been accurately transmitted. This is consistent with the claim that the Bible is the Word of God, but it does not decisively prove the claim.

External Evidence

Some Christians have argued for the truth of Scripture on the basis of various lines of external evidence. For example, archaeological discoveries have confirmed many events of the Bible. The excavation of Jericho reveals that the walls of this city did indeed fall as described in the Book

---

1. See chapters 5 and 12 of Brian Edwards, *Nothing but the Truth* (Darlington, UK: Evangelical Press, 2006).
2. Josh McDowell and Bill Wilson, *A Ready Defense* (Nashville, TN: Thomas Nelson Publishers, 1993), p. 42–55.

of Joshua.[3] Indeed, some passages of the Bible, which critics once claimed were merely myth, have now been confirmed archeologically. For example, the five cities of the plain described in Genesis 14:2 were once thought by secular scholars to be mythical, but ancient documents have been found that list these cities as part of ancient trade routes.[4]

Archaeology certainly confirms Scripture. Yet it does not prove that the Bible is *entirely* true. After all, not every claim in Scripture has been confirmed archeologically. The Garden of Eden has never been found, nor has the Tower of Babel or Noah's ark (as of this writing). So at best, archaeology demonstrates that *some* of the Bible is true.

Such consistency is to be expected. Yet, using archaeology in an attempt to *prove* the Bible seems inappropriate. After all, archaeology is an uncertain science; its findings are inevitably subject to the interpretation and bias of the observer and are sometimes overturned by newer evidence. Archaeology is useful, but fallible. Is it appropriate to use a *fallible* procedure to judge what claims to be the *infallible* Word of God? Using the less certain to judge the more certain seems logically flawed. Yes, archaeology can show consistency with Scripture but is not in a position to *prove* the Bible in any decisive way because archaeology itself is not decisive.

Predictive Prophecy and Divine Insight

A number of passages in the Bible predict future events in great detail — events that were future to the writers but are now in our past. For example, in Daniel 2 a prophecy predicted the next three world empires (up to and including the Roman Empire) and their falls. If the Bible were not inspired by God, how could its mere human writers possibly have known about events in the distant future?[5]

---

3. Bryant Wood, "The Walls of Jericho," *Creation* 21 (2) March–May 1999, p. 36–40, http://www.answersingenesis.org/creation/v21/i2/jericho.asp#.

4. Bryant Wood, "The Discovery of the Sin Cities of Sodom and Gomorrah," *Bible and Spade* (Summer 1999), http://www.biblearchaeology.org/post/2008/04/16/The-Discovery-of-the-Sin-Cities-of-Sodom-and-Gomorrah.aspx.

5. Even this begs the question to some degree. A critic could (hypothetically) argue that some people have the ability to perceive distant future events through some as-yet-undiscovered mechanism (be it psychic powers or whatever). The Christian knows better; he knows that God *alone* declares the end from the beginning (Isaiah 46:9–10). But the Christian knows this because it is what the Bible says. So only by presupposing the truth of the Bible could we cogently argue that *only God* can know the future.

The Bible also touches on matters of science in ways that seem to go beyond what was known to humankind at the time. In Isaiah 40:22 we read about the spreading out (expansion) of the heavens (the universe). Yet secular scientists did not discover such expansion until the 1920s. The spherical nature of the earth and the fact that the earth hangs in space are suggested in Scriptures such as Job 26:10 and Job 26:7 respectively. The Book of Job is thought to have been written around 2000 B.C. — long before the nature of our planet was generally known.

Such evidence is certainly consistent with the claim that the Bible is inspired by God. And some people find such evidence convincing. Yet, persons who tenaciously resist the idea that the Bible is the Word of God have offered their counterarguments to the above examples. They have suggested that the predictive prophetic passages were written after the fact, much later than the text itself would indicate. Examples of apparent scientific insight in the Bible are chalked up to coincidence.

Moreover, there is something inappropriate about using secular science to judge the claims of the Bible. As with archeological claims, what constitutes a scientific fact is often subject to the bias of the interpreter. Some people would claim that particles-to-people evolution is a scientific fact. Although creationists would disagree, we must concede that what some people *think* is good science does not always coincide with the Bible.

The Bible does show agreement with some of what is commonly accepted as scientific fact. But what is considered scientific fact today might not be tomorrow. We are once again in the embarrassing position of attempting to judge what claims to be infallible revelation from God by the questionable standards of men. Again, how can we judge what claims to be *inerrant* revelation by a standard that is itself uncertain and ever-changing? This would be like using something we merely suspect to be about three feet long to check whether a yardstick is accurate. Using the less certain to judge the more certain just doesn't make sense. At best, such things merely show consistency.

The Standard of Standards

The above lines of evidence are certainly consistent with the premise that the Bible is true. Many people have no doubt found such evidence quite convincing. Yet we must admit that none of the above lines of evidence quite proves that the Bible must be the inerrant Word of God. Critics have their counterarguments to all of the above. If we are to know *for certain* that the Bible is true, we will need a different kind of argument — one that is absolutely conclusive and irrefutable. In all the above cases, we took as an unstated premise that there are certain standards by which we judge how likely something is true. **When we stop to consider what these standards are, we will see that the *standards themselves* are proof that the Bible is true.**

Putting it another way, only the Bible can make sense of the standards by which we evaluate whether or not something is true. One such set of standards are the laws of logic. We all know that a true claim cannot contradict another true claim. That would violate a law of logic: the law of non-contradiction. The statements "The light is red" and "The light is not red" cannot both be true at the same time and in the same sense. Laws of logic thus represent a standard by which we can judge certain truth claims. Moreover, all people seem to "know" laws like the law of non-contradiction. We all assume that such laws are the same everywhere and apply at all times without exception. But why is this? How do we *know* such things?

If we consider the biblical worldview, we find that we can make sense of the laws of logic. The Bible tells us that God's mind is the standard for all knowledge (Colossians 2:3). Since God upholds the entire universe and since He is beyond time, we would expect that laws of logic apply everywhere in the universe and at all times. There can never be an exception to a law of logic because God's mind is sovereign over all truth. We can know laws of logic because we are made in God's image and are thus able to think in a way that is consistent with His nature (Genesis 1:27). So when we take the Bible as our worldview, we find that laws of logic make sense.

But if we don't accept the Bible as true, we are left without a foundation for laws of logic. How could we know (apart from God) that laws of logic work *everywhere*? After all, none of us has universal knowledge. We have not experienced the future nor have we traveled to distant regions of the universe. Yet we assume that laws of logic will work in the future as they have in the past and that they work in the distant cosmos as they work here. But how could we possibly know that apart from revelation from God?

Arguing that laws of logic have worked in our past experiences is pointless — because that's not the question. The question is: how can we know that they will work in the future or in regions of space that we have never visited? Only the Christian worldview can make sense of the universal, exception-less, unchanging nature of laws of logic. Apart from the truth revealed in the Bible, we would have no reason to assume that laws of logic apply everywhere at all times, yet we all do assume this. Only the Christian has a good reason to presume the continued reliability of logic. The non-Christian does not have such a reason in his own professed worldview, and so he is being irrational: believing something without a good reason. The unbeliever has only "blind faith" but the Christian's faith in the Bible makes knowledge possible.

The Foundation of Science

Another standard we use when evaluating certain kinds of claims is the standard of science. The tools of science allow us to describe the predictable, consistent way in which the universe normally behaves. Science allows us to make successful predictions about certain future states. For example, if I mix chemical A with chemical B, I expect to get result C because it has always been that way in the past. This happens the same way every time: if the conditions are the same, I will get the same result. Science is based on an underlying uniformity in nature. But why should there be such uniformity in nature? And how do we know about it?

We all presume that the future will be like the past in terms of the basic operation of nature. This does not mean that Friday will be exactly like Monday — conditions change. But it does mean that things like gravity will work the same on Friday as they have on Monday. With great precision, astronomers are able to calculate years in advance the positions of planets, the timing of eclipses, and so on — only because the universe operates in such a consistent way. We all know that (in basic ways) the universe will behave in the future as it has in the past. Science would be impossible without this critical principle. But what is the foundation for this principle?

The Bible provides that foundation. According to the biblical worldview, God has chosen to uphold the universe in a consistent way for our benefit. He has promised us in places such as Genesis 8:22 that the basic cycles of nature will continue to be in the future as they have been in the past. Although specific circumstances change, the basic laws of nature (such as gravity) will continue to work in the future as they have in the past. Interestingly, only God is in a position to tell us on His own authority that this will be true. According to the Bible, God is beyond time,[6] and so only He knows what the future will be. But we are within time and have not experienced the future. The only way we could know the future will be (in certain ways) like the past is because God has told us in His Word that it will be.

Apart from the Bible, is there any way we could know that the future will be like the past? So far, no one has been able to show how such a belief would make sense apart from Scripture. The only nonbiblical explanations offered have turned out to be faulty. For example, consider the following.

Some people argue that they can know that the future will be like the past on the basis of past experience. That is, in the past when they assumed that the future would be like the past, they were right. They then argue that this past success is a good indicator of future success. However, in doing so they arbitrarily assume the very thing they are supposed to be proving: that the future will be like the past. They commit the logical fallacy of begging the question. Any time we use past experience as an indicator of what will probably happen in the future, we are relying on the belief that the future will be (in basic ways) like the past. So we cannot merely use past experience as our reason for belief that in the future nature will be uniform, unless we *already knew* by some other way that nature is uniform. If nature were not uniform, then past success would be *utterly irrelevant* to the future! Only the biblical worldview can provide an escape from this vicious logical circle. And that is another very good reason to believe the Bible is true.

We Already Know the God of the Bible

Since only the Bible can make sense of the standards of knowledge, it may seem perplexing at first that people who deny the Bible are able to have knowledge. We must admit that non-Christians are able to use laws of logic and the methods of science with great success — despite the fact that such procedures only make sense in light of what the Bible teaches. How are we to explain this inconsistency? How is it that people deny the truth of the Bible and yet simultaneously *rely* upon the truth of the Bible?

The Bible itself gives us the resolution to this paradox. In Romans 1:18–21 the Scriptures teach that God has revealed Himself to everyone.

6. E.g., 2 Peter 3:8; Isaiah 46:9–10.

God has "hardwired" knowledge of Himself into every human being, such that we all have inescapable knowledge of God. However, people have rebelled against God — they "suppress the truth in unrighteousness" (Romans 1:18). People go to great lengths to convince themselves and others that they do not know what, in fact, they must know. They are denying the existence of a God who is rightly angry at them for their rebellion against Him.

But since all men are made in God's image, we are able to use the knowledge of logic and uniformity that He has placed within us,[7] even if we inconsistently deny the God that makes such knowledge possible. So the fact that even unbelievers are able to use logic and science is a proof that the Bible really is true. When we understand the Bible, we find that what it teaches can make sense of those things necessary for science and reasoning. God has designed us so that when believers read His Word, we recognize it as the voice of our Creator (John 10:27). The truth of the Bible is inescapably certain, for if the Bible were not true, we couldn't know anything at all. It turns out that the worldview delineated by the Bible is the only worldview that can make sense of all those things necessary for knowledge.

Conclusion

The truth of the Bible is obvious to anyone willing to fairly investigate it. The Bible is uniquely self-consistent and extraordinarily authentic. It has changed the lives of millions of people who have placed their faith in Christ. It has been confirmed countless times by archaeology and other sciences. It possesses divine insight into the nature of the universe and has made correct predictions about distant future events with perfect accuracy. When Christians read the Bible, they cannot help but recognize the voice of their Creator. The Bible claims to be the Word of God, and it demonstrates this claim by making knowledge possible. It is the standard of standards. The proof of the Bible is that unless its truth is presupposed, we couldn't prove anything at all.[8]

---

7. Babies do not "learn" uniformity in nature. They are born already knowing it. When a baby burns his hand on a candle, he does not quickly do it again because he rightly believes that if he does it again it will hurt again. The baby already knows that the future reflects the past.

8. This fact has been recognized and elaborated upon by Christian scholars such as Dr. Cornelius Van Til and Dr. Greg Bahnsen.

Chapter 2

Is the Old Testament Reliable?

Brian Edwards

❀❀❀❀❀❀❀❀❀❀❀❀❀❀❀❀❀❀❀

Why Read the Bible?

Some years ago, I informed my congregation that over the next few months something would happen in our church that the world would find strange. In the first place, I proposed to preach on a book that was more than 3,000 years old, and second, I knew the whole congregation would be there each week to listen. And they were there — for the 30 weeks as we worked our way through the Old Testament Book of Deuteronomy.

Across the world every week, millions of Christians listen to thousands of sermons from the Bible, a book that begins at the dawn of history itself. Why do they listen? The answer is that Christians believe the Bible to be both reliable and relevant to the need of 21st-century people to learn about their God and how they should live to please Him.

But must they have blind, unreasonable faith to believe the Bible to be true? Or are there sound reasons that the Bible, and specifically for this chapter, the Old Testament, can be accepted as reliable in every part?

What the Bible Writers Believed

The Old Testament writers believed their message was God-breathed and, therefore, utterly reliable. More than 400 times from Exodus 4:22 to Malachi 1:4, they declared, in just three Hebrew words, "Thus says the LORD."

To emphasize this divine authority many of the prophets received God's message through a powerful experience. For example, the prophet Jeremiah recorded that at the beginning of his ministry, "The LORD put forth His hand and touched my mouth, and the LORD said to me: 'Behold, I have put My words in your mouth' " (Jeremiah 1:9).

The prophets so identified themselves as God's spokesmen that they frequently spoke as though God Himself were speaking. In Isaiah 5:1–2 the prophet spoke of God in the third person — *He* — but in verses 3–6 Isaiah spoke for God in the first person — *I*. Isaiah had become the actual spokesperson for God. No wonder King David spoke of the word of the Lord as "perfect" (2 Samuel 22:31; see also Proverbs 30:5. The NIV translates this word as "flawless").

The New Testament writers did not doubt that the Old Testament prophets spoke for God. Peter and John saw the words of David in Psalm 2, not as the opinion of a king in Israel, but as the Word of God: "You spoke by the Holy Spirit through the mouth of your servant, our father David" (Acts 4:25; NIV). Similarly, Paul accepted Isaiah's words as God speaking to men: "The Holy Spirit spoke rightly through Isaiah the prophet to our fathers" (Acts 28:25).

The New Testament writers were so convinced all the words of the Old Testament Scripture were inspired by God that they even claimed, "Scripture says," when the words quoted came directly from God. For example, "The Scripture says to the Pharaoh" (Romans 9:17).

Clearly, the Lord Jesus Himself believed the words of the Old Testament were God-breathed. In John 10:34 (quoting from Psalm 82:6), He based His teaching upon a single phrase: "I said, 'You are gods.' " In Matthew 22:43–44 He quoted from Psalm 110:1 and emphasized a single word, "Lord," to reveal Himself as the Son of God.

Where Are All the Gods?

The entire history of Israel covered by the Old Testament took place under the shadow of at least four major empires across the Fertile

Crescent: Egypt, Assyria, Babylonia, and Persia. Their influence is seen throughout the Old Testament record, and the religious life of each of these powers was dominated by a vast pantheon of gods and goddesses. The Egyptian collection included at least 1,500 gods, a number nearly matched by the Assyrians, Babylonians, and Persians. They had gods for the land and sea, hills and valleys, planets and seasons, birth and death, and everything in between. The pantheon of the Greeks and Romans who carried us into the New Testament was equally numerous. Their collection included the same gods with different names as centuries and empires rolled by.

In staggeringly marked contrast to this polytheism, the Israelites, from their earliest history, were taught to believe in one God and one alone. Moses fixed this truth in the mind of the nation: "Hear, O Israel: The LORD our God, the LORD is one" (Deuteronomy 6:4). Other ancient peoples of the world were polytheistic, so where did this "strange" idea come from? And why did the prophets of Israel hold to monotheism so

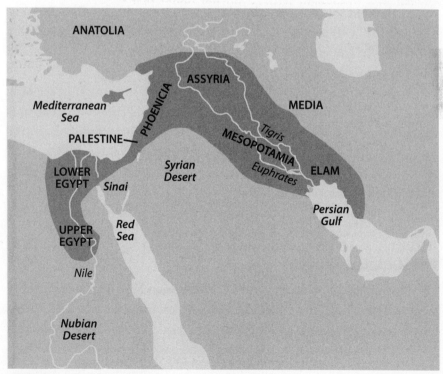

The Fertile Crescent and the main empires

firmly? The often-quoted idea that Israel garnered its religious ideas from the surrounding nations is completely toppled by the fact that Israel stood alone as a people who believed there was only one God, the God of the whole universe. Jonah's God of "heaven, sea, and land" (Jonah 1:9) was a radical idea to the sailors on the Phoenician ship as well as to the citizens of Nineveh.

Tell It Like It Is

Another unique feature of the Old Testament is its ruthless honesty in the records of Israel. In the ancient world, bad things were not recorded. If a king lost a battle, either government spin would turn it into a victory or else the defeat would simply be left unstated in the records. The 50-year struggle between the Egyptians and the Hittites, in which both sides were frequently bested in the fight, is vividly recorded in the temple of Ramesses II at Abu Simbel as a great victory for the pharaoh. Similarly, when recording the ancient dynasties of Egypt, this king deliberately omitted the dynasty of Amenhotep IV, who was considered the "heretic king" for elevating the god Aten above all others in the pantheon.[1] The Romans followed suit with purposeful omissions from the record, and they had a phrase for it: *damnatio memoria* (the damnation of memory). To record it was to perpetuate it; to ignore it meant that it never happened.

Contrast this with the authenticity of the Old Testament. If Israel lost a battle, it was recorded. When Israel's hero King David committed a terrible double crime of adultery and murder, that was also recorded. Even the godly King Hezekiah, in whose reign a spiritual revival took place, is on record as failing in his latter days and committing an act of foolish pride that brought disaster on the nation in years to come (2 Kings 20:12–18).

Why did the Israelites buck the majority vote of the nations and refuse to censor their history?

Tell It Like It Will Be

The fulfillment of biblical prophecy has always been a great embarrassment to the critics of the Bible, and their only escape route is to believe that the prophecies were written long after the event predicted. One significant problem with this conjecture is that no one has been able to explain how

---

1. See The Egyptian King List in the British Museum, London (EA117), www.britishmuseum.org.

the "prophetic con men" managed to pull off their "deception" so consistently, convincingly, and completely over so many centuries!

One writer on this subject has concluded that "the number of prophecies in the Bible is so large and their distribution so evenly spread through both Testaments and all types of literary forms that the interpreter is alerted to the fact that he or she is dealing with a major component of the Bible."[2] With that amount available, we can only toe the water here.[3]

The prophets of God challenged the false prophets of the nations to tell something prophetic: " 'Present your case,' says the LORD. 'Bring forth your strong reasons,' says the King of Jacob. 'Let them bring forth and show us what will happen; let them show the former things, what they were, that we may consider them, and know the latter end of them; or declare to us things to come' " (Isaiah 41:21–22).

The punishment for a prophet who gave false predictions was death. Conversely, the prophet Ezekiel, when prophesying of the coming destruction of Jerusalem, could claim with confidence, "When this comes to pass — surely it will come — then they will know that a prophet has been among them" (Ezekiel 33:33). For an Israelite it was unimaginable that a prophet would write up his "prophecy" after the event! A prophet would be stoned for such deceit.

The Prophecy of Nahum

The small Book of Nahum in the Bible contains a clear prophecy of the final destruction of Nineveh, the capital of the powerful Assyrian empire. If the prophet had written his prophecy after the event, it is hardly likely that the Jews would have been so gullible as to have accepted the retrospective prophecy of a prophet they knew to be still among them.

The argument most favored by scholars who will not accept Bible prophecy is that the author, under the pseudonym of Nahum, wrote many years beyond the lifetime of any who could have witnessed the fall of Nineveh. The problem with this argument is that Nahum records the precise way in which this impregnable city would eventually fall: primarily through fire and water (see Nahum 1:10, 2:4, 6–8, 3:8, 13, 15). Archaeologists have discovered how accurate his descriptions are, and some of the

---

2. Walter Kaiser, *Back Toward the Future* (Eugene, OR: Wipf & Stock Publishers, 2003), p. 20.

3. For more detail on this subject, see Brian Edwards, *Nothing but the Truth* (Darlington, England: Evangelical Press, 2006), p. 76–96.

fire-burnt palace reliefs can be seen in the British Museum in London.[4] The city was so utterly destroyed in 612 B.C. that two centuries after its destruction, the Greek historian Xenophon sat on top of the ruins and had no idea what city it had been. It would be another 2,246 years before the site was positively identified!

Attempts to deny Nahum's accurate prophecy of the destruction of Nineveh in 612 B.C. are more difficult to accept than believing real prophecy took place.

The Prophecies About Christ

The clearest and most challenging evidence of the reliability of the Old Testament is its consistent promise of the coming of the Messiah. Not even the most liberal critic of the Bible will doubt that Micah 5, Zechariah 9, Psalm 22, and Isaiah 53, to take four examples among many, were written centuries before Christ was born. Yet the details of His birth, triumphal entry, crucifixion, and burial are too close to doubt the connection. The suggestions that either Jesus deliberately arranged to fulfill the prophecies (including His place of birth and the soldiers casting lots for His clothes) or that the accounts were written two or three centuries after the events have themselves long been consigned to the stuff of myth.[5]

The Voice of Silent Stones

Archaeology is rubbish, but sometimes it turns up gold. Archaeology searches through yesterday's trash to discover how people lived, worked, fought, and died, as well as what they believed. The mantra that "archaeology disproves the Bible" is simple to refute if only people would check out the evidence. Archaeology is a big subject, so we can focus only on a

---

4. British Museum, London, England, Accession no. WA 124785, for example.
5. See, for example, *Redating the New Testament* by John A.T. Robinson (London: S C M Press, 1976), where Robinson (a liberal critic) concludes the entire New Testament was completed before 70 A.D.

few illustrations. But remember that the purpose of archaeology, as James Hoffmeier comments, is not to prove the Bible but to improve it.[6] By this he means that archaeology can throw new light on old accounts and help us understand the Bible better.

Many details of the Bible, once rejected as fanciful at best or in error at worst, are now accepted by biblical scholars. Here are three of many.

David Who?

Critics once claimed King David did not ever exist since they could find no record of him outside the Bible. The common idea was that sometime after the Persians came to power in the sixth century B.C., he and Solomon were invented by Jewish scribes in order to boost the morale of the Jews in exile.

In July 1993 at Tel Dan in northern Israel, a broken basalt inscription was found, which is dated by archaeologists to the eighth century B.C. The inscription claims that the king of Damascus (Ben-Hadad of Syria) killed the king of Israel (that would be Jehoahaz) and the king of the "house of David" (that would be Joash of Judah). The account is found in 2 Kings 13:1–25. This means that the dynasty of King David was known 250 years before the scribes supposedly invented him in the sixth century B.C.![7] Few now deny the existence of David as a figure of history.

The King Who Never Existed

For a long time the only reference to an Assyrian king by the name of Sargon was found in Isaiah 20:1. It was therefore assumed that no such king existed and that the writer had made up the name. In 1843 Paul-Emil Botta, the French vice-consul and archaeologist in Mosul (northern Iraq), uncovered the great city of Khorsabad, and Sharru-kin (Sargon) is now one of the best known Assyrian kings in the ancient world.

Be Patient, Herr Hitzig

In 1850 German scholar Ferdinand Hitzig wrote a commentary on the Book of Daniel and boldly declared that Belshazzar was "a figment of

---

6. James K. Hoffmeier, *The Archaeology of the Bible* (Oxford: Lion Hudson, 2008), preface.

7. George Athas, *The Tel Dan Inscription* (London: T & T Clark, 2003). See also K.A. Kitchen, *On the Reliability of the Old Testament* (Grand Rapids, MI: Eerdmans Publishing Company, 2003), p. 92.

the writer's imagination."[8] Hitzig's reasoning was that the only references in known history to a king called Belshazzar were found in the Book of Daniel.

Four years later, the British Consul in Basra, J.E. Taylor, discovered four identical time capsules from building works of King Nabonidus of Babylon in which he offered a prayer for himself and "Belshazzar my firstborn son, the offspring of my heart." Today, no one doubts the existence of Belshazzar.

Some archaeological discoveries may *appear* to clash with the biblical record. Yet conclusive archaeology consistently confirms the Bible. For example, evidence of the conquest of Canaan in the time of Joshua is slowly coming to light.[9] Also, the absence of evidence of the Hebrews in the land of Goshen has been answered by the Egyptologist Kenneth Kitchen, who asks what evidence we would expect to find from a people who, 3,500 years ago, lived in mud brick houses in an area frequently flooded. In fact, virtually all Egypt's administrative records of the Delta area have been lost.[10]

On the other hand, a comparison of the names of foreign kings known from inscriptions and those in the Bible is "impeccably accurate."[11] In brief, it is simply false to claim that "archaeology disproves the Bible" when every year something new is turned up out of the ground that authenticates the biblical record. While there are still some unresolved issues, nothing in archaeology contradicts the Bible.

The Big Picture

Oxford lecturer Richard Dawkins dismissed the Bible as "a chaotically cobbled-together anthology of disjointed documents."[12] Any well-taught Bible student will know that far from being "chaotically cobbled-together," one of the hallmarks of the Bible as a trustworthy book is its progressive unfolding of one great theme from beginning to end.

---

8. Ferdinand Hitzig, *Das Buch Daniel* (Leipzig: Weidman, 1850).

9. Hoffmeier, *The Archaeology of the Bible*. p. 76.

10. Professor Kitchen comments, "Those who squawk intermittently 'No trace of the Hebrews has ever been found' (so, of course, no exodus) are wasting their breath." Kitchen, *On the Reliability of the Old Testament*, p. 246.

11. Ibid., p. 62

12. Richard Dawkins, *The God Delusion* (London: Transworld Publishers, Bantam Press, 2006), p. 237.

We know the second part of the Bible focuses on Jesus Christ, but it is not always appreciated that the first part of the Bible is also consistently about Christ. While the Old Testament explores many subjects, the grand theme is Christ. Jesus called attention to the numerous Old Testament passages that spoke of Him (Luke 24:27, 44).

The first reference to Christ is made to Adam and Eve in the Garden of Eden. Shortly after they fell, God promised that the day would come when the offspring of a woman would crush Satan (Genesis 3:15). The whole of the Old Testament nudges history closer to the fulfillment of that promise. We have no space here to explore this in detail,[13] but the record of Noah and the Flood, the life of Abraham and the patriarchs, the accounts of Joseph and Israel in Egypt, the Exodus, Sinai and the moral and ceremonial law under Moses, the monarchy from Saul to Zedekiah, and all the prophets in between, nudge the big picture forward until the climax: "when the fullness of the time had come, God sent forth His Son" (Galatians 4:4). Every book, even the small ones like Ruth and Esther, plays its part in the big picture.

This perfect harmony of the 39 books in the Old Testament is as unique as it is remarkable and stands as one of the great witnesses to the divine authorship, not only of the books, but of the record they relate.

What the Wise Men Say

Many able archaeologists and Old Testament scholars, both past and present, have accepted the historical accuracy of the Old Testament record.

Robert Dick Wilson was professor of Semitic philology at Princeton Theological Seminary during the 1920s. His knowledge of languages (he learned 26 languages, both ancient and modern) was phenomenal and his understanding of the biblical text equally so. He concluded, "No man knows enough to assail the truthfulness of the Old Testament. . . . I try to give my students such an intelligent faith in the Old Testament Scriptures that they will never doubt them as long as they live."[14]

---

13. For more detail on this theme see Edwards, *Nothing but the Truth*, chapter 3, "The Master Plan."

14. Robert Dick Wilson, *Is the Higher Criticism Scholarly?* (Philadelphia, PA: The Sunday School Times Company,1922). See also Robert Dick Wilson, *A Scientific Investigation of the Old Testament* (Philadelphia, PA: Sunday School Times, 1926; reprinted by Solid Ground Christian Books, Vestavia Hills, AL), p. 8.

Kenneth Kitchen, professor emeritus of Egyptology and Honorary Research Fellow at the School of Archaeology, Classics, and Oriental Studies, University of Liverpool, England, has made the point that in the ancient world, "people did not write 'historical novels' with authentic research . . . in Near Eastern antiquity, as we do today."[15]

James Hoffmeier, Professor of Old Testament and Ancient Near Eastern History and Archaeology at Trinity Evangelical Divinity School, while borrowing a phrase from his mentor Alfred Hoerth that archaeology "improves" rather than "proves" the Bible, nevertheless rigorously defends the historical accuracy of the Old Testament.[16]

Donald J. Wiseman, who, until his death in 2009, was professor emeritus of Assyriology at the University of London, has claimed that archaeology, "correctly understood, always confirms the accuracy of the Bible."[17]

Alan Millard, Rankin professor emeritus of Hebrew and ancient Semitic languages at the University of Liverpool, wisely reminds us that archaeology can never prove or disprove the important message of the Bible, but it does "provide a good basis for a positive approach to the biblical records" and thus "enable its distinctive religious message to stand out more boldly."[18]

While archaeology can never "prove the Bible true" in that the Bible's most important message is about God's promise of the Savior Jesus Christ, the accuracy of its historical data confirms the integrity of its message.

---

15. Kitchen, *On the Reliability of the Old Testament*, p. 188.
16. Hoffmeier, *The Archaeology of the Bible.* Preface and throughout this excellent volume.
17. In private conversation with the author, and this faithfully represents his view.
18. Alan Millard, *Treasures from Bible Times* (Belleville, MI: Lion, 1985), p. 14.

Chapter 3

Is the New Testament Reliable?

Brian Edwards

(❀❀❀❀❀❀❀❀❀❀❀❀❀❀❀❀❀❀❀)

In the 17th century William Googe, preaching at Blackfriars in London, spent 32 years and 1,000 sermons on the New Testament Book of Hebrews. That may appear excessive, but he did this because he and his congregation believed the New Testament to be both reliable and relevant to their day. It still is. Every week, millions of Christians in tens of thousands of congregations listen to sermons based upon the life, death, and Resurrection of Jesus Christ and the work and teaching of His followers. Can we trust the New Testament as a reliable record of what actually happened, and do we possess what was actually written in the first century?

What the Writers Believed

Two important verses in the New Testament are 2 Timothy 3:16 and 2 Peter 1:21. The first tells us where the Scriptures came from — they came from God — and the second informs us how they came to us — through men moved by God. In their immediate context, of course, these verses refer to the Old Testament, but this inspiration is also what these men claimed for themselves and for each other. Let's quickly examine some of the evidence.

Paul wrote to the Corinthian Christians "not in words which man's wisdom teaches but which the Holy Spirit teaches" (1 Corinthians 2:13), and similarly, Peter encouraged the young churches to recall "the words which were spoken before by the holy prophets, and of the commandment of us, the apostles of the Lord and Savior" (2 Peter 3:2). The translators handled well an unusual form of Greek in these passages; the emphasis is not that the Apostles merely passed on the commands that Christ had given during His earthly ministry but that they now spoke the words of Christ Himself.

In his first letter, Peter was even more direct. He claimed that the Old Testament prophets spoke of the coming of Christ by the power of "the Spirit of Christ who was in them," and then he turned his attention to the apostles "who have preached the gospel to you by the Holy Spirit sent from heaven" (1 Peter 1:11–12). What the Holy Spirit was to the prophets, so He was to the Apostles; the authority of the prophets is equal to the authority of the Apostles.

Paul challenged the Thessalonians, "You know what commandments we gave you through the Lord Jesus" (1 Thessalonians 4:2). Earlier in the same letter, Paul had reminded his readers how they first responded to his message: "When you received the word of God which you heard from us, you welcomed it not as the word of men, but as it is in truth, the word of God" (2:13).

Because Paul was convinced that his teaching carried the authority of God, he claimed that his preaching was the standard of the truth and that other preachers could be tested and measured by it (Galatians 1:6–12). Paul's gospel was not "according to man," but was received "through the revelation of Jesus Christ" (Galatians 1:11–12; see also Ephesians 3:3). For this reason, obedience to Paul's teaching became the measure of a spiritual life: "If anyone thinks himself to be a prophet or spiritual, let him acknowledge that the things which I write to you are the commandments of the Lord" (1 Corinthians 14:37).

What's the Problem?

A few phrases used by Paul present a problem to some. In 1 Corinthians 7:10 he claimed, "Now to the married I command, yet not I but the Lord." Paul meant nothing more than that on the particular subject with which he was dealing, Christ had already left instructions — see for example Matthew 19:1–9. On the other hand, when Paul declared in 1 Corinthians 7:12, "But to the rest I, not the Lord, say," he meant that on this part of the subject Christ had nothing directly to say. We can understand verse 25 in the same way. The phrase, "I think I also have the Spirit of God," found in verse 40, is not a statement of doubt. Paul is either making a mocking jibe at those in Corinth who claimed to be full of spiritual gifts and wisdom (1 Corinthians 14:37), or else he is making a positive statement in the same way that we might affirm the truth of a statement with the positive claim, "I think I know what I am talking about."

How Their Letters Were Received

Paul did not expect his letters to be read once and then destroyed. The letter addressed to the Colossian church was to be read and passed on to the church at Laodicea; similarly, the letter he had written to Laodicea (long ago lost) was to be read at Colossae (Colossians 4:16). The Apostle was so insistent that his letter to the Thessalonian church should be read by everyone that he placed them under an obligation to the Lord Himself to make sure that "all the holy brethren" had it read to them (1 Thessalonians 5:27). There is no doubt that after the death of the Apostles, the early Church leaders accepted the Apostles' letters, and no others, as equal in authority to the Old Testament.[1]

Peter gave Paul's letters the same authority as the Old Testament Scriptures (2 Peter 3:16), just as Paul gave the words of Christ recorded in the Gospels equal authority with the Old Testament. For example, in 1 Timothy 5:18, Paul introduced both Deuteronomy 25:4 and Luke 10:7 by saying, "the Scripture says." Therefore, when we use the "all Scripture" in 2 Timothy 3:16 to refer to both Old and New Testaments, we are following the example of the Apostles.

The Authority Christ Gave to His Disciples

The words of Matthew 16:18–19 (and Matthew 18:18) have often been the cause of debate and argument, but the passage is straightforward. The promise, "I will give you the keys of the kingdom of heaven, and whatever you bind on earth will be bound in heaven, and whatever

---

1. Brian H. Edwards, *Why 27?* (Darlington, England: Evangelical Press, 2007), p. 89–106.

you loose on earth will be loosed in heaven," must be understood in the Jewish context. When scribes were admitted to their office, they received a symbolic key of knowledge (see Luke 11:52). The duty of the scribes was to interpret and apply the law of God to particular cases. When the scribes bound a man, they placed him under the obligation of the Law, and when they loosed him they released him from the obligation.

Similarly, the Lord had been training His disciples to be stewards of His teachings. In this promise in Matthew 16:19, He referred to their future writing and preaching as scribes of the New Testament and promised divine help to His disciples in those tasks. In John 14:26 He gave His disciples two promises: a divinely aided understanding and a divinely aided memory. "But the Helper [Counselor], the Holy Spirit, whom the Father will send in My name, He will teach you all things, and bring to your remembrance all things that I said to you." John 16:13 adds to this a divinely aided knowledge: "He will tell you things to come."

In order that the disciples might recall accurately all that Christ had said and done, instruct the Christian church in the way of truth, and write of things still in the future, Christ promised the help of the Holy Spirit. The Apostles would be writing with no less authority than the Old Testament prophets. This is confirmed in Revelation 22:6: "The angel said to me, 'These words are trustworthy and true. The Lord, the God of the spirits of the prophets, sent his angel to show his servants the things that must soon take place' " (NIV).

The Authority of Christ Himself

Nowhere did Christ more plainly express His belief in the authority of Scripture than in Matthew 5:18: "For assuredly, I say to you, till heaven and earth pass away, one jot or one tittle will by no means pass from the law till all is fulfilled." Later in His ministry, Jesus applied the same authority to His own words: "Heaven and earth will pass away, but My words will by no means pass away" (Matthew 24:35).

Written or Oral?

It is often assumed that the records in the Gospels circulated only as oral traditions for some 40 years. One critic's claim is typical: "It is incontrovertible that in the earliest period there was only an oral record of the

narrative and sayings of Jesus."[2] Thus, it was concluded that the Gospels are not history as we know it. But consider the following.

Get That Down

Although the Jewish rabbis and Greek and Roman philosophers preferred oral teaching, we know that students of both kept notes of the instruction they received. Notice the "writing tablet" in Luke 1:63. It was also common for civil servants and others (like Matthew, Zacchaeus, and the man in Luke 16:6) to use a "notebook" for their work. This was an early form of book made of parchment sheets fastened together with a primitive spiral bind. The Greek language borrowed the Latin name for it, which is *membranae*. This is exactly the word translated "the books" in 2 Timothy 4:13. Paul used a notebook.[3]

The Gospels record 21 Aramaic words used by Jesus, and we may therefore assume that Jesus generally taught in Aramaic. Professor Alan Millard comments, "The simplest explanation for the presence of these

2. W.G. Kümmel, trans. *Introduction to the New Testament* (London: SCM Press, 1975), p. 55.
3. Alan Millard, *Reading and Writing in the Time of Jesus* (Sheffield: Sheffield Academic Press, 2000), p. 63.

terms in the Greek text is accurate reporting."[4] In Galilee, where Hebrew was little used, Jesus may have taught in Greek. A leading Jewish authority on the rabbis of this time concludes, "We would naturally expect the logia [teaching] of Jesus to be originally copied in codices."[5]

We are not suggesting that all the Gospels were written "on the hoof" as the disciples accompanied Jesus, but it would be natural to expect some listeners to write down His teaching and parables. This would be fully in keeping with what we know of the literacy and note-taking of first-century Palestine. There is no reason the Gospel writers would not have had access to written records.

And Get It Down Now!

The idea that the Gospels and epistles were not written down until two or three centuries after the death of Jesus is yesterday's "scholarship." Ignatius, who was martyred around the year A.D. 115, wrote of the Apostles' letters and the Gospels as the "New Testament."[6] This was typical of all the early Church leaders who acknowledged only the four Gospels for the life and teaching of Jesus. By A.D. 150 the Muratorian Canon listed the books accepted by the "universal church," and it includes the four Gospels and all 13 letters of Paul.[7]

In 1972 a liberal scholar, John A.T. Robinson, published a detailed study of each of the books of the New Testament and concluded that every one must have been completed before the year A.D. 70.[8] In addition he condemned the "sheer scholarly laziness" of those who assume a late date for the New Testament and added, "It is sobering too to discover how little basis there is for many of the dates confidently assigned by modern experts to the New Testament documents."[9]

We may confidently claim that the Gospels and letters of the New Testament were written down by the traditionally accepted authors who lived in the first century.

4. Millard, *Reading and Writing in the Time of Jesus*, p. 142.

5. S. Lieberman in Millard, *Reading and Writing in the Time of Jesus*, p. 211.

6. Ignatius, Epistle to the Philadelphians 5, and Epistle to the Smyrnaeans 7:4.

7. Edwards, *Why 27?* p. 89–90.

8. J.A.T. Robinson, *Redating the New Testament* (London: SCM Press, 1972). Conservative Christians agree that all of the New Testament was completed by the close of the first century A.D.

9. Robinson, *Redating the New Testament*. p. 341.

Authentic Narratives

The Gospel records bear all the hallmarks of authentic eyewitness accounts. Here are three examples.

Philip told Nathanael about Jesus by stating, "We have found Him of whom Moses in the law, and also the prophets, wrote — Jesus of Nazareth, the son of Joseph" (John 1:45). No one writing in the second or third century would have invented that. Nazareth is not even mentioned in the Old Testament, and the Jews never associated it with the coming Messiah. The most natural introduction would have been "Jesus of Bethlehem" — since that town had strong Messianic connections (Micah 5:2). Besides, why say, "the son of Joseph," when well before the second century, only the heretics doubted that Jesus was really the Son of God? The only explanation for these "second century gaffes" is that the New Testament accurately records what Philip actually said.

One day, Jesus visited the home of Lazarus, Mary, and Martha. John reported that "Mary took a pound of very costly oil of spikenard, anointed the feet of Jesus, and wiped His feet with her hair. And the house was filled with the fragrance of the oil" (John 12:3). Why does the author even mention the fragrance of the oil? Surely, there is no great theological truth to be learned from this statement; however, the mention of this detail testifies to the account's authenticity. C.S. Lewis stated, "The art of inventing little irrelevant details to make an imaginary scene more convincing is a purely modern art."[10] He added, "As a literary historian, I am perfectly convinced that whatever else the Gospels are, they are not legends. I have read a great deal of legend and I am quite clear they are not the same sort of thing."[11]

If later writers wanted their readers to believe that Jesus is the Son of God and Lord of life, then His journey to Golgotha appeared to be a disaster. He stumbled and fell and was too weak to carry the crossbeam; and why make up that seemingly despairing cry from the Cross: "My God, My God, why have You forsaken Me?" (Matthew 27:46). So many details of Christ's final week — the entry into Jerusalem, the beating and Crucifixion, and the claim of a resurrection — opened Christians up to ridicule. The Jews were offended, the Greeks mocked, and the

---

10. C.S. Lewis, "What Are We to Make of Jesus Christ?" Essay. 1950.
11. Ibid.

' graffiti of a donkey-headed man on a cross. Why make it

A witness has a right to be believed unless he is proved to be false. And if the quality of his life matches the high morality of his teaching, then we must have strong reasons before we malign the integrity of his account.

The Stones Cry Out

As with the Old Testament, archaeology continually confirms the accuracy of the New Testament historical record.

Augustus Issued a Decree

The account of the Roman census recorded in Luke 2 is well known. What is not so well known is that it was assumed by some that a Roman emperor would never issue an order for a census where "all went to be registered, everyone to his own city." Then, a papyrus decree was discovered in Egypt that was an order for a Roman census in Egypt at the time of Trajan in A.D. 104, which mirrors the order of Augustus recorded in Luke 2. The Prefect Gaius Vibius Maximus ordered all those in his area to return to their own homes for the purpose of a census.[12]

Pilate Who?

Believe it or not, it was at one time suggested that Pilate was not a real figure of history because the only known reference to him came from the New Testament. Then in the late 1950s an inscription was found at Caesarea that dedicated a theater built by Pilate to the honor of Tiberias. Although half the stone tablet is destroyed, the rest is clear: "The Tiberius which Pontius Pilate, the Prefect of Judea dedicated." The stone had been recycled to be used as part of a stairway for the remodelled theater in the third century.[13] But that is not all. The British Museum in London displays a small bronze coin minted by Pontius Pilate while he was governor of Judea; it carries the date of the 17th year of Tiberius, which would be A.D. 30/31 — perhaps in use the very year of the Crucifixion of Jesus.[14]

12. Papyrus 904 in the British Library, London.
13. Yosef Porath, "Vegas on the Med: A Tour of Caesarea's Entertainment District," *Biblical Archaeological Review* (September/October 2004): p. 27.
14. British Museum accession no. CM 1908.01–10–530.

Polytarchs

Dr. Luke and the Polytarchs

At the time of Paul's travels, each city had its own town council, known by different titles from town to town; only a contemporary and careful writer would record them accurately. An example of the accuracy of Luke (the writer of Acts) as a historian was found in 1877 when a block of marble — rescued from becoming builder's rubble at Thessalonica — proved to be an inscription of the civic leaders in the city sometime in the second century. They are referred to as *polytarch*s. This is exactly the word translated as "rulers of the city" in Acts 17:6.[15]

A Final Word from Sir William

Much more about the stones could be added, but let a scholar have the last word. Sir William Ramsay was a bucket-and-spade archaeologist who spent his life digging around in modern-day Turkey, the land of Paul's travels. He was a bright man with three honorary fellowships from Oxford and nine honorary doctorates from British, continental, and American universities. He was at one time professor at Oxford and Aberdeen Universities, was awarded the Victorian medal of the Royal Geographic Society in 1906, and was a founding member of the British Academy. He was knighted in 1906 for his service to archaeology.

After a lifetime of painstaking research as a historian and archaeologist, this was his conclusion: "You may press the words of Luke in a degree beyond any other historian's and they stand the keenest scrutiny and the hardest treatment." He added, "Christianity did not originate in a lie; and we can and ought to demonstrate this as well as believe it."[16]

---

15. British Museum accession no. GR1877.5–11.1.
16. William Ramsay, *The Bearing of Recent Discovery on the Trustworthiness of the New Testament* (London: Hodder and Stoughton, 1915), p. 89.

Chapter 4

Did the Physical Resurrection of Christ Really Happen?

Tommy Mitchell

❀❀❀❀❀❀❀❀❀❀❀❀❀❀❀❀❀❀❀

The defining issue of Christianity is, "Did Jesus Christ rise from the grave?" In essence, was the Resurrection of Jesus an actual bodily resurrection or merely a spiritual manifestation of some sort? Since the day Jesus rose from the dead, detractors have tried to deny the reality of His Resurrection because, as stated in Romans 1:4, a genuine resurrection proves His deity. The Christian needs to be fully persuaded that the Resurrection was a real event, and believers must be able to defend that truth because salvation itself depends upon the reality of the Lord physically rising from the dead. Indeed, according to Romans 10:9, belief in the Resurrection of Jesus is necessary for salvation.

First, we need to distinguish between Christ's Resurrection and all other resurrections recorded in the Bible. When others were raised from the dead, the miracle was performed by a prophet or by Jesus through the power of God. Furthermore, those raised would again die someday, so it may be best to identify these miracles as resuscitations to distinguish them from Christ's Resurrection. Jesus rose from the grave through His own power, according to John 10:18, and He rose never to die again.

The Resurrection reveals that God placed His "seal of approval" on Jesus and His work. Jesus claimed to be God (John 8:58, 10:30) and predicted that He would rise from the dead (John 2:19). If He were a false teacher, and God still raised Him from the dead, then God would have given credibility to a liar. Since God cannot lie (Hebrews 6:18), He would not do this. The Resurrection shows that God was in complete agreement with Christ's message.

The Resurrection not only proves that Jesus is truly God but also guarantees that He, as the last Adam, has successfully paid the price of sin for the descendants of the first Adam. Paul clearly reveals the essential connection between Christ's Resurrection and our salvation in 1 Corinthians 15:17–18. "And if Christ is not risen, your faith is futile; you are still in your sins! Then also those who have fallen asleep in Christ have perished." Thus, without a real physical resurrection, we have no hope. We are still dead in our trespasses. Further, Paul tells us that without Christ rising physically, we have no reason to live for anything other than ourselves: "If the dead do not rise, 'Let us eat and drink, for tomorrow we die!'" (1 Corinthians 15:32).

The relationship of the Resurrection to our salvation is further explained in Romans 4:25 where Paul tells us that Jesus died for our sins and was raised for our justification. In other words, Christ's sacrifice for our sins was sufficient, and the fact that He rose from the dead proves He has the power to save us from death and eternal damnation. The Son of God put on human flesh and blood so that He could shed that blood as a sacrifice for our sins. His death and Resurrection had to be literal, physical events in order for Him to ensure that we, as physical beings, can be saved from the penalty for sin.

So is there a way we can really know that Christ rose from the dead? How can we assess the claim that someone was dead for three days and then was raised back to life? After all, as Christians we cannot claim that resurrections are common in our present everyday experience. How can we know that it happened in the past? As with all historical events, we must rely upon eyewitness testimony. With creation, the only eyewitness was God, and He has provided His eyewitness account in Genesis. With Christ's Resurrection, God made sure there were a number of eyewitnesses whose testimonies were recorded in the New Testament. Even before the testimonies of these people were written down, the news of the Resurrection spread like wildfire and turned the world upside-down. As we prepare to give an answer for the hope that is in us (1 Peter 3:15), we need to carefully analyze the accounts of those who attested to the Resurrection. Those accounts include the testimonies of both Christians and non-Christians, recorded in the Bible and even in the writings of first-century secular historians.

Historical Sources

For the Christian, the primary source of information about Christ and His life and death is the Bible itself. But is it appropriate to base our claim about the physical Resurrection of Jesus on a religious book? In reality, the Bible is more than just a religious book. While it does contain poetry, allegory, and other literary forms, it is predominantly a book of history — the true history of the world.

The skeptic often objects to the use of the Bible as a source of information, claiming that the Bible is full of errors or contradictions. However, in these cases the burden of proof for these alleged errors falls on the skeptic. In the end these allegations can be dealt with by a proper interpretation and understanding of the texts in question.

The reliability of the Bible as a historical document has been demonstrated over and over. Historians and archaeologists continually affirm the accuracy of the Bible in matters of history. Further, the number of ancient manuscripts of the Bible far exceeds that of other ancient documents. Thus, if we can gain knowledge about ancient events from sources for which there are relatively few manuscripts, then why should we not use a source for which there is far greater documentation?

Beyond the Bible, we can find information from several other sources. The non-Christian writers Josephus, Lucian, and Tacitus, among others, wrote of Christ's Crucifixion and the early days of Christianity. Much can be learned from investigating the works of these men.

Of course, the Bible is not *merely* any old history book. It claims to be written by inspiration of Almighty God, and it demonstrates that claim in any number of ways (such as making knowledge and science possible — see chapters 24 and 25). Given that the Bible has demonstrated itself to be the Word of God, by what external standard could we judge its claims? Who is in a position to tell God that He is wrong about anything? Since God is the source of all knowledge (Colossians 2:3), it is impossible for

Him to be wrong about anything. The Bible is therefore the standard by which all other claims must be judged. It follows then that the Bible's account of the death and Resurrection of Christ is the most reliable account possible. Other accounts and evidences are merely confirmatory.

Did Christ Really Die?

If we are to investigate the Resurrection of Jesus, it must first be established that He really died. After all, a resurrection can only be authentic if the person was actually dead.

In the case of Christ's death, the Bible records that He was beaten and scourged terribly by the Roman soldiers even before He was nailed to the Cross. The nature of this type of beating was quite gruesome and involved being beaten and whipped. The whipping would have left Christ's flesh mangled and torn, and there would have been considerable blood loss. Recall that He was too weak to carry His own Cross (Matthew 27:32).

He was then taken by the soldiers, and His hands and feet were nailed to the Cross. In agony, He struggled to take each breath. He willingly laid down His life as He submitted to the beatings and Crucifixion. So sure were the Roman soldiers that Jesus was dead that they did not feel it necessary to break His legs, as was customary in crucifixion. The final indignity was that His side was pierced by one of the soldiers.

Given all that had taken place, it is inconceivable that Christ survived the Crucifixion. The historical events of the Crucifixion have been studied closely by physicians, and the conclusion is always that Christ did, indeed, die from this process.

Further, the Roman historian Tacitus, writing in the late first century, records, "Consequently, to get rid of the report, Nero fastened the guilt and inflicted the most exquisite punishments on a class hated for their disgraceful acts, called Christians by the populace. Christ, from whom the name had its origin, suffered the extreme penalty during the reign of Tiberius at the hands of one of our procurators, Pontius Pilatus." Therefore, the testimony many decades later is that Christ did indeed die from this "extreme penalty." Any believable report to the contrary would surely have surfaced by the time of Tacitus's writings, but there was none.

Even with the evidence noted, some have suggested that Jesus did not die on the Cross but merely passed out or slipped into a coma-like state and was subsequently taken down from the Cross while alive. This is known as the "swoon theory."

The swoon theory is implausible for several reasons. First, it is unlikely that anyone could have survived all that Christ endured. Second, the Roman soldiers were experts at executions. It is unreasonable to suggest they could not determine if a victim was dead. After all, their job was to kill the person, and they performed this duty on a consistent basis. Finally, and perhaps most importantly, someone who had endured such horrific punishment and survived would be incapacitated for an extended period of time. If Jesus had only passed out on the Cross, He would not have been physically capable of moving the stone that sealed the tomb. Further, when He appeared to His disciples, His physical appearance would have been that of a person severely injured and in great pain rather than the mighty death conqueror. Seeing Christ in that state would not have inspired the disciples to preach with the boldness that cost them their lives.

The Empty Tomb

The empty tomb is crucial to the claim that Christ rose physically. If the body of Jesus were still in the tomb, then the Resurrection was disproven from the start. The evidence from Scripture is that no one disputed the empty tomb. Some merely desired to suppress the knowledge of it.

The Gospels relate the finding of the empty tomb. Multiple witnesses, including Mary Magdalene, Mary, Salome, Peter, John, and others, saw Christ's tomb empty. It was noted that the stone was rolled away and the burial garments of Christ were found inside the tomb. All four Gospels contain the account of this event. The body was missing.

When Mary Magdalene and the others went to the tomb to prepare the body of Jesus, they were told by the angel, "He is not here; for He is risen, as He said. Come, see the place where the Lord lay. And go quickly and tell His disciples that He is risen from the dead" (Matthew 28:6–7). These women were told that Jesus was raised from the dead. This implies an actual physical resurrection.

No historical report relates that a body was still in the tomb. Simply put, if the body were there, Jesus did not rise. The authorities could have easily put this entire issue to rest by merely producing the dead body of

Jesus. Moreover, there is no historical documentation, from either the Bible or other ancient documents, that even suggests that a body could be produced. Enemies of Christianity through the ages would relish the evidence of a body in the tomb. Such evidence would be the death knell of Christianity.

The best argument raised by those who opposed Christ was that His body was stolen by His disciples while the soldiers guarding the tomb were asleep. What folly is such a suggestion! First of all, immediately after the Crucifixion we find the disciples fearful and cowering. It is unrealistic to expect them to be able to evade or overpower the Roman guards at the tomb, break the seal, roll away the stone, and steal the corpse of Jesus. Further, what would be their motive for such a brazen act? The Bible describes that the disciples cowered in fear because they did not yet even grasp the fact that the Messiah must die and rise from the dead, even though Jesus had foretold His Resurrection (Luke 18:31–34). Thus, they would have no reason to even think of such a scheme. Why would they risk death to steal the body of their dead leader? How could they possibly benefit from such an endeavor? No, this could not be the reason the tomb was empty.

Perhaps the strongest refutation of the argument that the disciples merely stole the body is their bold witness after the Resurrection. These men were willing to die for their faith in their risen Lord. At no time did any of the disciples deny Christ even in the midst of their terrible trials and ordeals. If they had stolen the body, would they really be willing to die to conceal this act? Many people in history have willingly died for beliefs based on the testimony of others, but the disciples willingly suffered and most of them died because of something they had witnessed with their own eyes.

Lastly, one of the most compelling evidences for the empty tomb was the action of the chief priests and elders when told of the empty tomb. Instead of producing the body or embarking on an extensive search for the corpse, they merely told the soldiers to say that the disciples had stolen the body: "When they had assembled with the elders and consulted together, they gave a large sum of money to the soldiers, saying, 'Tell them, "His disciples came at night and stole Him away while we slept" ' " (Matthew 28:12–13). Notice that even the best argument of the day contradicts itself. How could the soldiers know who stole the body if they were asleep when the alleged theft occurred?

Eyewitness of the Disciples and the Women

The Bible records multiple appearances of Christ after He rose from the dead. The circumstances and descriptions of these appearances leave little doubt that what is being described are actual encounters with Christ in a physical, albeit glorified, body.

The first appearance was to Mary Magdalene as recorded in John 20. She initially did not recognize Him, thinking He was the gardener, but she soon realized He was the Savior. In Matthew 28, we find Christ's appearance to the other women as they left to tell the disciples about the empty tomb. They held Him by the feet and worshiped Him. Obviously, as they were able to touch Him, they did not see an apparition but a physical body.

The notion that women were the first witnesses powerfully supports the idea that the Gospel writers and early Church did not invent the Resurrection. At the time, the testimony of a Jewish woman was not allowed in court,[1] so it makes no sense if one is creating a story, to claim that women were the first eyewitnesses. It would be far more believable to claim that well-respected men like Joseph of Arimathea or Nicodemus were the first to discover the empty tomb. The fact that women were the first witnesses of the empty tomb and of the risen Lord testifies to the authenticity of the account.

Next, Jesus appeared to two disciples on the road to Emmaus (Mark 16:12–13; Luke 24:13–31). These two disciples walked and talked with Him along the way. In the evening, they sat down to eat. As they were handed the bread, they recognized Him: "Then their eyes were opened and they knew Him; and He vanished from their sight" (Luke 24:31).

He then came into the midst of ten disciples as they were hiding for fear of the Jews. John 20:20 reveals, "When He had said this, He showed them His hands and His side. Then the disciples were glad when they saw the Lord."

Thomas was not present at this appearance. When told of the meeting, Thomas said, "Unless I see in His hands the print of the nails, and put my finger into the print of the nails, and put my hand into His side, I will not believe" (John 20:25).

Eight days later, Christ again appeared to the disciples, this time with Thomas present. He told Thomas, "Reach your finger here, and look at My hands; and reach your hand here, and put it into My side. Do not be unbelieving, but believing" (John 20:27). How could this be a reasonable request unless Jesus appeared to them in an actual physical body?

Then, Jesus appeared to the disciples by the Sea of Galilee where He cooked fish and they dined together. The Lord was later seen again by the disciples on a mountain in Galilee (Matthew 28:16–17).

The Bible records that Christ also appeared to a group of more than 500 at one time and later to James: "After that He was seen by over five hundred brethren at once, of whom the greater part remain to the present, but some have fallen asleep. After that He was seen by James, then by all the apostles" (1 Corinthians 15:6–7).

Do these reports really stand as evidence for a bodily resurrection? As historical accounts they do seem credible and reliable, indicating the

---

1. Norman L. Geisler, *Baker Encyclopedia of Christian Apologetics* (Grand Rapids, MI: Baker, 1999), p. 648.

disciples encountered the physically risen Lord. The later b
these men shows that the only reasonable conclusion is that they ..
encountered the physically resurrected Christ.

After Jesus was crucified, these men were very afraid, hiding from the
Jews and fearing for their own safety. What would cause them to suddenly
become bold in their witness, preaching fearlessly, even at the risk of tor-
ture and death? History records that most of the disciples were ultimately
martyred for their faith. The only plausible reason for this is that they
truly had encountered the risen Messiah.

Those who question or deny the Resurrection cannot explain the
change in these men. If Christ had merely passed out on the Cross, would
an encounter with a horribly injured man be enough to embolden the
disciples to become great men of God? If the tomb were empty because
the disciples had stolen the body, would the disciples be willing to die for
a lie? Would not at least one of them expose the lie to save his own skin?
What would the religious leaders of the day have given to put down the
followers of Christ? No, the only answer is that the disciples knew that
Jesus had died and that they had seen Him alive again.

It could be argued that many people have been willing to die for a
cause, so the change in the disciples in itself is not proof for the Resurrection.
Further, the objection is raised that fanatics of all types have been willing
to die for their particular beliefs. Of course, but the real issue is not whether
the person willing to die *believes* their faith to be true, but whether they
know it is true or false. The disciples were in a position to know whether
the Resurrection actually occurred. If they had perpetrated a hoax, they
would not have been willing to suffer and die for their fraud. Their sacrifice indicates that they actually believed the Resurrection was real.

Witness of Paul

While the testimony of the disciples is compelling, the conversion of
the Apostle Paul would seem to be even more so. Saul of Tarsus, later
called Paul, greatly persecuted the early Church, persecuting and impris-
oning the faithful. He said, "I am indeed a Jew, born in Tarsus of Cilicia,
but brought up in this city at the feet of Gamaliel, taught according to the
strictness of our fathers' law, and was zealous toward God as you all are
today. I persecuted this Way to the death, binding and delivering into

prisons both men and women" (Acts 22:3–4). If there were an enemy of the early Church, it was Saul of Tarsus.

So what would make this man, this "Hebrew of Hebrews" (Philippians 3:5), become perhaps the boldest Christian who ever lived? The answer is simple. He had an encounter with the risen Christ. On the road to Damascus, Paul's life changed forever. As he testified, "Now it happened, as I journeyed and came near Damascus at about noon, suddenly a great light from heaven shone around me. And I fell to the ground and heard a voice saying to me, 'Saul, Saul, why are you persecuting Me?' So I answered, 'Who are You, Lord?' And He said to me, 'I am Jesus of Nazareth, whom you are persecuting' " (Acts 22:6–8).

Here was a man with no sympathy for the early Church that he persecuted and imprisoned. He had no love for Christ and certainly no reason to fabricate an account of meeting the resurrected Christ. On the road to Damascus, Paul believed that he had, indeed, met the Savior. As a result of that encounter, Paul was transformed from the greatest persecutor of the early Church to a man who suffered greatly for the cause of Christ (2 Corinthians 11:22–29).

Witness of James

Paul stated that Jesus appeared to James (1 Corinthians 15:7). While there are a handful of men named James in the New Testament, Paul likely was referring to the half-brother of Jesus, the biological son of Mary and Joseph. The Gospels indicate that Jesus had several brothers, including "James, Joses, Simon, and Judas" (Matthew 13:55), and that they "did not believe in Him" during His ministry (John 7:5).

James later became a leader of the Church at Jerusalem and at the so-called Jerusalem council (Acts 12:17, 15:13). According to tradition, he was martyred for his faith in Christ by being thrown off the temple and then beaten to death. What could so drastically change the life of an unbelieving person who actually grew up with Jesus? The only legitimate explanation is that he knew his brother had died, but then he saw Him alive again.

The Writings of Josephus

Josephus was a first-century Jewish military leader-turned-historian when captured by the Romans. His works have provided much eyewitness information about the destruction of Jerusalem in A.D. 70. Further, his writings have given us some insight into the early days of Christianity, including an extra-biblical account of Christ:

> Now, there was about this time Jesus, a wise man, if it be lawful to call him a man, for he was a doer of wonderful works — a teacher of such men as receive the truth with pleasure. He drew over to him both many of the Jews, and many of the Gentiles. He was [the] Christ; and when Pilate, at the suggestion of the principal men amongst us, had condemned him to the cross, those that loved him at the first did not forsake him, for he appeared to them alive again the third day, as the divine prophets had foretold these and ten thousand other wonderful things concerning him; and the tribe of Christians, so named from him, are not extinct at this day.[2]

Josephus

Incidentally, we can consider Josephus a "hostile witness" since he was not a Christian.

A Real Physical Resurrection?

Skeptics have tried to discount the idea of the physical Resurrection of Jesus. In spite of the historical evidence supporting the event, they seek to explain away the fact that Christ rose bodily.

Some have argued that the passages in Scripture relating to the Resurrection are not to be taken literally, that is, as real history, but should be understood as fables. They argue that these accounts were never meant to be mistaken for historical narrative.

Others have suggested that the Resurrection accounts have been embellished over time. It is said that the disciples never meant to claim there was a real physical resurrection but that the early Church kept adding to the original account.

Neither of these alternative ideas account for the changed lives of Paul, James, and the disciples. Only an encounter with the risen Christ provides an adequate explanation.

Some have tried to explain the post-Resurrection accounts by suggesting that the disciples had an hallucination. Again, this type of theory

---

2. Flavius Josephus, *The Antiquity of the Jews*, Book XVIII, chapter 3, "Sedition of the Jews against Pontius Pilate A.D. 19–33," lines 63–64.

fails for multiple reasons. For one, hallucinations occur in individuals, not in groups of ten men, who would not have had exactly the same hallucination at the same time and on multiple occasions. Furthermore, the group of 500 certainly would not have had a "group vision." Also, the empty tomb cannot be accounted for by the hallucination theory since so many people had viewed it.

Does Scripture Dispute a Bodily Resurrection?

Some have argued that the Bible itself denies the physical Resurrection of Christ. Several verses have been misused to support this claim. Not surprisingly, when more closely examined these verses do not support the claims made by detractors.

1 Corinthians 15:44

The most commonly cited verse to support the contention that the Bible does not claim the bodily Resurrection is 1 Corinthians 15:44, which says, "It is sown a natural body, it is raised a spiritual body. There is a natural body, and there is a spiritual body." The issue in this passage is the nature of the "spiritual body" that is raised. Some claim the verse teaches that there will not be a physical resurrection but a spiritual one.

In this verse the term "spiritual body" does not refer to an immaterial, nonphysical body. Furthermore, the concept of a "natural body" does not just mean a physical body. This verse is meant to provide a contrast between the "natural" body, which is driven by fleshly and sinful desires, and the "spiritual" body, which is holy and led by spiritual desires. Although Christians have a new spiritual nature, we still must battle against the flesh.

1 Peter 3:18

"For Christ also suffered once for sins, the just for the unjust, that He might bring us to God, being put to death in the flesh but made alive by the Spirit." This verse is occasionally used to suggest that the Resurrection was only spiritual, but it does not state what the critics claim it does.

Nowhere does this verse deny a physical resurrection. It states that He died physically. So the critic must read into this passage what is not there. Moreover, Peter knew full well that Jesus rose physically. Following the Resurrection, he was among the group of disciples who watched Jesus eat and heard Him say, "See My hands and My feet, that it is I Myself; touch Me and see, for a spirit does not have flesh and bones as you see that I have" (Luke 24:39, NASB).

John 20:19

> Then, the same day at evening, being the first day of the week, when the doors were shut where the disciples were assembled, for fear of the Jews, Jesus came and stood in the midst, and said to them, "Peace be with you."

Some have proposed that this verse proves that Christ was raised only in spirit form rather than physically. The claim is based on Christ's appearance in a room with closed doors. Thus, His body, they say, must not have had a material nature. However, the verse does not actually claim that Jesus passed through a door or a wall. It merely notes that He entered a room with a closed door. Even if the door was locked, simply by His will Christ could have overcome the lock and simply entered the room through the door. Furthermore, even in His physical body prior to His death and Resurrection, He was able to walk on water, so for Him to do the miraculous was no surprise.

In this instance, Jesus was so concerned to make sure the disciples knew He had physically risen that He ate in front of them (Luke 24:43). Later, meeting them in Galilee, He again ate in front of them. Ghostly apparitions do not eat.

The critic might object to using the information in the Bible as evidence for the Resurrection. But since the Bible has demonstrated its truthfulness time and again, such an attitude of distrust is irrational. The critic's objection to the Bible is due to an arbitrary philosophical bias, not logical argumentation or hard evidence. Even secular scholars largely acknowledge the historical accuracy of the Bible. So the critic has no basis in reality for objecting to its claim of the Resurrection of Christ. The critic may not emotionally like the claim, but he cannot refute it on scholarly, intellectual grounds.

Why Is the Resurrection Important?

"Blessed be the God and Father of our Lord Jesus Christ, who according to His abundant mercy has begotten us again to a living hope through the resurrection of Jesus Christ from the dead, to an inheritance incorruptible and undefiled and that does not fade away, reserved in heaven for you" (1 Peter 1:3–4).

Do we really need to understand that Christ's Resurrection was physical and not merely spiritual? Is this much ado about nothing? Can't we just love Jesus and let it go at that? Can we not just acknowledge that Christ took the punishment we deserved, regardless of whether He rose physically or spiritually? The answer is no.

Put simply, without the physical Resurrection of the Lord Jesus, there is no Christianity. As Paul said, if Christ is not risen, then our faith is futile (1 Corinthians 15:17). There is no salvation without the physical Resurrection of Christ, and one cannot be saved without believing it. Romans 10:9 states, "That if thou shalt confess with thy mouth the Lord Jesus, and shalt believe in thine heart that God hath raised him from the dead, thou shalt be saved" (KJV). As Christians, we are to be always prepared to give an answer for the hope that is in us (1 Peter 3:15), namely, the hope of eternal life. Only the Lord's victory over death, proven by His Resurrection, can guarantee us that heavenly inheritance. We need to prepare ourselves to defend this doctrine as we witness to others about the risen Lord and Savior.

Chapter 5

Is Genesis a Derivation from Ancient Myths?

Steve Ham

✿✿✿✿✿✿✿✿✿✿✿✿✿✿✿✿✿✿

When faced with the question as to whether the Bible accurately records ancient history in Genesis 1–11 or was derived from some other "ancient" document, we first need to apply a solemn reminder. God's Word has made the ultimate and justifiable claim for itself that none of these other ancient texts has made. The Bible repeatedly asserts to be the perfect Word of God (2 Timothy 3:16; 2 Peter 1:21; Psalm 19:7, 119:160). If the Bible borrowed from ancient mythologies, this claim would be called into question.

The Issue

All over the world we find cultural legends and myths that closely resemble certain accounts in Scripture, such as the creation, the Fall, the Flood, and the Tower of Babel accounts.[1] Oftentimes, these accounts are used as an *external* confirmation of the credibility of Scripture. If one accepts the account of Scripture that we are all of "one blood" (Acts 17:26), he should also accept the biblical account that all human heritage goes back to the city of Babel where all human population once lived after the

---

1. Stephanie Dalley, translator, *Myths from Mesopotamia: Creation, the Flood, Gilgamesh, and Others* (Oxford: Oxford University Press, 2009).

ɔal Flood of Noah's day. We would expect to find common accounts of history (such as the creation and the Flood) within the stories and traditions of today's people groups that once lived together in one place after the great Flood. Given years of cultural diversity as mankind spread throughout the world, it is also not surprising that these stories have taken on their own cultural influences in the retelling.

In the mid-1800s within the buried cities of the Ancient Near East (including Nineveh and Nippur in present-day Iraq), several excavations uncovered a whole library of tablets from earlier Mesopotamian times. Within these finds and upon the tablets were lists of kings, business archives, administrative documents, and a number of versions of the flood epic. Each version varied in language form and completion (most were only partially intact) with the most complete being the Babylonian collation of *The Gilgamesh Epic*.[2] On its 11th tablet was a narrative about the great Flood, and much of its detail shows similarities with the biblical account of the Flood. Rather than being used as a confirmation of biblical credibility, however, many have attempted to use these tablets as a reason to *doubt* the authority of God's Word because some of them supposedly predate the earliest times of biblical authorship (predating Moses). Some have concluded that with this supposed predating, along with storyline and some language similarity, the biblical accounts are a derivation from earlier Sumerian legends. Some have suggested the history in Genesis is also a form of earlier Jewish mythology in the same manner as the Middle Eastern texts.

Many have used these documents as reason to doubt the authority and inspiration of the Word of God. Some have used these documents to reject Moses as the writer of Genesis, and some have used these documents to suggest that Genesis itself is either myth, poetry, or even simply an argument (a theological polemic) used as a rebuttal of these supposedly older myths.

The Fallible Versus the Infallible

Only two conclusions can come from a study evaluating if the Bible is a derivation from ancient mythology. 1) If this is true, biblical claims of God's inspiration and His perfect Word are untrue, and the Bible cannot be trusted. 2) The Bible truly is the Word of God, and any other claim of authorship or external influence is false.

---

2. *The Epic of Gilgamesh*, translated by Andrew George (New York: Penguin Books, 1960).

How we view Scripture has great bearing on how we view the reliability of the gospel of Jesus Christ on which the whole of Christendom is centered. When we read the claims of Scripture, we are left with no room for compromise. The Bible claims *all* of Scripture comes from God and not of human will. The Bible also claims a perfection in God and of His Word, and any inconsistency or blemish is intolerable to biblical inerrancy and God's infallibility. At the end of the day, this comes down to the claims of fallible men versus the claims of the infallible God.

Today, some scholars seek to understand the Scripture through a "comparative" study approach, looking for parallels in texts and culture as a way of interpreting Scripture. This means the scholars use external documents to interpret Scripture in their light rather than starting with Scripture to shed light on the external documents. Like every other issue of biblical compromise, it comes down to starting points.

If the significance of finding these documents in Nineveh and Nippur has caused some to doubt the authority of Scripture, the issue can only be an interpretation problem. We should always remember the Bible is the inerrant and infallible Word of God, and it should be allowed to interpret itself and the evidence rather than permitting the evidence to interpret Scripture.

The Significance of the Find

The library of tablets from Nineveh and Nippur was an amazing find, and at the time the significance was not even known. In fact, not until decades later did the deciphered tablets show a version of the Flood account similar to what we find in Genesis. The two most significant items sharing any commonality to biblical history (even if loosely) were the versions of the flood epic and the list of Sumerian kings. Of particular interest is a list of pre-Flood kings.

While these documents have many similarities with biblical history, there are also many differences. In these contradictions biblical history sheds light on its own authentic history and authority. Only the Bible has a consistent logic to its account.

The Dating and Source Dependence of the Documents

The supposed dating of the tablets found range from 2200 to 620 B.C. God gave the Law to Moses during the wilderness wandering in the 15th century B.C. Dating these Sumerian documents as being written even up to 800 years before Moses wrote the account of Genesis does not automatically mean that Genesis was derived from these Sumerian records.[3]

Three possible reasons exist for the consistencies between these documents and the Bible:

1. These Sumerian documents were derived from the original Hebrew text (but are skewed and inaccurate).
2. The Hebrew text was derived from these documents (but was corrected in the process).
3. Both are separate accounts of commonly known history.

One cannot make a definitive choice between the first and third options, but the second option requires an irrational leap. When historical accounts are passed down, unless great care is taken to avoid it (such as has been taken with the biblical record), the records are usually embellished as time goes on, so the history becomes more and more distorted. The second option would require the writer to weed through numerous embellished and legendary accounts to produce the inspired record. Some might claim that God directed Moses throughout the process, but the author would need to sift through scores of texts in multiple languages just to find the scraps of inspired material in each. If one needs to invoke such divine intervention, it makes far more sense to accept the traditional view and obvious solidarity of God's whole inspired text.

Even as we look at the Babylonian flood epic, we find differences within the various Middle Eastern versions that have been uncovered. H.V. Hilprecht from the University of Pennsylvania in 1909 (Hilprecht was part of the University's Babylonian expeditions and excavations) uncovered the earliest fragment of the flood epic. After carefully uncovering and translating each cuneiform character, Hilprecht made the following statement: "In its preserved portion, it showed a much greater resemblance to the biblical deluge story than any other fragment yet published."[4]

Hilprecht's statement helps us understand the ongoing corruption of the Babylonian story compared to the authentic preservation of the biblical account and does not support the conclusion that the Near Eastern

3. Ira M. Price, *The Monuments and the Old Testament,* 2010 reprint (Valley Forge, PA: Judson Press, 1905).
4. H.V. Hilprecht, *The Babylonian Expedition of the University of Pennsylvania* (Philadelphia, PA: University of Pennsylvania, 1910), p. 35.

mythology should be attributed as the primary source of the biblical account. The inconsistencies within the texts themselves point to an unsurprising lack of reliability in using them as a gauge on the authenticity of the biblical account.

The Pre-Flood Kings

A brief look at just a few particulars of both the Sumerian kings list and the flood epics will show the many inconsistencies that forfeit any consideration of Babylonian myth as a source for Scripture.

The list of pre-Flood Sumerian kings has some curious similarities to the list of patriarchs in Genesis. For example, Genesis and the Sumerian list both refer to the Flood. Both refer to men of great ages, and when the differing numeric systems are considered, they provide similar totals. The lists, however, have three significant differences:

1. The ages and lengths of reigns of the Sumerian kings are much longer than that of the biblical patriarchs, as some of the Sumerian kings supposedly reigned for more than 30,000 years. After discovering the Sumerians used a sexagesimal system[5] rather than a decimal system of counting, the longer life spans in the Sumerian list are converted to a very similar number with the life spans of eight correlating patriarchs in the biblical account.

2. The Sumerian kings list has only eight in the list while the Bible gives 10 patriarchs before the Flood (including Noah). Although a close correlation exists between these lists, it seems the Sumerian list has omitted the first man and the man who survived the Flood (Adam and Noah). The similarities between the other eight men make this a reasonable consideration.

3. The Bible has a clear difference in the quality of information, the spiritual and moral superiority of the patriarchs, and the completeness of the list. The Genesis account explains in great detail the struggle of mankind with sin and the effects of the Curse. It highlights those who walked with God and also provides details about humanity apart from the patriarchs. Such detail is not found in the Sumerian kings list.

---

5. A sexagesimal system is based on the number 60 and allows for easy division into various fractions for trade and other purposes.

While a study of the Sumerian list is a fascinating journey in discovering the way Sumerians looked upon their ancestry and how their numeric and commercial systems worked, the quality of the biblical text is distinctly superior in completeness, information, and spiritual and moral quality. The biblical text does not reflect a borrowing from an inferior text. If anything, the very mention of this kings list that matches so closely the biblical account is a confirmation of biblical authenticity.

The Flood Epics

The Near Middle Eastern Flood epics have three main versions: the Sumerian Epic of Ziusudra, the Akkadian Atrahasis Epic, and the Babylonian Gilgamesh Epic. The Gilgamesh Epic is the most complete, with 12 tablets decipherable. The 11th tablet with the most complete flood account of the three versions.

After great bitterness over losing his friend Enkidu, Gilgamesh seeks Utnapishtim (the Babylonian equivalent of Noah) to give him the secret of immortality. Utnapishtim tells him of the gods' desire to flood the world because they could not sleep for the uproar of mankind. Ea, the god of wisdom, warned Utnapishtim in a dream to convert his house to a boat, take in the seed of all living creatures, and tell the people he was building a boat to escape the wrath of the god Enlil. Utnapishtim built the boat in seven days and took in family, kin, creatures both wild and tame, and all the craftsmen. The great flood came, and even the gods were terrified of it and fled. For six days and nights, the flood overwhelmed the world and on the seventh day grew calm. The boat rested on Mt. Nisir, and Utnapishtim sent out a dove, then a swallow, and then a raven. When the raven didn't return, he made a sacrifice, and the gods gathered like flies over it.

These flood epics reveal many internal inconsistencies, which rule them out from being the source of the Genesis text.

The Difference Is in the Detail

The Bible specifically states that Noah took two of every *kind* of land-dwelling animal and seven of some animals onto the ark. The Genesis account is clear and realistic when comparing the animals and the size of the ark. The Gilgamesh Epic is an unreliable account because it states Utnapishtim was to take the seed of all living creatures, both wild and tame, that he had available. This leaves us with no information about how many animals were likely on board the boat or whether all of the necessary kinds would have been represented for repopulation. The Bible is specific concerning the ark's animal cargo:

> You shall take with you of every clean animal by sevens, a male and his female; and of animals that are not clean two, a male and his female; also of the birds of the sky, by sevens, male and female, to keep offspring alive on the face of all the earth (Genesis 7:2–3; NASB).

The detailed biblical account explains that the Flood began as *all* the fountains of the great deep broke open, that it covered the whole earth to the extent of the highest mountains, and that it killed every man and land-dwelling, air-breathing animal of the earth (Genesis 7:21–22). The biblical detail shows that the whole earth was covered by water coming from both above and below and that it rained continuously for 40 days and nights and the waters continued to rise until the 150th day. The Gilgamesh Epic, while stating the devastation of the flood on humanity, does not specifically detail the full geographical extent and depth of the flood. Also, it is unreasonable to expect so much water coverage in just six days of rain.

The biblical dimensions of the ark are detailed and consistent with a vessel that could float in rough waters and could house the animals described. The dimensions of the boat in the Gilgamesh epic amount to more of a cube-shaped vessel with the beam equaling the length. Although we know it had seven stories (decks), it is impossible to determine the full size of the vessel. Logistically, this boat could not float in a stable manner in rough seas and would not be structurally reliable.

The Bible is consistently reliable on the account of the birds that were released. It is logical to send out a raven before a dove, given that ravens are scavengers while doves feed only on plants. The intervals of release of the dove are consistent with the expectation of having a drained land for vegetation and occupants, and this correlates with the dove returning with a freshly picked olive leaf and then the dove not returning at all. By contrast, the Gilgamesh epic mentions a dove, then a swallow, and finally a raven. There are no intervals mentioned to assess the appropriate time length for flights, and sending a raven last is questionable in that ravens may have been able to survive as scavengers.

The Character of the "Gods"

In the Gilgamesh Epic, the gods are impatient and impulsive. They do not like the uproar and babel of mankind and decide to destroy humanity. The gods have no justifiable moral reason to destroy humanity. In contrast, the God of the Bible sent the Flood on an already cursed world because of man's wicked heart that only desired evil. God's judgment in the light of sin is righteous and just.

The Babylonian gods lie and tell Utnapishtim to lie to other humans about the coming wrath. The Gilgamesh Epic promotes polytheistic mythology, whereas the Bible presents monotheistic theology. The many gods in the Gilgamesh Epic differ in ideas and motivations, and they seek to thwart each other. The God of the Bible is holy, pure, unchanging, and cannot lie. These are just a few of the character differences between the biblical God and the description of the gods in the Babylonian myth.[6]

Lastly, it is important to note that in the Gilgamesh Epic the god Ea tells Utnapishtim to save himself through the ark by means of deceiving the other gods. In the Bible, God Himself provides the plans for the ark as the means to save Noah and his family. Furthermore, Noah was a preacher of righteousness rather than deceit (2 Peter 2:5).

Even based solely on comparison between the perfect Word of God and the imperfect pagan myths, it is absurd to think the descriptions in the Babylonian texts could be the source of the Genesis account in the inspired Word of God.

Conclusion

It is not difficult to rule out the Ancient Near Eastern mythological texts from being the source of influence for the account of Genesis. While Genesis is reliable, they are not. While Genesis shows consistency of our God's righteous and sovereign character, the mythological texts show the gods as little more than squabbling people, deceiving each other and humanity and lacking sovereign control. While the Genesis Flood account

---

6. For more information, please see Nozomi Osanai, "A Comparative Study of the Flood Accounts in the Gilgamesh Epic and Genesis" at http://www.answersingenesis.org/home/area/flood/introduction.asp, accessed February 22, 2011.

gives enough credible information to allow for historical and geological confirmation, the mythological texts provide little that can be confirmed, and what is provided does not make sense logically or scientifically.

The similarities among Ancient Near Eastern mythologies and between the Gilgamesh Epic and the Bible make sense from a biblical worldview. Christians should not be surprised to see people groups all over the world with their own accounts of the creation, the Fall, the Flood, men of great ages, and even the Tower of Babel. The accounts can tell us people once had the same record or eyewitness of a common event handed down from a generation that was once congregated in the same place at the same time.

The Gilgamesh Epic tells a sad tale of a man (who was supposedly part god) looking desperately for everlasting life. This was a man who knew of great men of old who lived long lives and supposedly became gods, and he wanted to attain this status himself. He had a desperate desire to avoid death. A Christian can hear tales such as this and consider them in light of biblical truth. The Bible shows us that men did indeed live for longer periods of time, but as mankind became further distanced from a perfect original creation, life expectancies shortened. The Bible reveals the devastation of sin in the judgment of death, and mankind's continual need for a Savior. The Bible gives us the account of the world-wide Flood that covered the entire earth and shows both God's faithfulness in judgment and in salvation by protecting a line of humanity for the promised Messiah.

In the light of Scripture, we see confirmation in mythology around the world that the Bible is indeed God's Word and the only reliable truth. In the message of God's Word, we see Him stepping into this world and taking upon Himself the wrath we deserve. Only through the consistent Word of the Bible can we know salvation is only received through faith in Jesus Christ alone.

Chapter 6

Is the Trinity Three Different Gods?

Jobe Martin

Have you ever wondered about the doctrine of the Trinity? How could the God of the Bible be one God, but at the same time three Persons — Father, Son, and Holy Spirit? Doesn't the Bible emphatically state that God is one? These queries are common discussions among Christians and non-Christians alike.

The Bible should be accepted as the final authority for the believer. Therefore, we must look to Scripture to learn what God has revealed about Himself in His inspired Word. The famous passage known as the Shema (Hebrew: "hear") starts by stating, "Hear, O Israel: The LORD our God, the LORD is one! You shall love the LORD your God with all your heart, with all your soul, and with all your strength" (Deuteronomy 6:4–5). The Bible is quite clear: God is one!

The Bible is also clear that there are three persons who are each called God. This plurality of God is presented in 2 Corinthians 13:14: "The grace of the Lord Jesus Christ [the Son], and the love of God [the Father], and the communion of the Holy Spirit [the Holy Spirit] be with you all. Amen" (bracketed information added). With our finite minds it is impossible to fully comprehend the infinite God. It is also difficult for us to apprehend the concept that God is one being in three persons.

The Doctrine of the Trinity in the New Testament

The New Testament portrays each member of the Godhead as distinct persons in passages such as the Great Commission. In Matthew 28:18–20 Jesus said, "All authority has been given to Me in heaven and on earth. Go therefore and make disciples of all the nations, baptizing them in the name of the Father and of the Son and of the Holy Spirit, teaching them to observe all things that I have commanded you; and lo, I am with you always, even to the end of the age." Believers are to go into the world and make disciples and baptize them in the name (singular, not "names") of the Father, Son, and Holy Spirit. Jesus placed Himself and the Holy Spirit on the same level as the Father.

Matthew also portrays all three members of the Trinity as involved in the baptism of Jesus. "When He had been baptized, Jesus came up immediately from the water; and behold, the heavens were opened to Him, and He saw the Spirit of God descending like a dove and alighting upon Him. And suddenly a voice came from heaven, saying, 'This is My beloved Son, in whom I am well pleased' " (Matthew 3:16–17). In this passage the Father spoke from heaven and the Holy Spirit descended like a dove while Jesus was on the earth.

The Bible Names Each of the Three Persons of the Trinity as "God"

Virtually no one questions that the Father is described as God in the Bible. Paul wrote, "Then comes the end, when He delivers the kingdom to God the Father, when He puts an end to all rule and all authority and power" (1 Corinthians 15:24). Paul addressed the epistle of Romans to "all who are in Rome, beloved of God, called to be saints: Grace to you and peace from God our Father and the Lord Jesus Christ" (Romans 1:7).

Jesus identified Himself as God in John 10:30 when He stated, "I and My Father are one." He also declared His divinity during His temptation by the devil when He said, "It is written again, 'You shall not tempt the Lord your God' " (Matthew 4:7). This concept will be given more attention later in this chapter. Jesus is also called God by others.

Matthew claimed that the events surrounding the birth of Christ fulfilled Old Testament prophecies, including Isaiah 7:14, which states, "Behold, the virgin shall conceive and bear a Son, and shall call His name Immanuel." Matthew adds that Immanuel means "God with us" (Matthew

1:23). The writer of Hebrews wrote that the Father said to the Son, "Your throne, O God, is forever and ever" (Hebrews 1:8).

The Holy Spirit is also recognized as God. He is not merely an impersonal force similar to electricity, as some cults would like us to believe. When Peter condemned Ananias for lying, he said, "Ananias, why has Satan filled your heart to lie to the *Holy Spirit* and keep back part of the price of the land for yourself? While it remained, was it not your own? And after it was sold, was it not in your own control? Why have you conceived this thing in your heart? You have not lied to men, but to *God*" (Acts 5:3–4, emphasis added).

In the gospel of John, the Bible intimately links the Holy Spirit to both the Father and the Son: "But the Helper, the Holy Spirit, whom the Father will send in My name, He will teach you all things, and bring to your remembrance all things that I said to you" (John 14:26). In the next chapter Jesus added, "But when the Helper comes, whom I shall send to you from the Father, the Spirit of truth who proceeds from the Father, He will testify of Me" (John 15:26).

All Three Persons of the Trinity Are Eternal

The Scriptures listed above are just a few of many used to demonstrate that the God of the Bible is one God in three persons. Not only are each of the three persons of the Trinity identified as God, but each is said to possess eternality. Deuteronomy 33:27 explains to us that God the Father is eternal. "The eternal God is your refuge." In Micah's prophecy, which named Bethlehem as the birthplace of the Messiah, the Son is also shown to be eternal. "But you, Bethlehem Ephrathah, though you are little among the thousands of Judah, yet out of you shall come forth to Me the One to be Ruler in Israel, whose goings forth are from of old, from everlasting" (Micah 5:2). The eternality of the Holy Spirit is described when the author of Hebrews asked rhetorically, "How much more shall the blood of Christ, who through the eternal Spirit offered Himself without spot to God, cleanse your conscience from dead works to serve the living God?" (Hebrews 9:14).

The triune God of the Bible is utterly distinct from the false gods of this world. Jeremiah proclaimed Him as the only true Creator God:

> But the LORD is the true God; He is the living God and the
> everlasting King. At His wrath the earth will tremble, and the

nations will not be able to endure His indignation. Thus you shall say to them: "The gods that have not made the heavens and the earth shall perish from the earth and from under these heavens." He has made the earth by His power, He has established the world by His wisdom, and has stretched out the heavens at His discretion (Jeremiah 10:10–12).

Does the Old Testament Support the Doctrine of the Trinity?

A Grammatical Mistake in Genesis 1:1?

The very first sentence in the Bible appears to have a grammatical mistake in the original language. "In the beginning God created . . . ." The word translated as "God" is the word *elohim*, which is a plural noun.[1] But now we have a problem — the verb *created* is a third person singular verb. So it seems that in the first sentence of the Bible there is a grammatical mistake of using a plural noun with a singular verb. This would be like someone saying in English, "they was," which is not proper in English, nor is it proper in Hebrew.

God told us about Himself in the first sentence of the Bible. He is one being with a plurality of persons. Genesis 1:1 does not directly explain that God is a triunity, but it is consistent with this truth. Genesis 1:26 states, "Then God said, 'Let Us make man in Our image, according to Our likeness.' " Who is the "Us" and the "Our" in the passage? The next verse goes on to state, "So God created man in His own image; in the image of God He created him; male and female He created them" (Genesis 1:27). While verse 26 uses the pronouns "Us" and "Our," verse 27 uses the singular pronouns "His" and "He" to refer to the same God. As in Genesis 1:1 the word "God" in Genesis 1:26 is a plural noun, and the verb "said" is a third person singular verb. The God of the Bible reveals Himself as plural in persons but single in being.

---

1. Scholars have debated whether this term should be viewed as hinting at the plurality of persons of the Godhead or if it is used simply as "the majestic plural." Scott concluded, "More probable is the view that *ĕlōhîm* comes from *ĕlōah* as a unique development of the Hebrew Scriptures and represents chiefly the plurality of persons in the Trinity of the godhead." Jack Scott in Robert Laird Harris, Gleason Leonard Archer, and Bruce K. Waltke, *Theological Wordbook of the Old Testament*, electronic ed., 41 (Chicago, IL: Moody Press, 1999), 93c.

The Trinity in Isaiah

The prophet Isaiah made a statement that supports the doctrine of the Trinity: "Come near to Me, hear this: I have not spoken in secret from the beginning; from the time that it was, I was there. And now the Lord God [the Father] and His Spirit [the Holy Spirit] have sent Me [the Son]. Thus says the Lord, your Redeemer, the Holy One of Israel: I am the Lord your God, who teaches you to profit" (Isaiah 48:16–17, bracketed information added). All three persons of the Trinity are explicitly mentioned in this passage.

Jesus Is not God the Son?

Nearly every cult and false religion denies the doctrine of the Trinity. Two of the major cults that do this are Mormonism and Jehovah's Witnesses. The Jehovah's Witnesses believe that Jesus is not Jehovah God. Instead, they believe that He is a god but not the one and only true God. Jehovah's Witnesses have their own version of the Bible called the *New World Translation*. This version translates John 1:1 erroneously. While the inerrant Word of God states, "In the beginning was the Word, and the Word was with God, and the Word was God" (John 1:1), the *New World Translation presents* the last phrase of the verse this way: "and the Word was *a* god" (emphasis added). The article "a" is not in the original Greek. A rule in Greek grammar states that when an anarthrous (no article) predicate nominative is present it is for emphasis. The noun is "Word" and the predicate nominative is "God." Since no article is present before the predicate nominative, "God," the verse is testifying that the Word (Jesus) is God. By denying the Trinity and teaching that Jehovah God is supreme and Jesus is an inferior god on the order of Michael the Archangel, the Jehovah's Witnesses are actually polytheistic — they believe in multiple gods.

Mormonism is a religious system that believes in many gods and denies the Trinity. Here are some statements from Mormon writings:

> [T]here is an infinite number of holy personages, drawn from worlds without number, who have passed on to exultation and are thus gods.[2]

---

2. Bruce McConkie, *Mormon Doctrine*, (Salt Lake City, UT: Bookcraft, 1991), p. 576–577.

Abraham . . . Isaac . . . and Jacob . . . have entered into their exaltation, according to the promises, and sit upon thrones, and are not angels but are gods.[3]

"But both the scriptures and the prophets affirm that Jesus Christ and Lucifer are indeed offspring of our Heavenly Father and, therefore, spirit brothers."[4]

The founder of Mormonism, Joseph Smith, believed in many gods. Smith said, "I will preach on the plurality of Gods . . . I wish to declare that I have always and in all congregations when I have preached on the subject of Deity, it has been the plurality of Gods."[5] "Many men say there is one God; the Father, the Son and the Holy Ghost are only one God. I say that is a strange God anyhow — three in one, and one in three! It is a curious organization."[6]

Contrary to the beliefs of the Jehovah's Witnesses and Mormons, the Bible refers to Jesus as fully God. "For in Him [Christ] dwells all the fullness of the Godhead bodily" (Colossians 2:9, bracketed information added). Paul wrote that we should live in a godly manner, "looking for the blessed hope and glorious appearing of our great God and Savior Jesus Christ (Titus 2:13). Even "doubting Thomas," upon seeing the resurrected Lord, said to Jesus, "My Lord and my God!" (John 20:28). The fact is that Jesus is unequivocally called God in multiple passages.

Furthermore, Jesus identified Himself as God several times. Three times in John 8, Jesus declared that He was Almighty God. "Therefore I said to you that you will die in your sins; for if you do not believe that I am He, you will die in your sins" (John 8:24). The pronoun *He* is in italics in the New King James Version, meaning that it is not found in the Greek text but was added to the text by the translators to make it read better in English. Jesus proclaimed Himself to be the *I AM* who spoke to Moses out of the burning bush (Exodus 3:14). He does the same thing in John 8:28

---

3. *Doctrine and Covenants*, 132:37. Available online at http://lds.org/scriptures/dc-testament/dc/132?lang=eng, accessed March 9, 2011.

4. From *Ensign Magazine*, an official publication of the LDS Church in response to the question "How can Jesus and Lucifer be spirit brothers when their characters and purposes are so utterly opposed?" (June 1986): p. 25.

5. Joseph Smith, *Teachings of the Prophet Joseph Smith* (Salt Lake City, UT: Deseret Book Company, 1976).

6. Ibid., p. 372.

and John 8:58. The Jewish leaders understood exactly what He claimed, and they attempted to stone Him for claiming to be God (John 8:59).

The Jews tried to do the same thing in John 10 after Jesus declared, "I and My Father are one" (John 10:30). Jesus asked why they wanted to stone Him, and they replied, "For a good work we do not stone You, *but for blasphemy, and because You, being a Man, make Yourself God*" (John 10:33).

Conclusion

The Bible is quite clear — there is one true God, and He exists in three persons: God the Father, God the Son, and God the Holy Spirit. There is salvation in no other God. This Trinitarian God is eternal as stated in Isaiah:

> "You are My witnesses," says the Lord, "And My servant whom I have chosen, that you may know and believe Me, and understand that I am He. Before Me there was no God formed, nor shall there be after Me. I, even I, am the Lord, and besides Me there is no savior. I have declared and saved, I have proclaimed, and there was no foreign god among you; therefore you are My witnesses," says the Lord, "that I am God. Indeed before the day was, I am He; and there is no one who can deliver out of My hand; I work, and who will reverse it?" (Isaiah 43:10–13)

God the Father, in the power of God the Holy Spirit, through the agency of God the Son — Jesus Christ — created everything that exists. John 1, Colossians 1, and Hebrews 1 teach that the Lord Jesus is the Creator. Since He is our Creator, He has the right and the authority to be our Redeemer. Jesus said, "I am the way, the truth, and the life. No one comes to the Father except through Me. If you had known Me, you would have known My Father also; and from now on you know Him and have seen Him" (John 14:6–7).

The doctrine of the Trinity is not derived from pagan beliefs but was developed from the plain teaching of Scripture. God is one being in three persons. The following chart was developed by Bodie Hodge, Answers in Genesis, and provides numerous passages concerning the various attributes and works of each member of the Trinity.[7]

---

7. This chart is available online at http://www.answersingenesis.org/articles/2008/02/20/god-is-triune.

God . . .	The Father	The Son	The Holy Spirit
is the Creator	Genesis 1:1, 2:4, 14:19–22; Deuteronomy 32:6; Psalm 102:25; Isaiah 42:5, 45:18; Mark 13:19; 1 Corinthians 8:6; Ephesians 3:9; Hebrews 2:10; Revelation 4:11	John 1:1–3; Colossians 1:16–17; 1 Corinthians 8:6; Hebrews 1:2, 1:8–12	Genesis 1:2; Job 33:4; Psalm 104:30
is unchanging and eternal	Psalm 90:2, 102:25–27; Isaiah 43:10; Malachi 3:6	Micah 5:2; Colossians 1:17; Hebrews 1:8–12, 13:8; John 8:58	Hebrews 9:14
has a distinct will	Luke 22:42	Luke 22:42	Acts 13:2; 1 Corinthians 12:11
accepts worship	Too many to list	Matthew 14:33; Hebrews 1:6	—
accepts prayer	Too many to list	John 14:14; Romans 10:9–13; 2 Corinthians 12:8–9	—
is the only Savior	Isaiah 43:11, 45:21; Hosea 13:4; 1 Timothy 1:1	John 4:42; Acts 4:12, 13:23; Philippians 3:20; 2 Timothy 1:10; Titus 1:4, 2:13, 3:6; 2 Peter 1:11, 2:20, 3:18; 1 John 4:14	John 3:5; 1 Corinthians 12:3
has the power to resurrect	1 Thessalonians 1:8–10	John 2:19, 10:17	Romans 8:11
is called God	John 1:18, 6:27; Philippians 1:2, 2:11; Ephesians 4:6; 2 Thessalonians 1:2	John 1:1–5, 1:14, 1:18, 20:28; Colossians 2:9; Hebrews 1:8; Titus 2:13	Acts 5:3–4; 2 Corinthians 3:15–17
is called Mighty God	Isaiah 10:21; Luke 22:69	Isaiah 9:6	—
is omnipresent/ everywhere	1 Kings 8:27; Isaiah 46:10	Matthew 28:18–20	Psalm 139:7–10
is omnipotent/has power and authority	2 Chronicles 20:6, 25:8; Job 12:13; Romans 1:20; 1 Corinthians 6:14; Jude 1:25	John 3:31, 3:35, 14:6, 16:15; Philippians 2:9–11	1 Samuel 11:6; Luke 1:35
is omniscient/ all-knowing	Psalm 139:2; Isaiah 46:10; 1 John 3:20; Acts 15:8	John 16:3, 21:17	1 Corinthians 2:10–11

God . . .	The Father	The Son	The Holy Spirit
has the fullness of God in Him (not just "a part of God")	N/A	Colossians 2:9	—
gives life	Genesis 1:21, 1:24, 2:7; Psalm 49:15; John 3:16, 5:21; 1 Timothy 6:13	John 5:21, 14:6, 20:31; Romans 5:21	2 Corinthians 3:6; Romans 8:11
loves	John 3:16; Romans 8:39; Ephesians 6:23; 1 John 4:6, 4:16	Mark 10:21; John 15:9; Ephesians 5:25, 6:23	Romans 15:30
has ownership of believers	Psalm 24:1; John 8:47	Romans 7:4, 8:9	—
is distinct	Matthew 3:16–17, 28:19; John 17:1	Matthew 3:16–17, 4:1, 28:19; John 17:1	1 Samuel 19:20; Matthew 3:16–17, 4:1, 28:19
is Judge	Genesis 18:25; Psalm 7:11, 50:6, 94:1–2, 96:13, 98:9; John 8:50; Romans 2:16	John 5:21–27; Acts 17:31; 2 Corinthians 5:10; 2 Timothy 4:1	—
forgives sin	Micah 7:18	Luke 7:47–50	—
claimed divinity	Exodus 20:2	Matthew 26:63–64	—
is uncreated, the First and the Last, the Beginning and the End	Isaiah 44:6	Revelation 1:17–18, 22:13	—
lives in the believer	John 14:23; 2 Corinthians 6:16; 1 John 3:24	John 14:20–23; Galatians 2:20; Colossians 1:27	John 14:16–17; Romans 8:11; 1 Peter 1:11
has the title of deity, "I AM," pointing to the eternality of God	Exodus 3:14	John 8:58	—
is personal and has fellowship with other persons	1 John 1:3	1 Corinthians 1:9; 1 John 1:3	Acts 13:2; 2 Corinthians 13:14; Ephesians 4:30; Philippians 2:1
makes believers holy (sanctifies them)	1 Thessalonians 5:23	Colossians 1:22	1 Peter 1:2
knows the future	Isaiah 46:10; Jeremiah 29:11	Matthew 24:1–51, 26:64; John 16:32, 18:4	1 Samuel 10:10, 19:20; Luke 1:67; 2 Peter 1:21
is called "Lord of lords"	Deuteronomy 10:17; Psalm 136:3	Revelation 17:14, 19:16	—

Chapter 7

How Were People Saved Before Christ Died on the Cross?

Steve Fazekas

✿✿✿✿✿✿✿✿✿✿✿✿✿✿✿✿✿✿✿

Since the Gospel message is based on the death, burial, and Resurrection of Christ (1 Corinthians 15:1–4), many have wondered how people who lived prior to the Incarnation of Christ could have been saved. In Hebrews 11, sometimes known as the "gallery of faith" or the "faith hall of fame," we have a sampling of Old Testament saints whose lives pleased God. These heroes of the faith provide for us, even in these latter days, example after example of how to both live and die in times that are anything but receptive to the God of the Bible.

Yet a question continues to be raised over the faith of these heroes. Who or what was the source of the salvation and the object of the faith of men like Abel and Enoch? How did Joshua and Jeremiah exercise saving faith? How did redemption touch the lives of Ruth and Rahab?

Personal salvation by grace through faith in the atoning work of Christ on the Cross may not have been as clear at the time of Noah as it is to us today. The Lamb of God who takes away the sins of the world came to the nation of Israel approximately four hundred years after the Old Testament canon was closed. How then could there be a clear object of faith if the object had not yet appeared?

Abraham Was Saved by Grace Through Faith

The Apostle Paul dealt with an issue in Romans 4 that helps us answer this important question. He used the Old Testament to show salvation has always been by God's grace and can only be received through faith. While addressing those who thought they could save themselves by adhering to the Law of Moses, Paul made a brilliant argument.

> What then shall we say that Abraham our father has found according to the flesh? For if Abraham was justified by works, he has something to boast about, but not before God. For what does the Scripture say? "Abraham believed God, and it was accounted to him for righteousness." Now to him who works, the wages are not counted as grace but as debt.
>
> But to him who does not work but believes on Him who justifies the ungodly, his faith is accounted for righteousness. . . . Does this blessedness then come upon the circumcised only, or upon the uncircumcised also? For we say that faith was accounted to Abraham for righteousness. How then was it accounted? While he was circumcised, or uncircumcised? Not while circumcised, but while uncircumcised. . . . Therefore it is of faith that it might be according to grace, so that the promise might be sure to all the seed, not only to those who are of the law, but also to those who are of the faith of Abraham, who is the father of us all (Romans 4:1–16).

To demonstrate his point that salvation comes through faith instead of works, Paul referred to Abraham, the forefather of the Jewish people. He cited Genesis 15:6, which reveals that Abram (Abraham) "believed in the Lord, and He accounted it to him for righteousness." Circumcision was not introduced to Abraham and his descendants until Genesis 17 — more than ten years later.

Gospel Theme in the Old Testament

The Old Testament sets forth a gospel theme that people were saved from sin by grace through saving faith in the Lord and His promises. Several texts from the New Testament illustrate this premise.

> Of this salvation the prophets have inquired and searched carefully, who prophesied of the grace that would come to you,

searching what, or what manner of time, the *Spirit of Christ who was in them was indicating when He testified beforehand the sufferings of Christ and the glories that would follow.* To them it was revealed that, not to themselves, but to us they were ministering the things which now have been reported to you through those who have preached the gospel to you by the Holy Spirit sent from heaven — things which angels desire to look into (1 Peter 1:10–12, emphasis added).

This text reveals some important ideas. The "prophets . . . who prophesied" longed for the arrival of an era of grace. The "Spirit of Christ" within them was filling them with this great desire, witnessing through them and to them in advance of the work of Christ.

The prophetic message was often a gospel message since it told of the sufferings of the Messiah and the glories that would follow. The Spirit of Christ witnessed in advance about the sufferings and glories of Christ. The text indicates the prophets studied their own utterances and writings to plumb their depths. Yet according to this text, a Christ-led, Spirit-given understanding of this gospel theme was the core of the prophetic message.

The New Testament serves as the inspired commentary on the Old Testament, and it is an incredible blessing to have this in our hands. However, even before the completion of the New Testament, the Old Testament served as the Scripture for Israel, and it contained a gospel theme concerning the coming, sufferings, and glory of Messiah.

The second text underscoring the gospel theme of the Old Testament was spoken by Jesus Himself.

> Then He said to them, "O foolish ones, and slow of heart to believe in all that the prophets have spoken! Ought not the Christ to have suffered these things and to enter into His glory?" And beginning at Moses and all the Prophets, He expounded to them in all the Scriptures the things concerning Himself (Luke 24:25–27).

Here, Jesus spoke to a pair of His followers on the road to Emmaus. Notice the extent of His teaching. He began with Moses and the Prophets and opened to them in all the Scriptures the things pertaining to Himself, that is, His sufferings and His glory.

Later in the same chapter, Jesus spoke of His presence in the Old Testament Scriptures.

> Then He said to them, "These are the words which I spoke to you while I was still with you, that all things must be fulfilled which were written in the Law of Moses and the Prophets and the Psalms concerning Me." And He opened their understanding, that they might comprehend the Scriptures. Then He said to them, "Thus it is written, and thus it was necessary for the Christ

to suffer and to rise from the dead the third day, and that repentance and remission of sins should be preached in His name to all nations, beginning at Jerusalem" (Luke 24:44–47).

This text is loaded with gospel significance given by Jesus to His disciples. He referenced His presence in the Law of Moses, presumably the Pentateuch. He claimed the prophets testified about Him. He also showed that He could be found in the Psalms. Then Jesus collected these three areas and predicated them under one title — "the Scriptures." Again, the gospel significance of Old Testament content is remarkable. Central to the Lord's teaching about Himself in the Scriptures was the necessity of His suffering, His Resurrection, and His call to preach repentance for the remission of sins.

One final text illustrates the gospel theme found in the Old Testament, and it also spoke of things that took place before the Incarnation of Jesus upon this earth.

> But those things which God foretold by the mouth of all His prophets, that the Christ would suffer, He has thus fulfilled. Repent therefore and be converted, that your sins may be blotted out, so that times of refreshing may come from the presence of the Lord, and that He may send Jesus Christ, who was preached to you before, whom heaven must receive until the times of restoration of all things, which God has spoken by the mouth of all His holy prophets since the world began (Acts 3:18–24).

The Apostle Peter preached from Solomon's porch and called for the people to repent. He reminded the listening crowd that the suffering, Resurrection, and glory of the Messiah have been the major theme of the Scriptures.

The Scriptures teach that Jesus is its central theme. The primary message of the Bible is about His suffering, death, Resurrection, and glory.

Conclusion

So were there multiple ways of salvation prior to the coming of Jesus in space and time to die as a sacrifice for the sins of mankind? The answer must be a resounding "No." Paul explained in Romans 4 that salvation has always been and will always be by God's grace and received through faith alone.

Genesis 3:15 promised that Someone would come to clear up the sin problem created by our first father, Adam. As the seed of the woman, He would be the one to battle and defeat the serpent. Even Abel understood the nature of a bloody sacrifice and the death of a substitute, and because of his faith in God, he was regarded by God as righteous (Hebrews 11:4).

Thus, saturating all of Scripture, there is a gospel theme that showcases the suffering, Resurrection, and glory of the promised Savior, Jesus Christ. He is the central object of our faith and the fulfillment of all that the faithful who have preceded us down through the ages had believed in.

Chapter 8

Did Moses
Write Genesis?

Terry Mortenson and Bodie Hodge

❧❧❧❧❧❧❧❧❧❧❧❧❧❧❧❧❧❧❧

In the past few hundred years, the Bible has been under severe attack by scientific and philosophical skeptics of all sorts. In this scientific age the most-attacked book of the Bible has arguably been Genesis, particularly the first 11 chapters. Long-age geology, big-bang cosmology, secular archaeology, liberal theology, and philosophical attacks on miracles in the Bible have deceived many people to believe that the Bible is not true and therefore cannot be trusted.

One of the major attacks on the Bible in the past 300 years has been directed against Moses and his authorship of the Pentateuch, the first five books of the Old Testament (Genesis–Deuteronomy). Such attacks on these foundational books of the rest of the Bible come both from non-Christians as well as professing Christians.

Seminary courses, theology books, introductions to the Pentateuch in Bibles, and the secular media have promoted the man-made idea that Moses did not write the Pentateuch (also known as the Law or Torah). Instead, it is claimed that at least four different authors (or groups of authors) wrote various portions of these books over many centuries and then one or more redactors (editors) over many years combined and interwove everything together into its present form. For example, one translation of the Bible we surveyed said this in its introduction to the Pentateuch:

> Despite its unity of plan and purpose, the book is a complex work, not to be attributed to a single original author. Several sources, or literary traditions, that the final redactor used in his composition are discernable. These are the Yahwist (J), Elohist (E), and Priestly (P) sources which in turn reflect older oral traditions. . . .[1]

The introduction to the Old Testament in another Bible translation says that the J document was written by someone much later than Moses in the Southern Kingdom of Judah and the E document was written by someone in the Northern Kingdom of Israel.[2] Let's evaluate the arguments put forth in defense of this hypothesis.

The Documentary (or JEDP) Hypothesis

In this hypothesis, various sections of the Pentateuch are assigned to various authors who are identified by the letters J, E, D, and P. Hence, it is called the *documentary hypothesis* (or the *JEDP model*[3]). As this hypothesis was developed by a number of Jewish and theologically liberal Christian scholars in the late 17th to the late 19th centuries, there were a number of different proposals of who wrote what and when. But by the end of the 19th century liberal scholars had reached general agreement. The letters stand for:

> **J** documents are the sections, verses, or in some cases parts of verses that were written by one or more authors who preferred to use the Hebrew name *Jahweh* (Jehovah) to refer to God. It is proposed that this author wrote about 900–850 B.C.
>
> **E** documents are the texts that use the name *Elohim* for God and were supposedly written around 750–700 B.C.
>
> **D** stands for Deuteronomy, most of which was written by a different author or group of authors, perhaps around the time of King Josiah's reforms in 621 B.C.

---

1. *The New American Bible* (Nashville, TN: Memorial Bible Publishers, 1976), p. 1.
2. *The Dartmouth Bible* (Boston, MA: Houghton Mifflin, 1961), p. 8-9.
3. Some scholars rearrange these letters as JEPD, based on the order they believe the sections were written.

P stands for Priest and identifies the texts in Leviticus and elsewhere in the Pentateuch that were written by a priest or priests during the exile in Babylon after 586 B.C.

Then around 400 BC some redactors (i.e., editors) supposedly combined these four independently written texts to form the Pentateuch as it was known in the time of Jesus and modern times.

Development of the Documentary Hypothesis

Ibn Ezra was a very influential Jewish rabbi in the 12th century A.D. While he believed in the Mosaic authorship of the Pentateuch, he noticed that a few verses (e.g., Genesis 12:6, Genesis 22:14) had some phrases that seemed mysteriously out of place.[4] But he never pursued these mysteries to resolve them.[5]

About 500 years later, the famous Jewish philosopher Baruch (Benedict) Spinoza (1632–1677) picked up on what Ibn Ezra had stated and asserted that Ibn Ezra did not believe Moses wrote the Pentateuch. Others disagreed, pointing to other statements by Ibn Ezra that contradicted Spinoza's conclusion. In his book *Tractatus Theologico-Politicus* (1670), Spinoza, who was a pantheist and was subsequently excommunicated from the Jewish community and denounced by Christians, argued that Moses did not write the Pentateuch. Besides using the verses noted by Ibn Ezra, Spinoza offered a few other brief arguments against Mosaic authorship that were easily answered by Christian writers in the following few decades.[6]

Nevertheless, further attacks on the Mosaic authorship of the Pentateuch began taking hold in France through Jean Astruc, whose book

---

4. "Now the Canaanite was then in the land" (Genesis 12:6) and "as it is said to this day" (Genesis 22:14) might suggest that those phrases were written later than the rest of the verses they are in. In other words, they look like editorial comments.

5. Allan MacRae, *JEDP: Lectures on the Higher Criticism of the Pentateuch* (Hatfield, PA: Interdisciplinary Biblical Research Institute, 1994), p. 63.

6. Ibid., p. 63–64. Spinoza's arguments included these: 1) Numbers 12:3 says that Moses was the most humble man of his day, but a humble man would not write that about himself, 2) Moses is spoken of in the third person in the Pentateuch, which he would not do if he was the author, and 3) Moses could not have written his own obituary (Deuteronomy 34:5–6). In reply, even if the few verses (Genesis 12:6; 22:14, Numbers 12:3; Deuteronomy 34:5–6) are comments added by an inspired editor many years after Moses, that does not undermine the accuracy of the biblical testimony that Moses is the author of the Pentateuch. Second, modern authors often write about themselves in the third person, so this is nothing unusual.

Conjectures about the original memoirs which it appeared that Moses used in composing the Book of Genesis with certain remarks which help clarify these conjectures was published in 1753. He believed Moses was the author of the Pentateuch, but he unlocked the door for the skepticism of later scholars.

Astruc basically questioned, as others had before him, how Moses knew what happened prior to his own life, (i.e., the history recorded in Genesis). In other words, where did Moses get information on the patriarchs? Of course, there are several ways Moses could have obtained this information: divine revelation, previously written texts passed down through the generations, and/or oral tradition from his ancestors.[7] Regardless, under the guidance of the Holy Spirit (2 Peter 1:20–21), the books of Moses would be completely true and without error.

Astruc also noticed that *Elohim* (the Hebrew name for God in Genesis 1:1–2:3) was used in Genesis 1, but then the text switches to *Yahweh* (Jehovah) in chapter 2. Astruc claimed that these name changes indicated different sources that Moses used. Specifically, he thought that Genesis 1:1–2:3 was one creation account and Genesis 2:4–24 was a different creation account. Hence, we have the *Elohim* and *Jehovah* sections (or E and J documents).[8] Thus, the first assumption of the documentary hypothesis became established: the use of different divine names means different authors of the text.

The German scholar Johann Eichhorn took the next step by applying Astruc's idea to the whole of Genesis. Initially, in his 1780 *Introduction to the Old Testament*, Eichhorn said that Moses copied previous texts. But in later editions he apparently conceded the view of others that the J-E division could be applied to the whole of the Pentateuch which was written after Moses.[9]

Following Eichhorn, other ideas were advanced in denial of the Mosaic authorship of the first five books in the Old Testament. In 1802, Johann Vater insisted that Genesis was made from at least 39 fragments. In 1805, Wilhelm De Wette contended that none of the Pentateuch was

---

7. On this point, see Bodie Hodge, "How Was Moses Able to Read Pre-Tower of Babel Texts?" http://www.answersingenesis.org/home/area/feedback/2006/1027.asp, October 23, 2006.
8. MacRae, *JEDP*, p. 70–72.
9. MacRae, *JEDP*, p. 72–84.

written before King David and that Deuteronomy was written at the time of King Josiah.

From here, the door flew open to profess that other portions of the Law were not written by Moses. Not only was there a J-document, E-document and D-document, but then it was argued that Leviticus and some other portions of the Pentateuch were the work of Jewish priests, hence the P-documents.

And today, several variant views of documentary hypothesis exist, but perhaps the most popular is that of Julius Wellhausen proposed in 1895. Wellhausen put dates to the alleged four sources and none were earlier than around 900 B.C.[10] As noted Old Testament scholar Gleason Archer remarks, "Although Wellhausen contributed no innovations to speak of, he restated the documentary theory with great skill and persuasiveness, supporting the JEDP sequence upon an evolutionary basis."[11]

Even though a great many scholars and much of the public have accepted this view, is it really true? Did Moses have little or nothing to do with the writing of the Book of Genesis or the rest of the Pentateuch? Several lines of evidence should lead us to reject the documentary hypothesis as a fabrication of unbelievers.

Reasons to Reject the Documentary Hypothesis

There are many reasons to reject this skeptical attack on the Bible. First, consider what the Bible itself says about the authorship of the Pentateuch.

Biblical witness to Mosaic authorship

1. The chart below shows that the Pentateuch states that Moses wrote these books: Exodus 17:14; 24:4; 34:27; Numbers 33:1–2; Deuteronomy 31:9–11. In his rejection of Mosaic authorship, Wellhausen nowhere discussed this biblical evidence. It is easy to deny Mosaic authorship if one ignores the evidence for it. But that is not honest scholarship.
2. We also have the witness of the rest of the Old Testament: Joshua 1:8; 8:31–32; 1 Kings 2:3; 2 Kings 14:6; 21:8; Ezra 6:18; Nehemiah 13:1; Daniel 9:11–13; Malachi 4:4.

10. Josh McDowell, *A Ready Defense* (Nashville, TN: Thomas Nelson, 1993), p. 137–139.
11. Gleason Archer, *A Survey of Old Testament Introduction* (Chicago, IL: Moody Press, 1985), p. 89 (p. 95 in the 1994 edition).

3. The New Testament is also clear in its testimony: Matthew 19:8; John 5:45–47; 7:19; Acts 3:22; Romans 10:5; Mark 12:26. The divisions of the Old Testament were clearly in place in the Jewish mind long before the time of Christ, namely, the Law of Moses (first 5 books of the OT), the Prophets (the historical and prophetic books) and the Writings (the poetic books of Job, Psalms, Proverbs, etc.). So when Jesus referred to the Law of Moses, His Jewish listeners knew exactly to what He was referring.

Table 1 — Selected Passages Confirming Mosaic Authorship

Old Testament		
1	Exodus 17:14	Then the LORD said to Moses, "Write this for a memorial in the book and recount it in the hearing of Joshua, that I will utterly blot out the remembrance of Amalek from under heaven."
2	Numbers 33:2	Now Moses wrote down the starting points of their journeys at the command of the LORD. And these are their journeys according to their starting points:
	Joshua 1:7–8	Only be strong and very courageous, that you may observe to do according to all the law which Moses My servant commanded you; do not turn from it to the right hand or to the left, that you may prosper wherever you go. This Book of the Law shall not depart from your mouth, but you shall meditate in it day and night, that you may observe to do according to all that is written in it. For then you will make your way prosperous, and then you will have good success."
3	Joshua 8:31	as Moses the servant of the LORD had commanded the children of Israel, as it is written in the Book of the Law of Moses: "an altar of whole stones over which no man has wielded an iron tool." And they offered on it burnt offerings to the LORD, and sacrificed peace offerings. (See Exodus 20:24-25.)

	Joshua 23:6	Therefore be very courageous to keep and to do all that is written in the Book of the Law of Moses, lest you turn aside from it to the right hand or to the left.
4	1 Kings 2:3	And keep the charge of the LORD your God: to walk in His ways, to keep His statutes, His commandments, His judgments, and His testimonies, as it is written in the Law of Moses, that you may prosper in all that you do and wherever you turn.
5	2 Kings 14:6	But the children of the murderers he did not execute, according to what is written in the Book of the Law of Moses, in which the LORD commanded, saying, "Fathers shall not be put to death for their children, nor shall children be put to death for their fathers; but a person shall be put to death for his own sin." (See Deuteronomy 24:16.)
	1 Chronicles 22:13	Then you will prosper, if you take care to fulfill the statutes and judgments with which the LORD charged Moses concerning Israel. Be strong and of good courage; do not fear nor be dismayed.
6	Ezra 6:18	They assigned the priests to their divisions and the Levites to their divisions, over the service of God in Jerusalem, as it is written in the Book of Moses. (This is taught in the Books of Exodus and Leviticus.)
7	Nehemiah 13:1	On that day they read from the Book of Moses in the hearing of the people, and in it was found written that no Ammonite or Moabite should ever come into the assembly of God. (See Deuteronomy 23:3–5.)

8	Daniel 9:11	Yes, all Israel has transgressed Your law, and has departed so as not to obey Your voice; therefore the curse and the oath written in the Law of Moses the servant of God have been poured out on us, because we have sinned against Him.
9	Malachi 4:4	Remember the Law of Moses, My servant, which I commanded him in Horeb for all Israel, with the statutes and judgments.
New Testament		
10	Matthew 8:4	And Jesus said to him, "See that you tell no one; but go your way, show yourself to the priest, and offer the gift that Moses commanded, as a testimony to them." (See Leviticus 14:1–32.)
11	Mark 12:26	But concerning the dead, that they rise, have you not read in the book of Moses, in the burning bush passage, how God spoke to him, saying, "I am the God of Abraham, the God of Isaac, and the God of Jacob"? (See Exodus 3:6.)
12	Luke 16:29	Abraham said to him, "They have Moses and the prophets; let them hear them."
13	Luke 24:27	And beginning at Moses and all the Prophets, He expounded to them in all the Scriptures the things concerning Himself.
14	Luke 24:44	Then He said to them, "These are the words which I spoke to you while I was still with you, that all things must be fulfilled which were written in the Law of Moses and the Prophets and the Psalms concerning Me."
15	John 5:46	For if you believed Moses, you would believe Me; for he wrote about Me.
16	John 7:22	Moses therefore gave you circumcision (not that it is from Moses, but from the fathers), and you circumcise a man on the Sabbath.

17	Acts 3:22	For Moses truly said to the fathers, "The LORD your God will raise up for you a Prophet like me from your brethren. Him you shall hear in all things, whatever He says to you. (See Deuteronomy 18:15.)
18	Acts 15:1	And certain men came down from Judea and taught the brethren, "Unless you are circumcised according to the custom of Moses, you cannot be saved."
19	Acts 28:23	So when they had appointed him a day, many came to him at his lodging, to whom he explained and solemnly testified of the kingdom of God, persuading them concerning Jesus from both the Law of Moses and the Prophets, from morning till evening.
20	Romans 10:5	For Moses writes about the righteousness which is of the law, "The man who does those things shall live by them." (See Leviticus 18:1–5.)
21	Romans 10:19	But I say, did Israel not know? First Moses says: "I will provoke you to jealousy by those who are not a nation, I will move you to anger by a foolish nation." (See Deuteronomy 32:21.)
22	1 Corinthians 9:9	For it is written in the law of Moses, "You shall not muzzle an ox while it treads out the grain." Is it oxen God is concerned about? (See Deuteronomy 25:4.)
23	2 Corinthians 3:15	But even to this day, when Moses is read, a veil lies on their heart.

Take note of some the references back to Moses' work. For example, John 7:22 and Acts 15:1 refer to Moses giving the doctrine of circumcision. Yet John also reveals that this came earlier — in Genesis, with Abraham. Nevertheless, it is credited to Moses because it was recorded in his writings. The New Testament attributes all the books from Genesis through Deuteronomy as being the writings of Moses. So to attack the Mosaic authorship of the first five books of the Old

Testament then is to attack the truthfulness of the rest of the biblical writers and Jesus Himself.

Moses' Qualifications to Write

Not only is there abundant biblical witness that Moses wrote the Pentateuch, Moses was fully qualified to write the Pentateuch. He received an Egyptian royal education (Acts 7:22) and was an eyewitness to the events recorded in Exodus to Deuteronomy, which contain many references or allusions to Egyptian names of places, people, and gods, as well as Egyptian words, idioms, and cultural factors. He also consistently demonstrated an outsider's view of Canaan (from the perspective of Egypt or Sinai).[12] And as a prophet of God he was the appropriate recipient of the written records or oral traditions of the patriarchs from Adam to his own day, which the Holy Spirit could use to guide Moses to write the inerrant text of Genesis. There is no other ancient Hebrew who was more qualified than Moses to write the Pentateuch.

Fallacious Reasoning of the Skeptics

A final reason for rejecting the documentary hypothesis and accepting the biblical testimony to the Mosaic authorship of the Pentateuch is the erroneous assumptions and reasoning of the liberal scholars and other skeptics.

1. They assumed their conclusion. They assumed that the Bible is not a supernatural revelation from God and then manipulated the biblical text to arrive at that conclusion. They were implicitly deistic or atheistic in their thinking.
2. They assumed that Israel's religion was simply the invention of man, a product of evolution, as all other religions are.
3. Based on evolutionary ideas, they assumed that "the art of writing was virtually unknown in Israel prior to the establishment of the Davidic monarchy; therefore there could have been no written records going back to the time of Moses."[13] This claim not only attacks the intelligence of the ancient Israelites, but also the Egyptians who trained Moses. Were the Egyptians incapable of teaching Moses how to read and write? Since the time the

12. Archer, *A Survey*, p. 114–123.
13. Ibid., p. 175.

documentary hypothesis was first proposed, archaeologists have discovered scores of written records pre-dating the time of Moses. It is hard to believe that Israel's ancient neighbors knew how to write, but the Jews could not.

4. Liberal Bible scholars allegedly based their theories on evidence from the biblical text and yet they evaded the biblical evidence that refutes their theories. Theirs was a "pick and choose" approach to studying the Bible, which is hardly honest scholarship in pursuit of truth.

5. They arbitrarily assumed that the Hebrew authors were different from all other writers in history — that the Hebrews were incapable of using more than one name for God, or more than one writing style regardless of the subject matter, or more than one of several possible synonyms for a single idea.

6. Their subjective bias led them to illegitimately assume that any biblical statement was unreliable until proven reliable (though they would not do this with any other ancient or modern text) and when they found any disagreement between the Bible and ancient pagan literature, the latter was automatically given preference and trusted as a historical witness. The former violates the well-accepted concept known as Aristotle's dictum, which advises that the benefit of the doubt should be given to the document itself, rather than the critic. In other words, the Bible (or any other book) should be considered innocent until proven guilty, or reliable until its unreliability is compellingly demonstrated.

7. Although many examples have been found of an ancient Semitic author using repetition and duplication in his narrative technique, skeptical scholars assume that when Hebrew authors did this, it is compelling evidence of multiple authorship of the biblical text.

8. The skeptics erroneously assumed, without any other ancient Hebrew literature to compare with the biblical text, that they could, with scientific reliability, establish the date of the composition of each book of the Bible.[14]

9. To date, no manuscript evidence of the J-document, E-document, P-document, D-document, or any of the other supposed fragments

---

14. The points are explained in Archer, *A Survey*, p. 109–113.

have ever been discovered. And there are no ancient Jewish commentaries that mention any of these imaginary documents or their alleged unnamed authors. All the manuscript evidence we have is for the first five books of the Bible just as we have them today. This is confirmed by the singular Jewish testimony (until the last few centuries) that these books are the writings of Moses.

Is JEDP/Documentary Hypothesis the Same Thing as the Tablet Model of Genesis?

These two ways of dividing Genesis are not the same at all. The Tablet Model is based on the Hebrew word *toledoth*, which appears 11 times in Genesis (2:4; 5:1; 6:9; 10:1; 11:10; 11:27; 25:12; 25:19; 36:1; 36:9; 37:2) and helps to tie the whole book together as a single history. Our English Bibles translate *toledoth* variously as "this is the account" or "these are the generations" of Adam, Noah, Shem, etc. Scholars disagree about whether each *toledoth* follows or precedes the text with which it is associated, though we are inclined to agree with those scholars who conclude the former. In this case, the name associated with the *toledoth* is either the author or custodian of that section (see for example, Table 2 below). Regardless, the 11 uses of *toledoth* unite the book as a history of the key events and people from creation to the time of Moses.

Unlike the JEDP model, the Tablet Model shows a reverence for the text of Genesis and attention to these explicit divisions provided by the book itself. These divisions represent either oral tradition or written texts passed down by the Genesis patriarchs to their descendants,[15] which

---

15. All people need to know where they came from, where their place in history is, or they will be very confused people. Every culture, no matter how "primitive" (by our arrogant Western standards), teaches history to their children (how accurate that history may be is a separate question). It is therefore most unreasonable to think that the Genesis patriarchs would not record and pass on the history they had to the next generation. And studies of non-literate people groups have shown that they have much better memories for maintaining the accuracy of their oral traditions than people groups that rely primarily on written communication to learn and pass on information. See Kenneth E. Bailey, "Informal Controlled Oral Tradition and the Synoptic Gospels," *Themelios* 20.2 (January 1995): 4–11, (http://www.biblicalstudies.org.uk/article_tradition_bailey.html, accessed January 21, 2011), and "Oral Traditions — Oral Traditions as A Source and as a Method of Historical Construction," http://science.jrank.org/pages/10523/Oral-Traditions-Oral-Traditions-Source-Method-Historical-Construction.html, accessed January 21, 2011.

Moses then used to put Genesis into its final form under the inspiration of the Holy Spirit.

We think it very likely that Moses was working with written documents because the second *toledoth* (Genesis 5:1) reads "this is the book of the generations of Adam" where "book" is a translation of the normal Hebrew word meaning a written document. Also, the account of the Flood after the third *toledoth* (Genesis 6:9) reads like a ship's log. Only evolutionary thinking would lead us to conclude that Adam and his descendants could not write. Early man was very intelligent: Cain built a city (Genesis 4:17), six generations later people were making musical instruments and had figured out how to mine ores and make metals (Genesis 4:21–22), Noah built a huge boat for his family and thousands of animals to survive a year-long flood, etc.[16]

The biblical doctrine of the inspiration of Scripture does not require us to conclude that all the books of the Bible were written by God dictating to the human authors. Dictation was one means employed, very often in the prophetic books (e.g., the prophet says, "The Word of the Lord came to me saying"). But much of the Bible was written from the eyewitness experience of the authors (e.g., 2 Peter 1:16) or as a result of research by the author (e.g., Luke 1:1–4). And just as Christian authors today can quote truthful statements from non-Christian sources without thereby endorsing their wrong ideas, so the biblical authors could quote non-believers or non-biblical sources without introducing false statements into their divine writings (e.g., Joshua 10:13, 2 Samuel 1:18, Acts 17:28, Titus 1:12, Jude 14–15). So it is perfectly reasonable to think that Moses wrote Genesis from pre-existing, well-preserved oral tradition and/or written documents from the patriarchs.

Unlike those who affirm Mosaic authorship of Genesis and divide the text by the *toledoths*, JEDP adherents divide the text on the basis of the names of God that were used and say that, at best, Moses simply wove these texts together, often in contradictory ways. However, most JEDP advocates would say that Moses had nothing to do with writing Genesis or the rest of the Pentateuch, which were written much later by many authors and editors.

---

16. For more on this topic, see Henry Morris, *The Genesis Record* (Grand Rapids, MI: Baker Book House, 1976), p. 22–30, and Curt Sewell, "The Tablet Theory of Genesis Authorship," *Bible and Spade*, Vol. 7:1 (Winter 1994), http://www.trueorigin.org/tablet.asp.

Table 2 Breakdown of the Toledoth Sections from Genesis 1–11[17]

Beginning	End	Probable author of original work from which Moses drew
Genesis 1:1	Genesis 2:4a	Adam by direct divine revelation, so not connected with Adam's name
Genesis 2:4b	Genesis 5:1a	Adam
Genesis 5:1b	Genesis 6:9a	Noah
Genesis 6:9b	Genesis 10:1	Shem, Ham, and Japheth
Genesis 10:2	Genesis 11:10a	Shem
Genesis 11:10b	Genesis 11:27a	Terah
Genesis 11:27b	Genesis 25:12a	Abraham
Genesis 25:12b	Genesis 25:19a	Ishmael
Genesis 25:19b	Genesis 36:1a	Esau
Genesis 36:1b	Genesis 36:9a	Jacob?
Genesis 36:9b	Genesis 37:2	Jacob
Genesis 37:2b	Genesis 50:26	Joseph

Answering a Few Objections

A number of objections have been raised by the proponents of the documentary hypothesis. Space allows us to respond to only a few of the most common ones. But the other objections are just as flawed in terms of logic and a failure to pay careful attention to the biblical text.

> 1. Moses couldn't have written about his own death, which shows that he didn't write Deuteronomy.

The death of Moses is recorded in Deuteronomy 34:5–12. These are the last few verses of the book. Like other literature, past and present, it is not uncommon for an obituary to be added at the end of someone's work after he dies, especially if he died very soon after writing the book. The obituary in no way nullifies the claim that the author wrote the book.

In the case of Deuteronomy, the author of the obituary of Moses was probably Joshua, a close associate of Moses who was chosen by God to

---

17. The record of Esau's descendants contains a *toledoth* before and after it, which is problematic for either view of the connection of the *toledoth* to the text. Perhaps it signifies that the account of Esau (Gen 36:1–9) was inserted into the account written by Jacob (Gen 25:19b–37:2), since Jacob (not Esau) was the son of promise in the Messianic line from Adam.

lead the people of Israel into the Promised Land (for Moses was not allowed to because of his disobedience), and who was inspired by God to write the next book in the Old Testament. A similar obituary of Joshua was added by an inspired editor to the end of Joshua's book (Joshua 24:29–33).

2. The author of Genesis 12:6 seems to imply that the Canaanites were removed from the land, which took place well after Moses died.

Abram passed through the land to the place of Shechem, as far as the terebinth tree of Moreh. And the Canaanites were then in the land. (Genesis 12:6).

So the argument is that an author *after* Moses had to have written this statement to know that the Canaanites were removed in the days of Joshua who began judging the Canaanites for their sin after Moses died.

Two things can be said in response. First, Moses could have easily written this without knowing that the Canaanites would be removed after his death, because due to warring kingdoms or other factors, people groups did get removed from territories. So it was just a statement of fact about who was living in the land at the time of Abraham. But also, it could also be a comment added by a later editor working under divine inspiration. The editorial comment would in no way deny the Mosaic authorship of the Book of Genesis. Editors sometimes add to books by deceased authors and no one then denies that the deceased wrote the book.[18]

3. Genesis 14:14 mentions the Israelite region of Dan, which was assigned to that tribe during the conquest led by Joshua after Moses died. So Moses could not have written this verse.

Now when Abram heard that his brother[19] was taken captive, he armed his three hundred and eighteen trained servants who were

---

18. Though modern editors do this usually in a footnote, we cannot demand the same literary convention be applied to the ancient editors.

19. Just as "son of" in Hebrew doesn't always mean a literal father-son relationship, so the Hebrew word translated here as "brother" doesn't always mean a literal brother, but can refer more generally to a familial or tribal relative. In this case, Lot was Abraham's brother's son, i.e., Abraham's nephew.

born in his own house, and went in pursuit as far as Dan. He divided his forces against them by night, and he and his servants attacked them and pursued them as far as Hobah, which is north of Damascus (Genesis 14:14–15).

Genesis 14:14 mentions Dan. However, Dan in this context is not the region of Dan, that Israelite tribe's inheritance given when the Jews took the Promised Land, but a specific ancient town of Dan, north of the Sea of Galilee that was in existence long before the Israelites entered the land. Jewish historian Josephus, just after the time of Christ, says:

> When Abram heard of their calamity, he was at once afraid for Lot his kinsman, and pitied the Sodomites, his friends and neighbours; and thinking it proper to afford them assistance, he did not delay it, but marched hastily, and the fifth night attacked the Assyrians, near Dan, for that is the name of the other spring of Jordan; and before they could arm themselves, he slew some as they were in their beds, before they could suspect any harm; and others, who were not yet gone to sleep, but were so drunk they could not fight, ran away."[20]

This specific place was known to Abraham as one of the springs of Jordan. It is possible that Rachel was already aware of that name, as it meant "judge," and used it for the son of her handmaiden (Genesis 30:6). It seems Rachel viewed this as the Lord finally turning the tide in judgment and permitting her a son. In the same way, this was where the Lord judged his enemies through Abraham.

But again, even if "near Dan, for that is the name of the other spring of Jordan" was added by a later inspired editor, this would not mean that it was inaccurate to say the Moses wrote Genesis.[21]

---

20. Revised Works of Josephus, chapter 10: "The Assyrian army pursued and defeated by Abram — Birth of Ishmael — Circumcision instituted, 1912–1910 B.C., Taken from: The Online Bible, by Larry Pierce.

21. But let's assume for moment that it was referring to the region Dan, where Israelites, who were from the tribe of Dan, settled. Would this be a problem for Moses? No. It was Moses who wrote where the allotments would be! In Numbers 34:1–15, Moses described the general vicinity of the borders of the various tribes. So this would actually be further confirmation of Mosaic authorship, had this been referring to descendants of Israelite Dan's territory.

4. The author of Genesis 36:31 obviously knew about kings in Israel which took place well after Moses, so Moses could not have written this.

Such a claim is without warrant. Moses was clearly aware that this had been prophesied about the nation of Israel when the Lord told Abraham (Genesis 17:6) and Jacob (Genesis 35:11) that Israel would have kings. Also, Moses himself prophesied in Deuteronomy 17:14–20 that Israel would have kings. So knowing that kings were coming was already common knowledge to Moses.

Conclusion

There is abundant biblical and extra-biblical evidence that Moses wrote the Pentateuch during the wilderness wanderings after the Jews left their slavery in Egypt and before they entered the Promised Land (about 1445–1405 B.C.). Contrary to the liberal theologians and other skeptics, it was not written after the Jews returned from exile in Babylon (ca. 500 B.C.). Christians who believe Moses wrote the Pentateuch do not need to feel intellectually intimidated. It is the enemies of the truth of God that are failing to think carefully and face the facts honestly.

As a prophet of God, Moses wrote under divine inspiration, guaranteeing the complete accuracy and absolute authority of his writings. Those writings were endorsed by Jesus and the New Testament Apostles, who based their teaching and the truth of the gospel on the truths revealed in the books of Moses, including the truths about a literal six-day creation about 6,000 years ago, the Curse on the whole creation when Adam sinned, and the judgment of the global, catastrophic Flood at the time of Noah.

The attack on the Mosaic authorship of the Pentateuch is nothing less than an attack on the veracity, reliability, and authority of the Word of Almighty God. Christians should believe God rather than the fallible, sinful skeptics inside and outside the Church who, in their intellectual arrogance, are consciously or unconsciously trying to undermine the Word so that they can justify in their own minds (but not before God) their rebellion against God. As Paul says in Romans 3:4, "Let God be true but every man a liar."

Chapter 9

Did Miracles
Really Happen?

Paul Taylor

❀❀❀❀❀❀❀❀❀❀❀❀❀❀❀❀❀❀

The Christian encyclopedic website Theopedia has defined a miracle as "any action in time where the normal operation of nature is suspended by the agency of a supernatural action."[1]

Essentially, a miracle is an unusual manifestation of God's power designed to accomplish a specific purpose. The consistent Christian recognizes that God's power is constantly displayed in the clockwork operation of the universe. The Bible teaches us that it is Christ's power that holds everything together (Hebrews 1:3). Yet we would not call that power a miracle because it is the *normal* way God upholds the universe. A miracle must be unusual if it is to be called a miracle.

A miracle is not necessarily a violation of the laws of nature. God could demonstrate His power by using the laws of nature in an unusual way. For example, God used wind (a natural phenomenon) to drive back the water of the Red Sea, allowing the exodus of the Israelites (Exodus 14:21). Although there is no obvious violation of physics, who could doubt that the parting of the Red Sea constitutes a miracle? At the very least, the timing of the event was miraculous. Of course, if God wants to

---

1. http://www.theopedia.com/Miracle, accessed March 3, 2011.

suspend a law of nature, He is free to do so. They are His laws after all. But we should be careful about assuming God has suspended a law of nature to perform any particular miracle. After all, we do not even know all the laws of nature.

Most definitions given for the word *miracle* are interestingly partial. The popular Christian author and broadcaster C.S. Lewis wrote this in the introduction to his book on the subject: "I use the word *Miracle* to mean an interference with Nature by supernatural power."[2] On the same page, he footnoted this definition with an explanation.

> This definition is not that which would be given by many theologians. I am adopting it not because I think it an improvement upon theirs but precisely because, being crude and "popular," it enables me most easily to treat those questions which "the common reader" probably has in mind when he takes up a book on Miracles.[3]

Lewis used his book to argue that miracles exist. To do so, he made use of a concept from outside nature — the supernatural.

The 18th-century secular philosopher David Hume had a different approach. He defined a miracle as "a transgression of a law of nature by a particular volition of the Deity, or by the interposition of some invisible agent."[4] He went on to argue that the evidence will always be stronger for natural laws than for miracles, and hence he concluded that the wise man should always favor natural law instead of a miracle. Hence, miracles do not happen. Hume's definition goes beyond the standard definition of a miracle. Nonetheless, even if we accept his restricted definition, his argument does not stand.[5]

---

2. C.S. Lewis, *Miracles* (London: Harper Collins, 1947), p. 5.
3. Ibid.
4. David Hume, *An Enquiry Concerning Human Understanding*, Section X, "Of Miracles," Part I, Section 90 In a footnote).
5. In a sense, Hume attempted to define miracles out of existence. However, according to the guidelines he set forth, one should conclude the Resurrection really did happen, since it would be far more miraculous to accept an alternate theory of the Resurrection, than it would to accept God raised His Son from the dead. For example, it would be a far greater miracle for more than 500 people to hallucinate the same thing than it would for Jesus (a man who regularly worked miracles according to those who saw Him and predicted His own Resurrection) than it would for God to raise Christ to life. See chapter 4 for more information on the Resurrection.

The arguments used by both Hume and Lewis have been critiqued as using circular reasoning. Circular reasoning is the logical fallacy whereby the conclusion to an argument is assumed as a presupposition. The notion that miracles are impossible because they would (potentially) go beyond the laws of nature is not a rational argument. It merely presupposes the very thing it is supposed to be proving. The tacit assumption in the argument is that anything that goes beyond the laws of nature is impossible. But this is simply a restatement of the presupposed conclusion that there are no miracles (under Hume's definition).

Some have suggested the creationist argument is also circular, since it assumes the inerrancy of Scripture. However, the inerrancy of Scripture can be argued without assuming up front that violations of natural law ever occur. In fact, the very existence of laws of nature makes no sense apart from Scripture, as we have written elsewhere. David Hume was stumped by this very issue; he could not come up with a rational basis for induction (the temporal consistency of laws of nature) apart from the Christian worldview. Our presupposition that the Bible is true is therefore justified by the existence of uniform laws of nature, regardless of whether or not such laws are immutable. Therefore, it makes complete sense, logically and consistently, to look for the way miracles are described in the Bible and, using our presupposition that the Bible is true, see what case can be made for their existence.

The Word "Miracle" in the Old Testament

Three Hebrew words are used to represent miracles in the Old Testament. These are 'ōth, mō-phēth, and pālā'.

1. 'ōth — The word 'ōth means "sign."[6] The word can be seen in the emphasized part of the following verses.

   Then God said, "Let there be lights in the firmament of the heavens to divide the day from the night; and let them be for *signs* and seasons, and for days and years" (Genesis 1:14, emphasis added).

   And the LORD set a *mark* on Cain, lest anyone finding him should kill him (Genesis 4:15, emphasis added).

---

6. James Strong, *Enhanced Strong's Lexicon*, electronic edition (Ontario: Woodside Bible Fellowship, 1995), s.v., #H266.

Neither of the above verses used *sign* to imply a miracle happened. Instead, the sign is there for a purpose. In Genesis 1, the signs are literal, as people have always used the stars for direction. In Genesis 4, the mark signifies that Cain is not to be killed.

However, in other verses, we do see 'ōth representing miracles. This illustrates that miracles were for a purpose — to demonstrate God's power.

> I will harden Pharaoh's heart, and multiply My *signs* and My wonders in the land of Egypt (Exodus 7:3, emphasis added).

This same word is translated as miracles in a number of places in some English versions.

> Because all those men which have seen my glory, and my *miracles*, which I did in Egypt and in the wilderness . . . (Numbers 14:22; KJV, emphasis added).

> And his *miracles*, and his acts, which he did in the midst of Egypt unto Pharaoh the king of Egypt, and unto all his land (Deuteronomy 11:3; KJV, emphasis added).

2. *mō-phēth* — If 'ōth is for miracles that display God's power, then *mō-phēth* implies miracles "exhibited by God to produce conviction."[7] The word *mō-phēth* is frequently translated as "wonders" and is often used in conjunction with 'ōth (e.g., "signs and wonders").

> And the Lord said to Moses, "When you go back to Egypt, see that you do all those *wonders* before Pharaoh which I have put in your hand" (Exodus 4:21, emphasis added).

> You have seen all that the Lord did before your eyes in the land of Egypt, to Pharaoh and to all his servants and to all his land — the great trials which your eyes have seen, the signs, and those great *wonders* (Deuteronomy 29:2–3, emphasis added)

3. *pālā'* — Less frequent as a word for miracles is *pālā'*, which refers to something marvelous or wondrous. Thus, when Gideon asked about where all the miracles had gone, which accompanied the

---

7. W. Wilson, *Old Testament Word Studies*, reprint (McLean, VA: Macdonald Publishing, 1870, 1990), p. 487.

children of Israel leaving Egypt, he put a different emphasis on the miracles than the previous two words would. He concentrated on the *display* of the miracles, rather than their *purpose*.

> Gideon said to Him, "O my lord, if the LORD is with us, why then has all this happened to us? And where *are* all His miracles which our fathers told us about, saying, 'Did not the LORD bring us up from Egypt?' But now the LORD has forsaken us and delivered us into the hands of the Midianites" (Judges 6:13).

In summary, the Old Testament uses three words for miracles — one stresses God's power, another is designed to produce conviction, and the other emphasizes the effect of the miracles.

The Word "Miracle" in the New Testament

Three New Testament Greek words need to be covered in this discussion.

1. *dunamis* (δύναμις) — The implication of this word is a sense of power. Vine stated that it "is used of works of a supernatural origin and character, such as could not be produced by natural agents and means."[8] This sense of power is why the word was taken into the English language in such concepts as *dynamo* or *dynamic*.

In many ways, this word is the equivalent of the Hebrew *pālā*. It is translated as miracles in such places as Acts 8:13, 1 Corinthians 12:10, and Galatians 3:5.

> Then Simon himself also believed; and when he was baptized he continued with Philip, and was amazed, seeing the *miracles* and signs which were done (Acts 8:13, emphasis added).

> Therefore He who supplies the Spirit to you and works *miracles* among you, does He do it by the works of the law, or by the hearing of faith? (Galatians 3:5, emphasis added).

2. *semeion* (σημεῖον) — This word means a miracle, sign, or wonder, so it is the New Testament equivalent of 'ōth. It seems to refer to

---

8. W.E. Vine, *Expository Dictionary of New Testament Words* (Mclean, VA: Macdonald Publishing, 1983), p. 757.

"an unusual occurrence, transcending the common course of nature."[9]

Now when Herod saw Jesus, he was exceedingly glad; for he had desired for a long time to see Him, because he had heard many things about Him, and he hoped to see some *miracle* done by Him (Luke 23:8, emphasis added).

For, indeed, that a notable *miracle* has been done through them is evident to all who dwell in Jerusalem, and we cannot deny it (Acts 4:16, emphasis added).

3. *teras* (τέρας) — *Teras* is not actually translated as miracles, but I have included it here, because it is translated as wonders and seems to be a New Testament equivalent of the Hebrew *mō-phēth*. As such, it frequently occurs with *semeion*, as the phrase "signs and wonders."

In summary, the use of words for miracles in the New Testament seems to be similar to that in the Old Testament. One word concentrates on pointing to God as the source of the miracle, another to the wondrous character of the miracle itself, and another to a declaration of God's power.

Armed with this set of biblical definitions for miracles, we should examine some actual miracles to see how God worked through them.

Occurrence of Miracles Throughout the Old Testament

If a biblical miracle is recognized as an occurrence that is clearly of a miraculous nature, identifies God as its source, and declares God's power, then we see miracles in nearly every book of the Bible. It is unrealistic for the purposes of this study to list every miracle.

Probably the most miraculous event of all would be God's creation of the heavens and the earth. During the creation week, God created through miraculous means. Our current natural laws were being set up as God miraculously created our universe and everything in it. Other miraculous events in Genesis would include the Flood, the confusion of languages at Babel, and the destruction of Sodom and Gomorrah.

The events during the life of Moses are especially significant. At the birth of the nation of Israel, God seemed to be emphasizing who He

9. Ibid., p. 757.

was and is and how powerful He is. The purpose of the plagues is interesting.

> But I am sure that the king of Egypt will not let you go, no, not even by a mighty hand. So I will stretch out My hand and strike Egypt with all My wonders which I will do in its midst; and after that he will let you go (Exodus 3:19–20).

The miraculous signs that were to be performed before Pharaoh were not specifically designed to instantly persuade Pharaoh. Indeed, God indicated that Pharaoh would not let the people go immediately. Instead, the signs were to demonstrate God's nature and power.

Throughout the rest of the Old Testament, we read about numerous miracles: water appearing in the hollow place in Lehi (Judges 15:19); the idol Dagon falling twice before the ark of the covenant (1 Samuel 5:1–12); a widow's son raised from the dead (1 Kings 17:17–24); Shadrach, Meshach, and Abed-Nego delivered from the fiery furnace in Babylon (Daniel 3:10–27); and Jonah swallowed by a big fish (Jonah 2:1–10). Although there are clusters of miracles, for example, at the time of Moses and at the time of Elijah and Elisha, there were many other times during the Old Testament period when God performed miracles.

Miracles of Jesus

In the New Testament, miracles took on an even more important role because of the presence of Jesus, the second person of the Trinity. Some miracles allude to the Lord's divine power as Creator. In John 2 Jesus not only turned water into wine, but also, according to the master of the feast, the wine was of the best quality. Wine is itself a complex mixture of chemicals. Good wine requires an aging process during which slow chemical changes are taking place in the mixture. Jesus miraculously created wine that had not undergone the normal aging process. It is not surprising He could do this since He created all the individual atoms in the first place.

Another creative miracle occurred in Matthew 14:13–21 when Jesus fed 5,000 people, starting with just five loaves and two fish. Not only was everyone fed, but also there were 12 baskets full of leftovers. Why was there so much leftover? The miracle demonstrated His power and emphasized new material had been created.

Three specific miracles performed by Jesus are generally considered to be Messianic miracles (i.e., miracles that would indicate the miracle-worker was the Messiah):

1. The healing of a leper (Matthew 8:2–4)
2. The casting out of a demon that caused a man to be mute and blind (Matthew 12:22–37)
3. The healing of a man born blind (John 9:1–41)[10]

A miraculous healing from leprosy was extremely rare. (Two special cases deserve mention. Miriam was given leprosy for seven days for speaking against Moses and was subsequently healed. Naaman was a Gentile Syrian healed of leprosy.) Instead, lepers were to be treated as unclean. In Jewish exorcism rituals, it was necessary to get the possessing demon to give its name. This could not happen if the demon caused dumbness. And although people who had become blind could be healed, the healing of a man born blind is of exceptional note. So there would seem to be strong evidence that these three miracles authenticate Christ's claim to be the Messiah.

Miracles subsequent to Christ's life and death also appear to authenticate Him as the Messiah since they were performed "in the name of Jesus." For example, when Peter and John healed a lame man, Peter said:

> Silver and gold I do not have, but what I do have I give you: In the name of Jesus Christ of Nazareth, rise up and walk (Acts 3:6).

Witnesses

Miracles were done for a specific purpose — pointing to God and demonstrating His power — and they were often performed before witnesses. The reactions and accounts of these witnesses are mentioned in Scripture. For those who take the Bible seriously, this is absolute proof these miracles happened. Indeed, if we started from the premise that miracles could not happen, this would undermine our belief in Scripture since so many important events were miracles worked by God.

Those who start with the presupposition that Scripture is not true have a difficult problem with miracles as well, because of the

---

10. Arnold Fruchtenbaum, *The Three Messianic Miracles*, available from Ariel Ministries: http://arielc.org/mm5/merchant.mvc?Screen=PROD&Store_Code=amc&Product_Code=pmbs035-DLD.pdf.

large number of miracles specified. Often, non-believers want to infer that miracles are listed for symbolic purpose. But if this were true, then the symbolism would be lost because otherwise reliable witnesses would actually be deceivers or deceived. It is not satisfactory to claim that good moral lessons are taught from events that never happened, related by people who lied or were deceived! It is difficult to accept that all these witnesses could be wrong when we look at the caliber of the witnesses, such as Abraham, Moses, Daniel, Luke, and especially Jesus. Even members of the Sanhedrin, who were strongly opposed to the gospel message, admitted Peter and John had performed a "notable miracle" (Acts 4:16).

Miracles and Evolution

It is increasingly difficult to understand how Christians, who believe in the New Testament miracles of Jesus, fail to believe the miracles of the creation week in Genesis. The genuine miracles in the New Testament are not offered as a proof of creation but as a necessary corollary. Those who believe creation happened exactly as God revealed in Genesis 1 have no problem accepting the later miracles.

We have seen how some of Christ's miracles point to His creative power. This makes complete sense when we realize the Bible describes Jesus as the Creator (see John 1, Colossians 1, and Hebrews 1). The theistic evolutionist, on the other hand, believes God stepped in at certain times during human history, but he has no precedent for miracles since he thinks everything gradually evolved over millions of years of prehistory. This is inconsistent thinking. A theology of miracles is problematic when isolated from God's creative actions in Genesis.

I am reminded of a statement made by a speaker I heard while I was at Nottingham University Christian Union in the late 1970s. He implored us to "get your theology right on Genesis. Then everything else will fall into place." I have witnessed this to be true time and time again. If we distrust God's Word in Genesis, then we will be inconsistent in how we interpret the Word of God and will have a tendency to distrust other portions of Scripture.

Chapter 10

How to Do "Foolproof" Apologetics

Jason Lisle

The Apostle Peter was emphatic that every Christian needs to be ready to defend the faith (1 Peter 3:15). In fact, defending the faith is an essential component of evangelism. Yet Christians often find this command difficult and intimidating because some highly educated people have argued that scientific evidence refutes the claims of the Bible. How can we answer such people unless we know a lot of science? It's understandable that many Christians feel inadequate to respond to the lofty rhetoric of the academic elite. But this need not be so. The Bible gives every one of us, regardless of age or formal education, the basic tools we need to defend the faith. You don't need an advanced degree in science or theology. Anyone can do it. We simply have to understand a few basic biblical principles.

The Ultimate Issue — Competing Worldviews

When we defend the Christian faith, we must avoid the temptation to get sidetracked on secondary issues, such as nuances of scientific arguments.[1] The goal is to quickly hone in on the heart of the matter — the debate is ultimately an issue of competing worldviews.

---

1. It is easy to get caught up in nuances of scientific evidence. And while there is a place for this, we must remember the "big picture"—that science itself presupposes a Christian worldview.

We all have a worldview (a way of thinking about life and the universe) that shapes our understanding of what we observe. But not all worldviews are equal. Non-Christian worldviews always have internal defects. Because they reject the Bible at their foundation, they end up being inconsistent, arbitrary, and ultimately irrational. With practice, anyone can learn to identify these flaws.

The Bible teaches that genuine knowledge begins with a reverential submission to God (Proverbs 1:7). So to have a worldview that is consistently rational, we must begin with God's Word as the foundation by which we evaluate the facts. Only God knows everything, so only He is in a position to tell us — on His own authority — what our starting point should be. Only the Bible provides a logical foundation for those things that are essential for knowledge.

The Requirements for Knowledge

In order for human beings to have genuine knowledge of any topic, certain things would have to be true, whether we recognize it consciously or not. For example, the human mind has to be capable of rational thought. The universe has to be orderly and comprehensible. Our sensations of the world around us have to be basically reliable.

The Christian worldview can make sense of all these things. The Christian understands that God made the human mind so that we could have the ability to think rationally. God made the universe and upholds it in a consistent, logical way. God created our senses so that we could accurately probe the world around us.[2]

Most people simply take these things for granted. They don't stop to consider how human beings are able to have knowledge of anything. Most people just blindly assume that our senses are reliable, that the mind is rational, and that the universe is orderly and understandable.

Few people think to ask, "Why should knowledge be possible?" The answer is not as obvious as it may seem. In fact, without God, we have no reason to expect an understandable universe.

So although there is a place for discussing scientific details, it is good to remember that science itself is based on a Christian worldview. We must patiently get the unbeliever to realize that he couldn't even do science if his evolutionary worldview were true.

---

2. Of course, our senses and minds do not always work perfectly due to the effects of sin.

If evolution were true, would there be any reason to think that mind would be capable of rational analysis? If the universe were just the aftermath of a big bang, why would we expect it to be orderly or comprehensible? If the universe is just matter in motion, then how could there be abstract laws, such as mathematics and logic, which are required for rational thinking? If any alternative to Christianity were true, then there would be no foundation for any of the things necessary for knowledge.[3]

This isn't to say that non-Christians cannot know anything. Obviously they can. But this is possible only because they are being inconsistent — implicitly relying on biblical principles while simultaneously denying the Bible.

This is the important thing to keep in the back of your mind during any discussion about worldviews and Christianity. In the end, we know that Christianity is true because, if it were not, then we couldn't know anything at all. This can be a difficult concept since most people are not used to thinking through such foundational issues. But it is something that we must learn to explain if our defense of the faith is to be effective.

Don't Answer . . .

King Solomon, the wisest man who ever lived, writing under the inspiration of the Holy Spirit (2 Timothy 3:16), gave us the strategy to expose the defects in non-Christian worldviews in two verses of Proverbs 26. First, verse 4 states, "Do not answer a fool according to his folly, lest you also be like him."

To be clear, the Bible is not engaging in name-calling by using the word fool — nor should we (Matthew 5:22). Rather, the Bible uses this word to describe anyone who has rejected God's revelation (Proverbs 1:7; Psalm 14:1). By rejecting the biblical God, the unbeliever has given up the foundational truths necessary for knowledge. His position is irrational — "foolish" in the Hebrew meaning of the word.

When an unbeliever tries to set the terms of the conversation by saying things like, "You can't use the Bible in your argument," or "Miracles

---

3. Like evolution, other non-Christian religions fail to account for those things necessary for knowledge. Although a complete discussion is beyond the scope of this article, it turns out that only the Christian worldview makes genuine knowledge possible. Non-Christian conceptions of God, when carefully analyzed, turn out to be mere idols that cannot do what the Living God does (Proverbs 1:7).

are not allowed as a legitimate explanation," he is embracing an illogical starting point for this thinking. It is inappropriate to agree to such terms.

According to the Bible, we should not "answer a fool according to his folly" or else we become like him. That is, we shouldn't embrace the unbeliever's starting point or else we too will end up just like him, holding a worldview in which knowledge doesn't make sense.

. . . Answer!

By reflecting back the absurd philosophy of the "fool," as in a mirror, we show him that his view is irrational.

The next verse in Proverbs 26 states, "Answer a fool according to his folly, lest he be wise in his own eyes."

At first glance, this verse may sound as if it contradicts the previous one, but the last part of each verse makes it clear that the sense is different. Verse 5 indicates that we should show the "fool" that he isn't as wise as he thinks he is by illustrating where his thinking leads. In other words, while we never embrace the unbeliever's starting point ("don't answer"), we can temporarily use his starting point ("answer"), for the sake of argument, to show that it leads to an absurd result.

For example, if evolution were true, we should have no reason to depend on our brain to know what is true because our brain is the result of chance mutations. This is an inconsistency.[4] By reflecting back the absurd philosophy of the "fool," as in a mirror, we show him that his view is not rational.

Examples of the "Don't Answer, Answer" Strategy

The "don't answer, answer" strategy is a powerful tool to use when defending the Christian faith. Consider those who say, "Christians are dishonest. They teach that God created the world only thousands of years ago, which is clearly false." First, using the "don't answer" side of the strategy, you'd reject the starting assumption of the critic and say something like

---

4. In the evolutionary worldview, one might argue that the brain has been preserved because it has survival value. But that does not equate to rationality. For example, a blade of grass has properties that allow it to survive; but that does not mean that a blade of grass is an intelligent, rational being. In the evolutionary worldview, the thoughts of the mind are merely chemical reactions — essentially the equivalent of weeds growing. Our thoughts may have survival value, but this does not translate to "truth."

DO NOT ANSWER A FOOL ACCORDING TO HIS FOLLY,

LEST YOU ALSO BE LIKE HIM.

We should never embrace the foolish presuppositions of an unbeliever.

Otherwise, we too will be reduced to foolishness (Proverbs 26:4).

ANSWER A FOOL ACCORDING TO HIS FOLLY,

LEST HE BE WISE IN HIS OWN EYES.

Without embracing the unbeliever's philosophy, we take it to its logical conclusion . . .

. . . so that he can see how absurd his position is (Prov. 26:5).

this: "I don't accept your claim that teaching creation is dishonest. We are equally convinced that evolution is untrue."

Then you'd go to the "answer" part of the strategy and show that the critic's position is inconsistent: "But for the sake of argument, even if we were lying, why would that be wrong according to your worldview? The idea that it's wrong to lie is a biblical concept. Lying is wrong because it's contrary to the nature of God. But in an evolutionary universe, on what

d I say that it's wrong to lie — particularly if it benefits my sur-
nderstand you agree with me that it's wrong to lie. But my point
is that such a belief makes sense only if the Bible is true."

Consider another common complaint, "How can you believe the
Bible in this age of science and technology? Science has proven that the
Bible is not true."

Using the biblical "don't answer, answer" strategy, you could reply:
"Science has not disproved the Bible; on the contrary, science has confirmed the Bible in many areas." You could give some examples at this
point, too.

Then you'd move to the "answer" part of the strategy: "But, for the
sake of argument, how would science even be possible in the first place,
unless the Bible's claims about God were true?" You then patiently explain
that the principles of science, such as the order and uniformity of nature
and the ability of the mind to understand the universe, all ultimately come
from the Bible.

Remembering that all knowledge is in Christ (Colossians 2:3), you
can quickly get to the heart of the matter and expose the irrationality in
any attack on Christianity. Using the "don't answer, answer" strategy of
Proverbs 26:4–5, you can efficiently expose the inconsistency of each
example of unbiblical reasoning (1 Corinthians 3:20).

Jesus tells us to build our house upon the rock — His teachings — not
the shifting sands of human opinion (Matthew 7:24–27). By standing on
the authority of the Bible, we can give a powerful and respectful defense
of the faith. God can bless our efforts and will use our defense to draw
many people to Himself.

1 Peter 3:15 — Four Keys to Being an Effective Apologist

1. "Sanctify Christ as Lord in your heart." Remember that all knowledge is in Christ (Colossians 2:3), and so our defense (apologetic)
   should be based unashamedly on the person of Christ as revealed
   in His Word. We can show that any system of thought, if it's not
   based ultimately on biblical revelation, is inherently irrational.
2. "Be ready always to give a defense." In obedience to our Lord, we
   should continually study the Bible and read about the common
   issues in apologetics so that we will be prepared. Thinking through

the issues and studying the Scriptures is a lifelong process that will continually improve our defense of the faith.

3. "To everyone who asks a reason of the hope that is in you." Remember that our job is to give a good defense for those who ask. We should not be discouraged if the person is not persuaded, as long as we have given a good, biblical faithful reason for our faith. Conversion is the job of the Holy Spirit (1 Corinthians 12:3).

4. "With gentleness and respect." Our defense should never be emotionally charged or derisive. Remember, even those who are in rebellion against God are made in His image and deserve respect.

Chapter 11

How Should We
Interpret the Bible?

Tim Chaffey

❦❦❦❦❦❦❦❦❦❦❦❦❦❦❦❦❦❦❦

A popular seminary professor recently wrote the following about the creation of Adam and Eve:

> Any evils humans experience outside the Garden before God breathes into them the breath of life would be experienced as natural evils in the same way that other animals experience them. The pain would be real, but it would not be experienced as divine justice in response to willful rebellion. Moreover, once God breathes the breath of life into them, we may assume that the first humans experienced an amnesia of their former animal life: Operating on a higher plane of consciousness once infused with the breath of life, they would transcend the lower plane of animal consciousness on which they had previously operated — though, after the Fall, they might be tempted to resort to that lower consciousness.[1]

So according to this professor, Adam and Eve were animals before God breathed the breath of life into them. At that point, they experienced

---

1. William A. Dembski, *The End of Christianity: Finding a Good God in an Evil World* (Nashville, TN: Broadman & Holman Publishing Group, 2009), p. 155.

ir former animal life" so that they would no longer remem-
l past.

his line up with the Word of God, which states that God
. Adam from the dust of the ground (Genesis 2:7) and Eve from
Adam's rib (Genesis 2:22)? Has the professor made a plausible interpreta-
tion of God's Word? Is his interpretive work what Paul had in mind when
he advised Timothy to be diligent in his efforts to accurately interpret the
Word of Truth (2 Timothy 2:15)?

The example above highlights the importance of being able to properly interpret the Bible. In this postmodern age, bizarre interpretations
are accepted because people believe they have the right to decide for
themselves what a passage means. In other words, meaning is in the eye
of the beholder, so you can decide truth for yourself.

This ideology flies in the face of Christ's example. He routinely
rebuked those who twisted the words of Scripture or misapplied them.
The Bible is God's message to man. We can have perfect confidence that
God is capable of accurately relaying His Word to us in a way that we can
understand. As such, it is crucial that we learn how to interpret properly
so that we can determine the Author's Intended Meaning (AIM) rather
than forcing our own ideas into the text. A given document means what
the author intended it to mean. The alternative would make communication futile. There would be no point in writing anything if the readers are
simply going to take what they want from the passage, rather than what
the writer intends. All communication is predicated on the presupposition that language conveys the author's or speaker's intention (unless, of
course, the person is trying to deceive us, which is something God does
not do since He wants us to understand His Word).

Interpretation

Hermeneutics (from the Greek word *hermēneuō,* which means to
explain or interpret) is the branch of theology that focuses on identifying
and applying sound principles of biblical interpretation. While the Bible
is generally plain in its meaning, proper interpretation requires careful
study and is not always an easy task. Consider that the Bible was written
over a period of roughly 2,000 years by 40 or more authors using three
languages (Hebrew, Aramaic, Greek). The authors wrote in different

genres and had different vocabularies, personalities, cultural back-grounds, and social standings. The Holy Spirit moved each of these men to produce His inspired, inerrant, and infallible Word (2 Timothy 3:16; 2 Peter 1:20–21), but He allowed their various writing styles and personalities to be expressed in its pages. It was written in a culture very different from our modern world and has been translated from its original languages. These are just some of the factors that must be taken into account as we interpret.

In fact, Bible colleges and seminaries often require their students to complete a course in hermeneutics. Numerous books have been written to explain these principles, and while Bible-believing Christians may disagree over particulars, there is general agreement about the major rules required to rightly divide the Word of Truth.

This is not to claim that only the scholarly elite can correctly interpret the Bible. Various groups have wrongly held this position. William Tyndale lived in the early 16th century when only certain people were allowed to interpret the Bible, which was only available in Latin, not the language of the common man. He sought to bring God's Word to the average person by translating it into English. Tyndale is credited with telling a priest that he could make a boy who drove a plough to know more of the Scripture than the priest himself.[2] The Bible was penned so that in its pages all people, even children, can learn about God and what He has done so that we can have a personal relationship with Him.

We must also battle against our pride, which tempts us to think that our own views are always right or that the beliefs of a particular teacher are necessarily right. We must strive to be like the Bereans who were commended by Luke for searching the Old Testament Scriptures daily to make sure that what Paul taught was true (Acts 17:11).

God desires for His people to know and understand His Word — that's why He gave it to us and instructed fathers to teach it to their children in the home (Deuteronomy 6:4–9). However, we must keep in mind several important points.

First, Christians must seek the guidance of the Holy Spirit while studying the Bible. It's not that the Bible requires any "extra-logical" or mystical insight to understand it. But we are limited in our understanding

---

2. http://www.tyndalesploughboy.org, accessed January 7, 2011.

and often hindered by pride. We need the Holy Spirit to help us to think correctly, lest we distort the Scriptures (2 Peter 3:16).

Second, a person can spend his or her entire life and still never come close to mining the depths of Scripture. The Bible is written in such a marvelous way that a child can understand the basic message, and yet the most educated theologians continue to learn new things from the Bible as they study it. There is always much more to learn, so we must humbly approach the Word of God.

Third, God has given the Church learned men and gifted teachers who have devoted their lives to studying God's Word. While these people are certainly not infallible, we shouldn't automatically reject the work of those who have gone before us.

Finally, since the Bible consists of written data, then in order to understand it, we must follow standard rules of grammar and interpretation. We will examine some of these rules and principles later, especially as they relate to Genesis.

Because people often confuse the two concepts, it must be pointed out that interpretation is different than application, although they are related. Interpretation answers the questions, "What does the text say?" and "What does the text mean?" Application follows interpretation and answers the question, "How can I apply this truth in my life today?" After all, the goal of studying the Bible is not to simply fill one's head with information but to learn what God wants for us to know so that we can live how He wants us to live.

Which Method Do We Use?

Bible-believing Christians generally follow a method of interpretation known as the historical-grammatical approach. That is, we try to find the plain (literal) meaning of the words based on an understanding of the historical and cultural settings in which the book was written. We then follow standard rules of grammar, according to the book's particular genre, to arrive at an interpretation. We seek to perform careful interpretation or exegesis — that is, to "read out of" the text what the author intended it to mean. This is in contrast to eisegesis, which occurs when someone "reads into" the text his own ideas — what the reader wants the text to mean. In other words, exegesis is finding the AIM (Author's

Intended Meaning) of the passage because its true meaning is determined by the sender of the message, not the recipient.

This hermeneutical approach has several strengths. It can be demonstrated that the New Testament authors interpreted the Old Testament in this manner. Also, it is the only approach that offers an internal system of "checks and balances" to make sure one is on the right track. As will be shown, other views allow for personal opinion to sneak into one's interpretation, which does not truly reflect what the text means.

Finally, this approach is consistent with how we utilize language on a daily basis while interacting with others. For example, if your best friend says, "I am going to drive to work tomorrow morning," you can instantly understand what he means. You know that he has a vehicle that he can drive to his place of employment, and that's exactly what he plans on doing early the next day.

If the postmodern approach is accurate and meaning is determined by the recipient of the message, then perhaps your friend is really just telling you that he likes pancakes. Communication becomes impossible in such a world, and it gets even worse if your friend was talking to you and several other buddies. One friend might think he was talking about his favorite color, another interpreted his words to mean that he doesn't believe in air, and another thought he meant that he was going to walk to work ten years later.

Words have a particular meaning in a particular context. When they are placed together in sentences and paragraphs, then a person must follow common-sense rules in order to derive the appropriate meaning. The sender of the message had a reason for choosing the words he did and putting those words together in a particular order and context. The same is true with the Bible. God had a reason for moving the writers of the Bible to use the words they did in the order they did. Our goal must be to ascertain the AIM.

Principles of Interpretation

Since the goal of interpreting the Bible is to determine the Author's Intended Meaning, we must follow principles derived from God's Word. The following principles do not comprise an exhaustive list but are some of the major concepts found in the majority of books on interpretation. In the next chapter, the quote from the introduction of this chapter will be examined to see if it properly applies these standard principles.

Carefully Observe the Text

It may seem rather obvious, but this principle is often overlooked. We must carefully observe what the text actually states. Many mistakes have been made by people who jump into interpretation based on what they think the text states rather than what it really does state.

As you read a particular verse or passage, pay close attention to different types of words that make up a sentence. Is the subject singular or plural? Is the verb tense past, present, or future? Is the sentence a command, statement of fact, or question? Is the statement part of a dialogue? If so, who is the speaker, and why did he make that comment? Can you note any repetition of words, which perhaps shows emphasis? What ideas are compared or contrasted? Can you identify any cause and effect statements or questions and answers? What is the tone of the passage; are emotional words used?

Failure to carefully observe the text has resulted in numerous misconceptions about the Bible. For example, many Christians have taught that Adam and Eve used to walk with God in the cool of the day. While it is possible that they did take walks with God in the garden, the Bible never claims this. Instead, God's Word reveals that *after they had sinned, Adam and Eve "heard the sound of the* LORD *God walking in the garden in the cool of the day,"* and they hid themselves from Him (Genesis 3:8).

Carefully observing the text can also protect you from making another common mistake. Just because the Bible contains a statement does not mean that it affirms the statement as godly. For example, much of the Book of Job consists of an ongoing dialogue between Job and four of his friends (Bildad, Eliphaz, Zophar, and Elihu). Some people have been careless by quoting certain verses from this book to support their own ideas, but we have to keep in mind that God told Eliphaz that what he, Bildad, and Zophar had spoken about Him was not right (Job 42:7). This ties in perfectly with our next principle.

Context Is Key

Perhaps no principle of interpretation is more universally agreed upon than the idea that understanding the context of the word, phrase, or passage is absolutely essential. *Context is defined as "the parts of a discourse that surround a word or passage and can throw light on its meaning."*[3]

You may have heard someone say that a particular verse has been pulled out of context. Critics of Scripture often take verses out of context when they attack the Bible. The reason is that they can make the Bible "say" just about anything if they do not provide the context. For example, the critic might ask, "Did you know that the Bible says, 'There is no God'?" Then he may go on to claim that this contradicts other passages, which certainly teach that God does exist.

How do we handle such a charge? We look at the context of the quoted words, which in this case comes from Psalm 14:1 (and is repeated in Psalm 53:1). It states, "The fool has said in his heart, 'There is no God.' " So, it's true that the Bible states, "There is no God," but it attributes these words to a foolish person. So the Bible is not teaching both the existence and non-existence of God, as the skeptic asserts.

If I asked you what the word "set" means, would you be able to provide me with the correct answer? No, it would be impossible because the word has more than 70 definitions in the 11th edition of *Merriam-Webster's Collegiate Dictionary*, and can be used as a verb, noun, and an adjective. Now if I asked you what the word "set" meant in the following sentence, you could easily figure it out: "His mind was set on solving the problem." In this sentence, the word means "intent" or "determined." But without the context, you would not know this.

The same thing is true with the Bible or any other written communication. The context clarifies the meaning of the word, phrase, sentence, etc. With the Bible, it is important to know the context of the particular passage you are studying. It is also important to understand the context of the entire book in which the passage is found and how that book fits into the context of Scripture.

We also need to recognize where the passage fits into the flow of history. It makes a huge difference in determining the writer's intent if we note whether the passage was pre-Fall, pre-Flood, pre-Mosaic Law, after the Babylonian exile, during Christ's earthly ministry, after His

3. Frederick C. Mish, editor in chief, *Merriam-Webster's Collegiate Dictionary, Eleventh Edition* (Springfield, MA: Merriam-Webster, 2008), s.v. "Context."

Resurrection, or after Pentecost. This is especially important when we reach the point of application. For example, just because God commanded Israel to sacrifice lambs at Passover doesn't mean we should do the same today. Jesus died on the Cross as our Passover Lamb (1 Corinthians 5:7) and was the ultimate fulfillment of the Passover sacrifice. Since the Bible was revealed progressively, there are instances where later revelation supersedes earlier revelation.

Ron Rhodes summarized these truths by stating, "No verse of Scripture can be divorced from the verses around it. Interpreting a verse apart from its context is like trying to analyze a Rembrandt painting by looking at only a single square inch of the painting, or like trying to analyze Handel's 'Messiah' by listening to a few short notes."[4]

Clarity of Scripture

Since the Bible is God's Word to man, He must expect us to understand it. As such, it makes sense that He would communicate His message to us in such a way that we can indeed comprehend it if we are serious about wanting to know the truth. The Apostle Paul told the Corinthians:

> Rather, we have renounced secret and shameful ways; we do not use deception, nor do we distort the word of God. On the contrary, by *setting forth the truth plainly* we commend ourselves to every man's conscience in the sight of God (2 Corinthians 4:2; NIV, emphasis added).

Proverbs 8:9 states that God's words "are all plain to him who understands, and right to those who find knowledge."

This principle was one of the key differences between the Reformers and Roman Catholics. The Reformers believed in the perspicuity (clearness) of Scripture, especially in relation to its central message of the gospel, and they believed each believer had the right to interpret God's Word. Roman Catholic doctrine held (and still holds) that Scripture can only be interpreted by the Magisterium (teaching office of the church).

Consider the words of Psalm 119, which is by far the longest chapter in the entire Bible, and every one of its 176 verses extols the superiority of

---

4. Ron Rhodes, "Rightly Interpreting the Bible," from http://home.earthlink.net/~ronrhodes/Interpretation.html, accessed January 12, 2011.

God's Word. "Your word is a lamp to my feet and a light to my path" (Psalm 119:105). "The entrance of Your words gives light; it gives understanding to the simple" (Psalm 119:130). God's Word should be a lamp to our feet and a light to our path, giving understanding to the simple. How could it be or do any of these things if it is not clear?

The principle of the clarity of Scripture does not mean that every passage is easily understood or that one does not need to diligently study the Word of God, but it does teach that the overall message of the Word of God can be understood by all believers who carefully and prayerfully study it. The principle also means that we should not assume or look for hidden meanings but rather assess the most straightforward meaning. Two of Christ's favorite sayings were "It is written" and "Have you not read?" Then He would quote a verse from the Old Testament. By these sayings, He indicated that the Scriptures are generally clear.

Compare Scripture with Scripture

Another key principle of hermeneutics is that we should use Scripture to interpret Scripture. Known by theologians as the "analogy of faith" or "analogy of Scripture," this principle is solidly based on the Bible's own teachings. Since the Bible is the Word of God and God cannot lie or contradict Himself (Numbers 23:19; Hebrews 6:18), then one passage will never contradict another passage. This principle is useful for several reasons.

First, not all Bible passages are equally clear. So a clear passage can be used to shed light on a difficult, not-so-clear passage. There are a number of obscure verses in Scripture, where you might wish the writer would have provided more details. First Corinthians 15:29 is a classic example. Right in the middle of the chapter on the Resurrection of Jesus and the future resurrection of believers, Paul asked, "Otherwise, what will they do who are baptized for the dead, if the dead do not rise at all? Why then are they baptized for the dead?" Several ideas have been suggested to explain what Paul meant about baptism for the dead, but because this is the only verse in all of Scripture that mentions this concept, we may not be able to reach a firm conclusion about its meaning.

However, by comparing this verse with other Scripture, we can reach definite conclusions about what it *does not* teach. We know that Paul did not instruct the Corinthians to baptize people for the dead,[5] because Paul and other biblical writers unequivocally taught that salvation is only by God's grace and can only be received through faith alone in Christ alone (Ephesians 2:8–9). We can also be sure that those who practice such a thing are not accomplishing what they hope to accomplish — the salvation of an unbeliever who has already died. Hebrews 9:27 states, "it is appointed for men to die once, but after this the judgment."

Second, by comparing Scripture with Scripture, we have a system of checks and balances to help us stay on the right track. There will likely be times when, for whatever reason, we incorrectly interpret a given passage. By studying other passages that shed light on the same issue, we can recognize our error. Many people are unwilling to change their original interpretation and hold on to contradictory beliefs. Some will even claim that the Bible contradicts itself when, in reality, they have misinterpreted one or both of the passages. It is crucial for us to humbly approach Scripture and realize that if we believe we have found a contradiction, then it is our interpretation that is flawed, not God's Word.

Since this principle provides a system of checks and balances, it can provide us with great certainty concerning a given interpretation. If we interpret a passage and then discover that every other passage on the topic seems to teach the same truth, we can be confident in the accuracy of our interpretation.

Classification of Text

While interpreting the Bible, we must never forget to understand the genre (literary style) of the passage we are studying. The Bible contains numerous types of literature, and each one needs to be interpreted according to principles befitting its particular style. Below is a chart identifying the basic literary style of each book of the Bible. Note that some books contain more than one style. For example, Exodus is written as history, but chapter 15 includes a song written in poetic language. Also, the books are sometimes divided into more categories, but for our purposes "History" includes the books of the Law, the historical books, and the four gospels; "Poetry" includes the Psalms and wisdom literature; "Prophecy"

---

5. The Latter-Day Saints (Mormons) have developed an entire doctrine called baptism by proxy in which current members of the group are baptized in place of the dead. They use this verse to support this practice.

includes the prophetic books; and "Epistles" are letters written to an individual or church by someone with apostolic authority.

History	Poetry	Prophecy	Epistles
Genesis	Job	Isaiah	Romans
Exodus	Psalms	Jeremiah	1 Corinthians
Leviticus	Proverbs	Lamentations	2 Corinthians
Numbers	Ecclesiastes	Ezekiel	Galatians
Deuteronomy	Song of Solomon	Daniel	Ephesians
Joshua		Hosea	Philippians
Judges		Joel	Colossians
Ruth		Amos	1 Thessalonians
1 Samuel		Obadiah	2 Thessalonians
2 Samuel		Jonah	1 Timothy
1 Kings		Micah	2 Timothy
2 Kings		Nahum	Titus
1 Chronicles		Habakkuk	Philemon
2 Chronicles		Zephaniah	Hebrews
Ezra		Haggai	James
Nehemiah		Zechariah	1 Peter
Esther		Malachi	2 Peter
Matthew		Revelation	1 John
Mark			2 John
Luke			3 John
John			Jude
Acts			

These distinctions are important to keep in mind while interpreting the Bible. Each classification uses language in a particular way. Historical books are primarily narratives of past events and should be interpreted in a straightforward manner. This does not mean that they never utilize figurative language. For example, after Cain killed his brother Abel, God said to Cain, "What have you done? The voice of your brother's blood cries out to Me from the ground. So now you are cursed from the earth, which has opened its mouth to receive your brother's blood from your hand" (Genesis 4:10–11). There are two obvious instances of figurative language in this passage: the ground "opened its mouth" and Abel's "blood cries out" from it. Nevertheless, these figures of speech are perfectly legitimate in historical writing, and it is easy to understand what they mean.

Poetry, prophecy, and the New Testament epistles all have their own particular nuances and guidelines for proper interpretation. Space does not permit a full treatment here, so just remember to recognize the book's (or passage's) genre and interpret accordingly.

Church's Historical View

Finally, it is important to know how those who have gone before us have interpreted a passage in question. Although our doctrine must be based squarely on the Word of God and not on tradition or what some great leader believed, we should allow ourselves to be informed by the work of others who have spent long hours studying God's Word. Most doctrines have been discussed, debated, and formulated throughout Church history, so we should take advantage of that resource.

Imagine studying a passage and reaching a conclusion only to discover that no one else in history has ever interpreted those verses in the same way. You would not necessarily be wrong, but you would certainly want to re-examine the passage to see if you had overlooked something. After all, you need to be very careful and confident in your interpretation before proposing an idea that none of the millions of interpreters have ever noticed before.

While Bible scholars and pastors often have access to resources that permit them to search out the teachings of our spiritual forefathers, this information can also be obtained by the average Christian. Consider borrowing a commentary from a pastor or taking advantage of some of the Bible software on the market, which allows you to quickly search for this information.

Application of the Hermeneutical Principles

Let's consider how well Professor Dembski's quote from the introduction fits the description of the creation of Adam and Eve as described in Genesis 2. Was he careful to observe the text, examine the context, assume the clarity of Scripture, compare Scripture with Scripture, properly classify the text, and compare his conclusions with those who have gone before him?

Here is the quote again:

> Any evils humans experience outside the Garden before God breathes into them the breath of life would be experienced as natural evils in the same way that other animals experience them. The pain would be real, but it would not be experienced as divine justice in response to willful rebellion. Moreover, once God breathes the breath of life into them, we may assume that the first

humans experienced an amnesia of their former animal life: Operating on a higher plane of consciousness once infused with the breath of life, they would transcend the lower plane of animal consciousness on which they had previously operated — though, after the Fall, they might be tempted to resort to that lower consciousness.[6]

Shortly before this quote, Dr. Dembski proposed that the world was full of death and suffering but that God created an oasis of perfection (the Garden of Eden) in which Adam and Eve were allowed to live.[7] Is this consistent with Scripture? Did he *carefully observe the text?*

In Genesis 2:7, the verse that describes the creation of Adam, we immediately run into a problem. It states, "And the LORD God formed man [Hebrew: *adam*] of the dust of the ground, and breathed into his nostrils the breath of life; and man became a living being." The following verse, Genesis 2:8, reveals that after God made Adam, He created the Garden of Eden and put Adam in it. So Dr. Dembski is right that Adam came from outside the garden and was subsequently moved into it. However, contrary to his claims, Adam was already fully human while he was still outside the garden. The immediate context reveals that Adam was made from the "dust of the ground," so he did not evolve from ape-like ancestors.

There are some other problems. According to Genesis 2:21–22, the first woman (Eve) was made from Adam's rib once Adam was in the garden and *after* he named the animals. She was not an animal who came from outside the garden, nor did she become fully human when she entered the garden or receive amnesia about the past the moment she entered it. So this interpretation does not pay attention to the details of the text of Genesis 2. Also, in the context, Genesis 1:31 indicates that everything God had made was "very good." This sharply contrasts with Dr. Dembski's view of a world that was already full of pain and "natural evils."

Dr. Dembski's interpretation also runs counter to the *clarity of Scripture* (at least in the early chapters of Genesis). A plain reading of the text reveals that Adam was made from the dust of the ground, placed in

---

6. Dembski, *The End of Christianity,* p. 155.
7. Ibid., p. 153.

the garden, told to name the animals, and put in a deep sleep during which God made the first woman from Adam's rib.

When we compare *Scripture with Scripture,* we find other reasons why Dr. Dembski's interpretation fails. The Bible consistently shows that death did not exist prior to Adam's sin.[8] Also, in Genesis 3:18–19 God explained that, as a result of Adam's sin and God's Curse, the ground would bring forth thorns and thistles (the ground that was cursed was outside the garden from which Adam and Eve were expelled), making Adam's work more difficult, and that Adam would eventually die. Yet, since Dr. Dembski apparently accepts a view of theistic evolution (the notion that God used evolutionary processes to bring man into existence),[9] he promotes the idea that thorns and death pre-existed Adam by hundreds of millions of years. He seeks to solve this dilemma by claiming that Adam's sin was retroactively applied to all of creation.[10] Nowhere does the Bible state anything like this. Throughout its pages, the Bible reveals there was no death before sin because death was brought into the world by man.

The literary style of Genesis, based on the *classification of the text,* was also ignored by Dr. Dembski. As will be demonstrated in the next section, Genesis was written as historical narrative, and it should be interpreted as such. Although many claim to believe in the historicity of the events in Genesis 1–11, they simply reclassify the text as something other than history. For example, some view it as poetic or mythological. It is not enough to simply claim that one believes Genesis is historically accurate. One must also recognize that it was written as historical narrative and interpret accordingly. The strange ideas proposed by Dr. Dembski reveal he does not interpret the early chapters as historical narrative.

Dr. Dembski's interpretation of these chapters is rather unique. It certainly has not been a standard or well-accepted position throughout

---

8. See Dr. Terry Mortenson's article "Young-Earth Creationist View Summarized and Defended" at http://www.answersingenesis.org/articles/aid/v6/n1/yec-view-summary. Accessed February 16, 2011.

9. Actually, Dr. Dembski is very confusing in his section on Adam and Eve (p. 155–159). Some statements seem to reject evolution, but many other statements seem to accept it. At the very least, he seems to indicate that theistic evolution is compatible with the theodicy he is proposing.

10. For a full refutation of Dr. Dembski's view, see Terry Mortenson's article "Christian Theodicy in Light of Genesis and Modern Science: A Young-Earth Creationist Response to William Dembski" at http://www.answersingenesis.org/articles/arj/v2/n1/dembskis-theodicy-refuted, accessed January 26, 2011.

Church history, and I only know of one other person who has discussed something similar.[11] While this principle of considering the Church's historical view does not disprove his view by itself, it illustrates the need to carefully examine his beliefs before accepting them.

Also, we should ask why Dr. Dembski has come up with this novel view. He answered that question when he wrote, "The young-earth solution to reconciling the order of creation with natural history makes good exegetical and theological sense. Indeed, the overwhelming consensus of theologians up through the Reformation held to this view. I myself would adopt it in a heartbeat *except that nature seems to present such strong evidence against it*."[12]

This statement reveals his motives. The young-earth creationist position is clearly presented in the text of Scripture, but he does not accept it because he believes scientists have shown the earth and universe to be billions of years old. As such, he does not allow the Bible to be the authority in this area. Instead, he has placed man's ever-changing views in a position to override the plain words of the God who knows all things, cannot lie, and has revealed to us how and when He created. By his interpretation, Dr. Dembski is reading into (eisegesis) the Bible what he would like it to mean, rather than reading out (exegesis) of the Bible what it actually teaches.

Several other problems could be cited, but these are sufficient to show that Dr. Dembski has failed to accurately interpret the passage about the creation of man. The early chapters of Genesis are written as historical narrative. When you follow the well-accepted principles of interpretation, then it is easy to see why, until the onslaught of old-earth philosophy in the early 1800s, Christians have predominantly believed that God created everything in six days approximately six thousand years ago.[13]

---

11. Because he also sought to reconcile the ideas of long ages and the biblical teaching that death came as a result of Adam's sin, Charles Spurgeon once briefly stated as a possibility the concept of death as a result of Adam's sin being retroactively applied to the death of animals for long periods of time prior to the Fall. Charles H. Spurgeon, "Christ, the Destroyer of Death" (preached on December 17, 1876), *The Metropolitan Tabernacle Pulpit, Vol XXII* (Pasadena, TX: Pilgrim, 1981), p. 698–699.

12. Dembski, *The End of Christianity*, p. 55.

13. For more information on this dramatic shift in interpretation of Genesis 1–11 in the early 1800s, see Terry Mortenson, *The Great Turning Point: The Church's Catastrophic Mistake on Geology — Before Darwin* (Green Forest, AR: Master Books, 2004).

Interpreting Genesis 1–11

By allowing man's ever-changing ideas about the past to override the plain words of Scripture, many people have proposed that Genesis 1–11 should be viewed as mythical, figurative, or allegorical, rather than historical narrative. Since these people believe in millions and billions of years of death, suffering, disease, and bloodshed prior to Adam's sin, they search for ways to reinterpret the Bible's early chapters in a manner that will allow their views. As a result, the accounts of creation, the Fall, the Flood, and the Tower of Babel are often reinterpreted or dismissed.

We must remember that our goal is to discover the AIM (Author's Intended Meaning) of the biblical text. Did God intend for these chapters to be understood in a figurative, mythical, or allegorical manner, or did He intend to tell us precisely (though not in all the detail we might want) what He did in the beginning and in the early history of the earth? The Bible provides abundant support for the conclusion that these chapters are indeed historical narrative.

First, although many commentators have broken Genesis into two sections (1–11 and 12–50), such a distinction cannot be found in the text. Some have even argued that the first 11 chapters represent primeval history and should be interpreted differently than the final 39 chapters. There are several problems with this approach. Genesis 12 would make little sense without the genealogical background provided in the previous chapter. Further, since chapter 11 includes the genealogy of Shem (which introduces us to Abraham), this links it to the genealogy in Genesis 10, which is tied to the one found in Genesis 5.

Second, Todd Beall explained another link between chapters 11 and 12, which demonstrates one should not arbitrarily insert a break in the text at this point. He wrote, "Genesis 12 begins with a *waw* consecutive verb, *wayomer* ('and he said'), indicating that what follows is a continuation of chapter 11, not a major break in the narrative."[14] Also, chapter 11 ends with mention of Abraham, and chapter 12 begins with Abraham.

Third, Genesis seems to be structured on the recurrence of the Hebrew phrase *eleh toledoth* ("This is the book of the genealogy of . . ." or

---

14. Todd S. Beall, "Contemporary Hermeneutical Approaches to Genesis 1–11" in Terry Mortenson and Thane H. Ury, *Coming to Grips with Genesis: Biblical Authority and the Age of the Earth* (Green Forest, AR: Master Books, 2008), p. 145.

"This is the history of . . ."). This occurs 11 times throughout the book: six times in Genesis 1–11 and five times in chapters 12–50. Clearly, the author intended that both sections should be interpreted in the same way — as historical narrative.

Fourth, the New Testament treats Genesis 1–11 as historical narrative. At least 25 New Testament passages refer directly to the early chapters of Genesis, and they are always treated as real history. Genesis 1 and 2 were cited by Jesus in response to a question about divorce (Matthew 19:4–6; Mark 10:6–9). Paul referenced Genesis 2–3 in Romans 5:12–19; 1 Corinthians 15:20–22, 45–47; 2 Corinthians 11:3; and 1 Timothy 2:13–14. The death of Abel recorded in Genesis 4 is mentioned by Jesus in Luke 11:51. The Flood (Genesis 6–9) is confirmed as historical by Jesus (Matthew 24:37–39) and Peter (2 Peter 2:4–9, 3:6), and in Luke 17:26–29, Jesus mentioned the Flood in the same context as He did the account of Lot and Sodom (Genesis 19). Finally, in Luke's genealogy of Christ, he includes 20 names found in the genealogies of Genesis 5 and 11 (Luke 3:34–38).

Conclusion

These are just some of the reasons why Genesis 1–11 should be understood as literal history. Jesus and the New Testament authors viewed it as such,[15] and the internal consistency of Genesis demonstrates its historical nature. Consequently, to interpret Genesis 1–11 in the same way Jesus did, you must treat the passage as historical narrative and follow the standard principles of interpretation. When you do this, it is clear that God created everything in six normal-length days approximately six thousand years ago.

---

15. For more on Christ's and the Apostles' view of Genesis 1–11, see chapters 11 and 12 in Mortenson and Ury, *Coming to Grips with Genesis.*

Chapter 12

What about the Factual Claims in *The Da Vinci Code*?

Tim Chaffey

❡❀❀❀❀❀❀❀❀❀❀❀❀❀❀❀❀❀❀

F ACT: . . . All descriptions of artwork, architecture, documents, and secret rituals in this novel are accurate."[1] Thus begins one of the best-selling and most controversial books in history. Dan Brown's action-thriller became a cultural phenomenon and triggered a firestorm of debate due to many of the statements about Jesus Christ.

The story involves a quest for a redefined holy grail. Rather than being the cup used by Christ during the Last Supper, Brown claims the grail is Mary Magdalene. According to the story, Jesus and Mary Magdalene were married, and she was pregnant with His child when He was crucified. The Apostles were jealous of Mary's role among the group, so she fled in fear to France where her descendants would eventually become French royalty. However, the Apostles changed Christ's message so they could make the Church patriarchal and suppress women. They tried desperately to destroy any documents or evidence that went against their claims.

---

1. Dan Brown, *The Da Vinci Code* (New York, Doubleday, 2003), p. 2. Pagination reflects electronic edition of the book. Brown stated, "One of the many qualities that makes The Da Vinci Code unique is the factual nature of the story. All the history, artwork, ancient documents, and secret rituals in the novel are accurate — as are the hidden codes revealed in some of da Vinci's most famous paintings," http://www.bookbrowse.com/author_interviews/full/index.cfm?author_number=226, accessed June 10, 2010.

Supposedly, a secret society called the Priory of Sion passed on the truth to its followers, which included an impressive list of scientists and scholars throughout history, such as Leonardo da Vinci and Isaac Newton.[2] Brown claims that da Vinci left clues in his artwork, especially *The Last Supper* painting. The book centers on the idea that sitting to the right of Jesus in the painting is Mary Magdalene rather than the Apostle John.

But it's just fiction, right? Everyone knows it's just a story, so why bother spending time refuting it? Yes, it's just fiction, but Brown's opening "FACT" purports that much of the story is true. His claims have deceived millions concerning the truth about the deity of Jesus Christ, His life, His ministry, and Church history.

How Factual Are Dan Brown's Facts?

Before examining the more important issues centering on Jesus Christ, it is important to understand that Brown plays fast and loose with even the most basic details. Although these issues are not crucial, they demonstrate Brown's uncanny ability to miss the truth or his willingness to twist the truth to tell his story. Here is a small sample of mistakes made by Brown on these lesser issues.

Claim in The Da Vinci Code	Reality
At President Mitterand's explicit demand, the pyramid at the Louvre consists of 666 panes of glass, which created a stir among conspiracy buffs who view 666 as the number of Satan (Brown, p. 18).	The Louvre's official website states there are 673 panes of glass.
The Dead Sea Scrolls were discovered in the 1950s (Brown, p. 198).	The Dead Sea Scrolls were discovered in 1947.
The documents found at Nag Hammadi were scrolls (Brown, p. 198).	The Nag Hammadi documents consisted of codices (bound books).

---

2. Although this is a major issue in the novel, space does not allow for a critique of Brown's claims about the Priory of Sion and the Knights Templar. The fact is that the Priory of Sion did not exist until May 7, 1956. It was founded in France by Pierre Plantard, who sought to lay claim to France's royal line. He also planted false documents, *Le Dossiers Secrets*, in the Bibliotheque Nationale (National Library) in Paris in an effort to support some of his wild claims, many of which have been repeated by Dan Brown.

Da Vinci's *The Last Supper* is described as a fresco ten times (Brown, p. 79, 198, 199, 200, 205, 206).	*The Last Supper* is a tempera, which is why it has undergone numerous restorations. Frescoes are quite permanent.
Da Vinci's *The Last Supper* did not show Christ's cup because da Vinci wanted to identify the "Holy Grail" as Mary Magdalene (Brown, p. 200).	*The Last Supper* was not painted to show Christ's announcement of the New Covenant (when He used the cup) but was painted to show the moment that Jesus announced His betrayer.
The Bible celebrates the Last Supper as the definitive arrival of the cup of Christ (Brown, p. 199).	The Bible never focuses on the so-called grail, nor does it instruct followers to search for it. This became a popular idea in medieval times.
Constantine made Christianity the state religion because it was growing in popularity and he was "a very good businessman" (Brown, p. 196).	Constantine did not make Christianity the state religion, but he did enact the Edict of Toleration (A.D. 311) and the Edict of Milan (A.D. 313), which legalized Christianity throughout the Empire. Theodosius made Christianity the state religion in A.D. 386 — more than half a century after Constantine.

Rewriting Church History

The Da Vinci Code repeats the common but erroneous belief that "History is always written by the winners" (Brown, p. 215). The idea is that an accurate view of history cannot really be known since the winners have distorted it to paint themselves in the best light. There is little question that this has happened, but is history always written by the winners? Even if it was, does it mean we cannot know what really happened? The well-known first-century historian Josephus was from the losing side. He was a Jewish military leader who was taken captive by the conquering Romans. As a captive of the Roman army, Josephus recorded many of the events he witnessed and is considered to be one of the most important early historians. Furthermore, although everyone does have a bias, it does not preclude the possibility that a historian has accurately reported what has actually happened.

Ironically, if Brown's claim were true, then it would necessarily refute his attempt to rewrite history. If true history is unknowable because it is only written by the winners, then how could Brown's characters dogmatically assert that Jesus was married to Mary Magdalene along with all of their other lies about Christ? Brown could only make these claims if he had an accurate historical record about such events, but his own claim makes this impossible.

Dan Brown has completely misrepresented and twisted Church history. It seems his real goal is to promote Gnosticism, a popular belief system in the second and third centuries. Gnostics believed the physical world was evil and that men needed to seek enlightenment by finding secret knowledge (Greek: *gnosis*).

So much of the revisionist history centers on the famous Council of Nicaea in A.D. 325. According to Brown, this is where Jesus was proclaimed as God by a "relatively close vote" (Brown, p. 197) and where the Bible was compiled. Once again, he is not even close to the facts.

Most of what we know about the Council of Nicaea came from the pen of the famous Church historian Eusebius. One of the debates at Nicaea did focus on the nature of Christ. Due to the teachings of Arius, some had come to believe that Jesus was a created being who in turn created everything else. This belief system, known as Arianism, was strongly opposed by Athanasius and many others. In the end, the 318 bishops were present when the Council voted, with 316 voting on the Nicene Creed, which affirmed Christ's full divinity and rejected Arianism. Two bishops, apparently in favor of Arianism, did not vote. This is not a "relatively close vote," as Brown claimed.

In one of the more ridiculous claims of the book, Brown's "Grail historian," Leigh Teabing, stated, "More than eighty gospels were considered for the New Testament. . . . The fundamental irony of Christianity! The Bible, as we know it today, was collated by the pagan Roman emperor Constantine the Great" (Brown, p. 195). It's true that Constantine convened the Council, but there is not a single mention from any primary document from the Council of Nicaea that supports the notion that the canon of Scripture was discussed.

There were never 80 competing gospels either. Only a handful of early Gnostic writings, dating to the second and third centuries, were called gospels, including *The Gospel of Truth*, *The Gospel of Thomas*, *The Gospel of Philip*, *The Gospel of the Egyptians*, and *The Gospel of Mary*, but they did not vie for inclusion in the canon — they were never even considered. This is a far cry from 80 gospels, and none of these were written by the person for whom they were named.

At one point in the novel, Teabing told Sophie to read from *The Gospel of Philip* in an effort to prove Jesus and Mary Magdalene were married. "And the companion of the Saviour is Mary Magdalene. Christ loved her more than all the disciples and used to kiss her often on the mouth. The rest of the disciples were offended by it and expressed disapproval" (Brown, p. 207). Teabing asserted, "As any Aramaic scholar will tell you, the word companion, in those days, literally meant spouse."

There are several problems with this claim. First, the document is very old and has several holes. There just happens to be a hole after "kiss her often" so that we do not know where Jesus allegedly used to kiss her, according to this document. It could have been the hand or forehead. Second, the document we have today was written in Coptic (from ancient Egypt), and even that was probably a translation of the Greek form of the document in which it was originally written. So it does not matter what an Aramaic scholar would tell us. But if it did, there are no Aramaic or Hebrew words that normally mean spouse.[3]

This leads us to another problem in the book. Dan Brown portrays Church history as one long assault against women and what he called "the sacred feminine," which was allegedly honored throughout ancient pagan cultures. The Church has certainly had its share of mistakes since its inception. After all, the Church is made up of sinful men and women who make mistakes. However, Christianity has done more to elevate women to equality than any other belief system because the Bible states that both male and female are made in God's image (Genesis 1:26–27).

Brown thinks he elevates women in his book by discussing "the sacred feminine" and "the goddess." The book's protagonist, Robert Langdon, told Sophie, "The ancients believed that the male was spiritually incomplete until he had carnal knowledge of the sacred feminine. Physical union with the female remained the sole means through which man could become spiritually complete and ultimately achieve *gnosis* — knowledge of the divine" (Brown, p. 261).

On the surface, this seems to elevate women above men, but look closer. It's hard to imagine something more demeaning to women. Imagine telling young men that the only way they could ever achieve

---

3. Dr. Craig L. Blomberg, "*The Da Vinci Code: A Novel*," *Denver Seminary Journal*, volume 7 (Denver, CO: Denver Seminary, 2004). Available online at http://www.denverseminary.edu/article/the-da-vinci-code-a-novel/, accessed June 14, 2010.

knowledge of the divine was to have sexual intercourse with women. Countless women would simply be used as a means to an end. Rather than endorsing the Bible's instruction to love one's wife as Christ loved the Church (Ephesians 5:25), *The Da Vinci Code* endorses using women as sex objects.

Dan Brown would have his readers believe that Christianity is to blame for suppressing women. However, consider the following statement from *The Gospel of Thomas*, a Gnostic text. "Simon Peter said to them, 'Let Mary [Magdalene?] leave us, for women are not worthy of life.' Jesus said, 'I myself shall lead her in order to make her male, so that she too may become a living spirit, resembling you males. For every woman who makes herself male will enter the kingdom of heaven' " (saying 114). This Gnostic text says that women cannot enter the kingdom of heaven unless they make themselves male — whatever that might mean.

The Bible, on the other hand, clearly teaches that both men and women are made in God's image (Genesis 1:26–27), we have all sinned and are all in need of redemption (Romans 3:23), and both men and women are saved by God's grace alone, received through faith alone, in Christ alone (Galatians 3:28; Ephesians 2:8–9). Each woman has been designed by God to fulfill His unique plan for her life. She does not need to become male in order to be saved. Like any man, she needs to repent of sin and have faith in Christ alone to be saved.

What about Brown's insistence that Jesus was married to Mary Magdalene? After all, marriage was instituted by God, so it couldn't have been wrong for Jesus to marry, could it? This is an interesting question because marriage is from God and it is not sinful for a man and woman to marry under the right circumstances (1 Corinthians 7:28). However, the Bible also indicates that when husband and wife come together, they become one flesh (Genesis 2:24). This would be problematic in Christ's case because He was sinless and could not become "one flesh" with some-one who was a sinner, which Mary clearly was (Luke 8:2).

Attacks on Jesus Christ

" 'What I mean,' Teabing countered, 'is that almost everything our fathers taught us about Christ is *false*' " (Brown, p. 198). *The Da Vinci Code* proposes a radical redefinition of Jesus Christ. Rather than Jesus being fully God and fully man, the Son of God, and the Second Person of the Trinity, Dan Brown claims that Jesus was only a man.

" 'My dear,' Teabing declared, 'until that moment in history [the Council of Nicaea], Jesus was viewed by His followers as a mortal prophet . . . a great and powerful man, but a man nonetheless. A mortal' " (Brown, p. 197).

We have already seen that the Council of Nicaea overwhelmingly affirmed the full deity of Jesus Christ. But where did the idea of Christ's divinity come from? Was it invented by the Church during Constantine's day to "expand their own power," as Brown claims (Brown, p. 197)?

The reason the bishops affirmed the deity of Jesus is because that is exactly what He claimed about Himself and what the New Testament authors taught. It was also the view of the early Church up until that time and ever since.

Jesus Claimed to Be God

Jesus affirmed His divinity on numerous occasions. In John 10:30 Jesus stated, "I and My Father are one." Look at the response by the Jews. They picked up stones to kill Him for apparent blasphemy. When He asked them why they wanted to stone Him, they replied, ". . . because You, being a Man, make Yourself God" (John 10:33).

In John 8:58 Jesus stated, "Most assuredly, I say to you, before Abraham was, I AM." Here Jesus identified Himself as the God of the Old Testament. Once again, the Jews knew exactly what He was doing, because they immediately took up stones to kill Him.

In John 18:4–6, when He was about to be arrested, Jesus once again applied God's name to Himself when He said, "I am *He*." The word *He* does not appear in the original. So Jesus again appropriated God's name for Himself, and this time, the troops and officers fell to the ground.

Jesus claimed to be able to forgive sins (Matthew 9:2; Luke 7:48). He healed people from paralysis (Mark 2:11), leprosy (Matthew 8:3), and blindness (John 9:6–7). He demonstrated His power over nature (Matthew 14:25, 32) and over death (Matthew 9:25; Luke 7:14–15; John 11:43–44). All of these miracles testify loud and clear that Jesus truly was and is God.

New Testament Claims Jesus Is God

The gospel of John starts with this statement: "In the beginning was the Word, and the Word was with God, and the Word was God" (John

1:1). Lest there be any confusion about the identity of the Word, John added, "And the Word became flesh and dwelt among us, and we beheld His glory, the glory as of the only begotten of the Father, full of grace and truth" (John 1:14). In fact, John revealed that he wrote his gospel so that "you may believe that Jesus is the Christ, the Son of God, and that believing you may have life in His name" (John 20:31).

After the disciples witnessed Jesus walk on water and calm the storm at sea, they declared, "Truly You are the Son of God" (Matthew 14:33). One day, Jesus asked His disciples what the people thought about Him. After a couple of responses, He asked them directly, "But who do you say that I am?" Peter responded, "You are the Christ, the Son of the living God" (Matthew 16:13–16). Peter repeatedly used the title "Lord Jesus Christ" in his letters (1 Peter 1:3; 2 Peter 1:8, 11, 14, 16) and identified Jesus as the Son of God (2 Peter 1:17). When Thomas (often called Doubting Thomas) saw Jesus after He had risen from the dead, he declared, "My Lord and my God!" (John 20:28).

The Apostle Paul regularly proclaimed that Jesus is God. In Romans 1:3 he called Jesus "our Lord," and the "Son" of God. In Colossians 2:9 he wrote, "For in Him [Jesus] dwells all the fullness of the Godhead bodily." In Philippians 2:10–11 he stated, "that at the name of Jesus every knee should bow, of those in heaven, and of those on earth, and of those under the earth, and that every tongue should confess that Jesus Christ is Lord, to the glory of God the Father."

Early Church Believed Jesus Is God

The words of Scripture are inspired by God and therefore infallible. So when the Bible proclaims that Jesus is God, that settles the matter. However, Dan Brown has alleged that the early Church was divided on whether or not Jesus should be seen as divine. Once again, Brown is in error. Here is a list of what several early Church fathers, prior to Nicaea, said about Jesus (dates are approximate).

Ignatius (A.D. 105): "God Himself being manifested in human form."[4]

---

4. Ignatius, *Epistle of Ignatius*, XIX, cited in Alexander Roberts and James Donaldson, editors, *Ante-Nicene Fathers*, Volume I, electronic edition (Peabody, MA: Hendrickson, 1994).

Clement (A.D. 150): "It is fitting that you should think of Jesus Christ as of God."[5]

Justin Martyr (A.D. 160): "The Father of the universe has a Son. And He . . . is even God."[6]

Irenaeus (A.D. 180): "He is God, for the name Emmanuel indicates this."[7]

Tertullian (A.D. 200): "Christ our God."[8]

Origen (A.D. 225): "And as no one ought to be offended, seeing God is the Father, that the Savior is also God."[9]

Novatian (A.D. 235): "He is not only man, but God also."[10]

Cyprian (A.D. 250): "Let us assuredly, as far as we can, please Christ our Lord and God."[11]

Methodius (A.D. 290): "He truly was and is, being in the beginning with God, and being God."[12]

Lactantius (A.D. 304): "We believe Him to be God."[13]

Arnobius (A.D. 305): "Christ performed all those miracles . . . by the inherent might of His authority; and as was the proper duty of the true God."[14]

More names could be added to this list, but these are sufficient to show that Christ's divinity was not concocted by Constantine and the Church in an attempt to grab power.

Finally, Dan Brown's character Teabing claimed, "Constantine's underhanded political maneuvers don't diminish the majesty of Christ's life. Nobody is saying Christ was a fraud, or denying He walked the earth and inspired millions to better lives" (Brown, p. 197). Stripping Jesus of divinity, thus making Him a liar many times over, does, in fact, "diminish the majesty of Christ's life." That's exactly what Brown has attempted to do in this novel, but God's Word will stand the test of time. Jesus said,

---

5. Ibid., Clement, *The Second Epistle of Clement*, I.
6. Ibid., Justin Martyr, *The First Apology*, LXIII.
7. Ibid., Irenaeus, *Against Heresies*, III.21.
8. Ibid., Tertullian, *Part Third*, VI.13
9. Ibid., Origen, *De Principiis*, I.2.
10. Ibid., Novatian, *A Treatise Concerning the Trinity*, XI.
11. Ibid., Cyprian, *The Epistles of Cyprian*, LXI.
12. Ibid., Methodius, *The Banquet of the Ten Virgins*; Or, *Concerning Chastity*, III. 6.
13. Ibid., Lactantius, *The Divine Institutes*, V.3.
14. Ibid., Arnobius, *The Seven Books of Arnobius*, I.44.

"Heaven and earth will pass away, but My words will by no means pass away" (Matthew 24:35).

Conclusion

Entire books have been written to refute the many errors and lies found in *The Da Vinci Code*. This brief summary has demonstrated that Dan Brown's novel is full of falsehoods, even though he has claimed that the historical details are entirely accurate. He missed the mark on dozens of simple facts that can be easily checked out. He has misrepresented Christian history and put it in the worst possible light. He has lied about the identity of Jesus Christ as the Son of God and slandered Him and His followers.

Christians can rest assured that they possess the accurate record of history in the Bible. Jesus is exactly who He claimed to be, the Son of God who came in the flesh to die for the sins of the world and to rise from the dead three days later. Contrary to Brown's claim that a man's way to the divine is through sexual intercourse with a woman, Jesus proclaimed that He is the only way to God and that no one can go to the Father except through Him (John 14:6). Jesus said, "Most assuredly, I say to you, he who hears My word and believes in Him who sent Me has everlasting life, and shall not come into judgment, but has passed from death into life" (John 5:24).

One day Jesus will return to this world He created, and those who have placed their faith in Him will be saved from judgment. Those who refuse His gracious offer of eternal life will suffer for eternity apart from Him. Dan Brown's words will pass away, but the words of Jesus will last forever.

Chapter 13

How Did We Get the Bible in English?

Herb Samworth

C an you imagine a world without books? In spite of the increase in communication by the Internet and other electronic media, the basic resource for knowledge remains the book. If we depend on books for information about the present life, how infinitely more important is it that we have the means of knowledge concerning life's ultimate issues?

The wonderful news is that God has given us this knowledge in a book that we know as the Bible. What a privilege to have such a text! What meaning could life have without its existence? Have you ever wondered how we got the Bible and the wonderful message of the gospel? We have it as a complete document, but it did not begin that way. The knowledge of how God gave us the Bible will enable us to appreciate it more.

The Origin of the Bible

The history of the Bible is the account of God communicating to mankind the knowledge of Himself and His grace and mercy. This process of communication from God to man is called revelation. Revelation is simply God revealing Himself to mankind. Because of man's sin, he is unable to grasp spiritual realities. However, the understanding of spiritual truths is absolutely necessary if man is to know God personally, experience the forgiveness of sins, and have the hope of eternal life. These are the ultimate issues of life, and man must have the means to know the answers to them.

The Bible opens with an inspired account of the creation of the world, including the creation of man in God's image. *Inspiration* is a theological word, but its basic meaning is that God enabled man to write in human language words that were identical in meaning to His own words. The process of inspiration was so controlled by the Holy Spirit that the final result was without mistakes.[1]

From the biblical evidence, Moses wrote the first five books of the Old Testament called the Pentateuch. Bible scholars believe that he began to write about 1450 B.C. However, many of the events Moses recorded took place more than centuries earlier. How could Moses know about the creation of the world and man? The simple answer is that God revealed it to him (of course, Moses likely used some preexisting texts to edit as well, e.g. Genesis 5:1). The Scriptures, not science, provide the authoritative account of the creation of the world.

By the time of Moses, human writing was still highly developed. Archaeologists have discovered writing on stone (called inscriptions), on clay tablets (using a wedge-form of writing called cuneiform), animal hides, wood, and other materials. Moses surely wrote in Hebrew, the language of the Israelites, and he probably wrote on animal hides in a scroll format.

God commanded Moses to place a copy of his writings in the ark of the covenant in the Holy of Holies (Deuteronomy 10:2). After the death of Moses, God gave Israel's new leader, Joshua, special instructions concerning these books. Joshua was to meditate on and obey their precepts. God not only promised him good success but also indicated that He would guide His people by this book.[2]

---

1. This process of inspiration is called organic because it takes into account the author's education, culture, and background. The organic view of inspiration is contrasted with the so-called mechanical or dictation view that the writer merely served as a penman to write the words. For an explanation of this view, see Basil Manly Jr., *The Biblical Doctrine of Inspiration* (Harrisonburg, VA: Gano Books, 1985), p. 68.

2. See Deuteronomy 31:26 and Joshua 1:8. In addition, note Deuteronomy 17:18 where the king was commanded to write out a personal copy of the Law. Taking the three texts together, we gain an understanding of the importance of God's Word in the life and worship of the nation of Israel. Note also that God commanded what books were to be included. This is the first instance of canonization or determining what books are truly Scripture.

As the history of Israel unfolded, additional books were built on the books of Moses. The writing of the Hebrew canonical Scriptures would not be completed until 420 B.C. with the Book of Malachi. These Scriptures were divided into a three-fold division: Law, Prophets, and Writings. Although the organization and order of the books in the Hebrew Scriptures are different from the English Bible, the content is exactly the same.

The Transmission of the Hebrew Text

During the following years, a special group of priests, called the scribes, was founded. Their responsibility was to make new copies of the Scriptures as the older copies wore out. The majority of these texts were copied on animal skins that had been tanned to produce leather, although they later would be copied on other materials including papyrus. The writing was in the form of a scroll.

Special rules directed the scribes in their work of copying the Scriptures. For example, before they could write the covenant name of God, translated into English as "Jehovah," they were required to wash their hands, use a special brush or pen dedicated only to writing that name, and then wash their hands after finishing writing the word. They were extremely careful to copy the words exactly, because the Scripture was the Word of God. They even devised a special means to count the number of words on a single panel to determine if the text had been copied accurately.

Jewish scribes had an interesting view of the copies of the Scriptures. Because they would use such care in copying them, they believed that a newer copy would be more accurate than an older copy. Most people tend to believe that the older copy would be more accurate because of the errors that could have crept into the text as it was copied over the years.

This view, that the newer copy was more accurate, led to a further question: what was to be done with the older manuscript, called the exemplar, from which the text had been copied? No one had the authority to destroy it because it was the Word of God. The solution was to have the scribes place the manuscript in a clay jar and then bury it. Thus, the processes of nature that God Himself had instituted would cause the copy to disintegrate. As a result of this practice, we do not have extremely old copies of the Hebrew Scriptures. Before the discovery of the Dead Sea Scrolls in 1947, the oldest extant manuscript copies of the Hebrew text were about one thousand years old. In comparison, we possess manuscripts of the Greek New Testament that are dated as early as A.D. 200 (and perhaps sooner).[3]

The Beginning of Translations

Around 200 B.C. a remarkable event illustrated how God prepared the world for the coming of the Messiah. That event was the translation of the Hebrew Scriptures into the Greek language. Although the exact details are unknown, the king of Egypt desired a copy of every known literary work for inclusion in the famed Library of Alexandria. To secure a copy of the Hebrew Scriptures, he invited 72 scribes from Israel to undertake the work of translation. Tradition states that each of the scribes was housed in a separate house to complete the task. Tradition also states that each scribe completed his work in 70 days, and all the copies were exactly the same!

Although the account of the translation has undoubtedly been exaggerated, we should not overlook the fact that for the first time the Word of God had been translated into another language. This translation was called the Septuagint, a word that means 70 in the Greek language. It became the Bible of the early Church, and many New Testament authors quoted from it rather than from the Hebrew text (and this makes sense considering the New Testament is written in Greek). For example, the Book of Hebrews uses the Septuagint to quote from the Old Testament.

Copies of this Greek translation soon made their way into all areas of the Roman Empire because most of the inhabitants spoke the Greek language. The knowledge of the Word of God in an accessible language paved the way for the preaching of the Gospel of Jesus Christ years later.

The Writing of the New Testament

There was a marked contrast between the amount of time required for the writing of the Old Testament books and the writing of the New Testament. It required nearly 1,000 years before the Old Testament was completed in comparison with the approximately 50 years for the writing of the New Testament. Scholars believe that the final books of the New Testament were completed by the Apostle John before the year A.D. 100 (some scholars even place it before A.D. 70).

---

3. The manuscript evidence for both the Hebrew Old Testament and the Greek New Testament is briefly but adequately surveyed by Neil Lightfoot in the third edition of *How We Got the Bible* (Grand Rapids, MI: Baker Books, 2003). Note especially chapters 3 and 12.

There was another contrast between the writing of the two testaments. The task of writing the Old Testament was given to the Jewish people, and the majority of its books were written in the land of Israel. The exceptions were the books written during the time of the Babylonian captivity such as Daniel, Ezekiel, and Esther or by Moses prior to entering the land or Job, which was written in the East (Job 1:3). Although the majority of the New Testament books were also written by Jewish authors, Luke's Gospel and Acts being the exceptions, they were written in different locations of the Roman Empire.[4] For example, Paul wrote his epistles from several cities, including Corinth and Rome.

The New Testament books were written and circulated as single units of composition. It is probable that the majority of them were written on papyrus. Later, they would be collected into groups such as the epistles of Paul, the Gospels, etc. Finally, they would be bound together as a single volume. They were originally written in a scroll format, but as they were transcribed and bound together, they would be placed into the codex or book format. There is evidence that helps us reveal that this format was first used by the Church about A.D. 100 to distinguish their writings from the Jewish synagogues.

Although the books had been written before A.D. 100, the process by which they were recognized as Scripture, known as canonization, took longer. Of course, a book was Scripture the moment it was written, but it took time for church people to realize this because they were spread about. It is an important fact that the Church did not formulate the canon; rather, they recognized it. Here is a chart that contrasts incorrect views of the canon with correct views of the canon:[5]

Incorrect View of Canon	Correct View of Canon
Church Determines Canon	Church Discovers Canon
Church Is Mother of Canon	Church Is Child of Canon
Church Is Magistrate of Canon	Church Is Minister of Canon
Church Regulates Canon	Church Recognizes Canon
Church Is Judge of Canon	Church Is Witness of Canon
Church Is Master of Canon	Church Is Servant of Canon

---

4. There has been some debate over Luke's ancestry and whether he was Jewish or not. His name tends to be more Greek by nature, but many Jews did live abroad. Much of this debate is centered on Romans 3:2.

5. Chart taken from Norman Geisler, *Systematic Theology*, Volume I (Minneapolis, MN: Bethany House, 2002), p. 530.

Several books, known as the *antilegomena*, were not immediately accepted as canonical. The word itself means "spoken against," and some were convinced these books were not Scripture. For example, many people thought the epistle of James should be excluded because James apparently taught a doctrine of justification by works in contrast to the Apostle Paul. Others rejected the Book of Hebrews because no human author was named. However, with time it was recognized that James and Paul taught the same doctrine of justification and many think that Hebrews did not contain the author's name because it was important to stress its divine origin.

Other excluded books were the *pseudepigraphia*. These books had supposedly been written by one of the Apostles or a well-known Christian. However, evidence demonstrated that the real author had only used the name of the Apostle to gain acceptance for the book. An example of the *pseudepigraphia* was the gospel of Peter.

Vernacular Translations

With the Scriptures, the Church was prepared to take the gospel to all nations. For a time, it was easy to preach the gospel because most people understood the Greek language. But as the boundaries of the Church expanded, it became apparent there were many who did not speak Greek. What was to be done?

There was precedence for what the Church did. The Hebrew Scriptures had been translated into Greek about 200 B.C. and had proven to be a great blessing to the Gentiles. Now the Scriptures, beginning with the New Testament, were translated into the vernacular languages of the day. Within a short time, people whose spoken language was Syriac, Latin, Coptic, or another language had copies of the Word of God in their own native tongue.[6]

A thrilling account of a vernacular translation is the history of two brothers, Cyril and Methodius, who were originally from Thessalonica. The Bishop of Rome sent them to evangelize the Slavs sometime in the ninth century. However, the Slavs did not have a written language. So Cyril designed an alphabet, called the *Cyrillic*, to translate the Bible into

---

6. The best resource of information for this work of translation remains Bruce Metzger, *The Early Versions of the New Testament: Their Origin, Transmission and Limitations* (New York: Oxford University Press, 1977). This work is indispensable for the history of early vernaculars, and remains the standard in the field.

the Slavonic language. This alphabet remains in use today as the alphabet of the Russian language. Not only did the brothers provide a great boon to the Slavonic people in giving them the Word of God, but also they made a lasting contribution to their culture.

The Dominance of the Latin Vulgate

For the people of Western Europe, the most significant translation was the Latin. Although Latin today is a "dead" language because it is not spoken, this was not the situation during the times of the early Church. A Latin translation had been done by unknown persons, but the date is uncertain. This translation was called the *Itala* or Old Latin. Because the scribes were careless in copying its manuscripts, the text soon became riddled with errors.

The Bishop of Rome, Damasus, about A.D. 380 realized the seriousness of the situation. He persuaded Jerome, the finest textual scholar of the time, to revise the New Testament. Jerome not only revised the New Testament but went to Bethlehem, studied Hebrew, and translated the entire Old Testament directly into Latin. The Old Testament of the Itala had been translated from the Septuagint. The task required 20 years, but Jerome completed it in A.D. 402. This translation was called the Vulgate because it was the form of Latin spoken by the majority of the people.[7]

The Vulgate became the Bible of the Western or Roman Church. Although it was not officially ratified until A.D. 1546 at the Council of Trent, it had long been the standard version of the Scriptures. Although Jerome wanted to exclude the Apocrypha,[8] Pope Damasus insisted that it be included. To show his displeasure, Jerome put it between the Old and New Testaments. As a result, books that the Jews considered non-canonical were included as Scripture.

Jerome also made some crucial errors in translating key New Testament words, especially the word *to justify*. In its New Testament

---

7. See Metzger, *The Early Versions of the New Testament*, for the details.
8. Although there are numerous apocryphal books, the term Apocrypha usually refers to those books added to the Roman Catholic canon during the Council of Trent (1546–1563) and consists of the following books: Wisdom of Solomon, Ecclesiasticus, Tobit, 1 Maccabees, 2 Maccabees, Judith, Baruch, and the Letter of Jeremiah. It also includes additional sections to Esther and two extra chapters in Daniel known as Susanna and Bel and the Dragon. Roman Catholics often refer to these books as deuterocanonical ("second canon"). Protestants do not believe the Apocrypha is inspired and therefore reject them as canonical.

usage, this word always means "to declare righteous" (a change of legal status). However, Jerome translated it as a word that means "to make righteous" (a change of moral fitness). As a result, the official teaching of the doctrine of justification by the Roman Catholic Church is that God justifies a person by making him or her righteous. This has tremendous implications as to how one becomes a Christian.[9]

The Translation of the Bible into English

In the West, national churches were branches of the Church of Rome. Although the people spoke different languages, the only available Bible was the Latin Vulgate. Practically speaking, this meant that the knowledge of God's Word was concealed from the majority of the people because they neither read nor understood Latin.

At this time God raised up a man to translate the Bible into the English language. That man was John Wycliffe, who lived from A.D. 1330 to 1384. In his work of translation, Wycliffe used the Vulgate because it was the only available text. Two translations into English were done. One followed closely the word order of the Vulgate and is difficult to read. The other, done primarily by John Purvey, is freer in its translation and thus easier to read.[10]

After Wycliffe's death in 1384, the English clergy declared English translations to be illegal at the Convocation of Oxford in 1408. No one was permitted to translate the Bible into English apart from the permission of a bishop. Thus, the English Bible would be officially illegal for nearly 130 years.

The Printing of the Greek New Testament

While this was occurring in England, God prepared the way for the Reformation of the 16th century. In 1453, Constantinople, where the headquarters of the Greek Church was located, fell to the Muslims. No longer could Greek Christians worship freely. Many of them migrated to

---

9. For the importance and proof of the above, see Philip Schaff, *The Creeds of Christendom, Volume II*, reprint edition (Grand Rapids, MI: Baker Books House, 1983). Note especially Chapters IV and VII of The Decrees and Canons of the Council of Trent.

10. A modern critical study of the person and work of John Wycliffe remains to be done. Much of the current literature appears to be in the interest of diminishing or even eliminating his role in the translation of the Bible into English. An example of this view of Wycliffe is found in G.R. Evans, *John Wycliffe: Myth & Reality* (Downers Grove: IL: IVP Academic, 2005). The subtitle of the book illustrates the author's presuppositions.

the West, bringing with them Greek manuscripts of the New Testament. Meanwhile in Europe a great cultural revival, known as the Renaissance, was underway. The key theme of the Renaissance was *ad fontes* ("to the sources"). As a result, a great revival of the Greek language occurred in Western Europe. During this time the art of printing by moveable type was perfected by Johannes Gutenberg.

These events combined so that by the early years of the 16th century the means to produce a printed edition of the Greek New Testament existed. In 1516 the first Greek New Testament, called the *Novum Instrumentum*, was issued from the press of Johannes Froben of Basel. This Greek New Testament had been edited by Erasmus of Rotterdam, the great humanist, who remained in the Roman Catholic Church even though he sided with some positions that many Protestants held. Many consider this book to be the most important book ever printed because it sparked the Reformation of the 16th century.[11]

For Erasmus to edit the Greek New Testament, it was necessary to obtain manuscript copies of the Greek text. He located five or six

---

11. The standard biography of Erasmus is Roland H. Bainton, *Erasmus of Christendom* (New York: Charles Scribner's Sons, 1969). For the influence of this book on the beginning of the Reformation, consult Roland H. Bainton, *Here I Stand: A Life of Martin Luther* (New York: Abingdon-Cokesbury Press, 1950).

manuscript copies in the monasteries around Basel that he used as the basis for the printed text. Most, if not all, of these texts had originally come from Constantinople. Manuscripts from that area formed what is called a text type or a text that had similar readings. This text type from Constantinople came to be known as the *Byzantine*. As a result, the Byzantine text type became the dominant one of the Middle Ages.[12]

The dominance of the Byzantine text type continued for nearly 350 years. All Reformation Bibles of the 16th century, including German, English, French, and others, were translated from this text type. This text type continued to be printed by the successors of Erasmus: Robert Stephanus and Theodore Beza. It reached its high water mark in 1633 in a Greek New Testament published by the Elzevirs of the Netherlands. In the book's introduction, we find the following words in Latin: "The reader now has the *text received* by all in which we give nothing changed or corrupted" (emphasis added). This became known as the *Textus Receptus* or the received text due to the publisher's blurb. For many, this version continues to remain the standard Greek text even in the 21st century, especially to those who favor the King James Version.

However, there were critics who were dissatisfied with the *Textus Receptus*. On the negative side, they pointed to the relatively few manuscripts that Erasmus had used to edit the Greek New Testament, and that those manuscripts were dated no earlier than the 10th or 11th centuries.

The following years saw the discovery of additional manuscripts. Some of these were dated earlier and were of a different text type than those used by Erasmus. Some originated in Egypt and were written in a script that used block capital letters. These were called *uncial* manuscripts, and while many of the readings agreed with the Byzantine text type, there were some significant differences. This new text type became known as the *Alexandrian* text.

The most important discoveries of manuscripts of the Alexandrian text type were the *Codex Sinaiticus* and the *Codex Vaticanus*. The *Codex Sinaiticus* is believed to be the oldest complete manuscript of the Greek New Testament and is dated as early as A.D. 350. The *Codex Vaticanus*, while not complete, agrees with the *Codex Sinaiticus*. Many scholars

---

12. See Bruce M. Metzger, *The Text of the New Testament: Its Transmission, Corruption, and Restoration* (New York: Oxford University Press, 1968) for the history of the printing and transmission of the Greek New Testament.

believe these two manuscripts were among the 50 Bibles commissioned by Constantine.

With the increase of the number of older Greek manuscripts, dissatisfaction with the *Textus Receptus* increased. There were calls for a new edition of the printed Greek New Testament that would include the textual variants found in the recently discovered manuscripts.

The Critical Greek New Testament

In 1881 a new edition of the Greek New Testament, edited by Bishop Brooke Foss Westcott and Fenton John Anthony Hort, was published by Cambridge University Press. The publication of this *Critical Greek New Testament* was not without controversy. Some hailed its publication as bringing textual studies into the 19th century while others claimed the variant readings from the Alexandrian texts (Codex Sinaiticus and others) allowed heresy to creep into the New Testament.[13]

The publication of the *Critical Greek New Testament* and the controversy it engendered remains a debated topic. However, its publication signaled the beginning of English translations using it as the textual base.

Modern English Versions

Concurrent with the publication of the *Critical Greek New Testament* was a new English translation called the *Revised Version* (RV) undertaken by a joint committee of British and American scholars. The *Revised Version* was published during the years 1881–1885. However, members of the American Committee disagreed with certain translations of the British Committee, and in 1901 they published the *American Standard Version* (ASV). Following the publication of these two versions has come a multiplicity of translations. Today, we are familiar with the *New American Standard Bible* (NASB), the *New Revised Standard Version* (NRSV), the *New International Version* (NIV), the *English Standard Version* (ESV), and many others. These translations all use the *Critical Greek New Testament* as their textual base.

What of the *Critical Greek New Testament* itself? Since the groundbreaking publication by Westcott and Hort in 1881, the text has been constantly updated. A major discovery has been Greek manuscripts

---

13 See Metzger, *The Text of the New Testament,* for the details of the printing of the *Critical Greek New Testament.*

preserved on papyrus. The majority of these manuscripts are from Egypt because the arid climate permitted their preservation. Many are dated to the second and third centuries and have readings that agree with the Alexandrian text type.[14]

How has the discovery of new Greek manuscripts influenced modern English versions? Several things should be remembered. First, God has providentially preserved the text of His Word, both in the Hebrew and Greek languages. Scholars possess about 3,400 Greek manuscripts of the New Testament alone. Second, the manuscripts demonstrate amazing agreement. While no one manuscript agrees completely with another, the differences amount to just one word in a thousand. Putting it another way, 999 out of every 1,000 words are in agreement in the Greek texts. It is possible to print these textual variants (differences between the words) on just two pages of a standard Greek New Testament. While these variants are important because we are dealing with the Word of God, not one of them calls into question a major doctrine of Scripture.

What does this mean practically? It demonstrates that the English Bible is trustworthy because God is trustworthy. If God chose to guide His people through His Word, we believe He has preserved that Word to guide our lives today.

An illustration will confirm the truth of the above statement. When the Dead Sea Scrolls were discovered in 1947, no one had been aware of their existence for nearly 2,000 years. Yet when those manuscripts were compared with the existing manuscripts of the Old Testament, the differences were inconsequential. The Bible is the record of God's grace in giving us the Word of Life and the record of His power in preserving it. Let us honor the God of Scripture by reading and trusting in Him through His written Word!

---

14 Lightfoot, *How We Got the Bible*, has a fascinating account of their discovery and importance.

Chapter 14

Polygamy in the Light of Scripture

Roger Patterson

✿✿✿✿✿✿✿✿✿✿✿✿✿✿✿✿✿✿✿✿

The Bible is an incredibly candid book when compared to the religious writings of other traditions. Rather than covering up the faults and flaws of its key figures, the Bible frequently shows us humanity in its deepest sin. A prime example of this is the transparent treatment of David's adulterous relationship with Bathsheba and his murder of Uriah (2 Samuel 11). These sinful actions had real consequences from which we can draw lessons, and David's repentance gives us a model to follow when we fall into sin. Likewise, the Bible records many instances of polygamy in the Old Testament, involving even some of the patriarchs of Israel.

Though our common usage of *polygamy* tends to be applied to a man with multiple wives, the word *polygamy* simply means multiple spouses. More accurately, *polygyny* would be one man with multiple wives, while *polyandry* would be one woman with multiple husbands. *Bigamy* is another word used for having two spouses. More recently, those who live in communities of open relationships have been called *polyamorous*, having multiple husbands, wives, boyfriends, and girlfriends in various arrangements. As we look at Scripture, none of these arrangements matches the structure of marriage given by God from the beginning.

The First Marriage

When God created the universe, He did things in a very specific manner. Those descriptions are provided for us in Genesis 1–2. At the end of His creative activity, God pronounced the things He had made as being "very good" (Genesis 1:31). In Genesis 2 we learn the details of the creation of mankind. After creating Adam from the dust of the ground, God presented the beasts of the field and the birds of the air to Adam to name. When Adam found no suitable helper, God formed the first woman from Adam's side.

> And the Lord God said, "It is not good that man should be alone; I will make him a helper comparable to him." Out of the ground the Lord God formed every beast of the field and every bird of the air, and brought them to Adam to see what he would call them. And whatever Adam called each living creature, that was its name. So Adam gave names to all cattle, to the birds of the air, and to every beast of the field. But for Adam there was not found a helper comparable to him.
>
> And the Lord God caused a deep sleep to fall on Adam, and he slept; and He took one of his ribs, and closed up the flesh in its place. Then the rib which the Lord God had taken from man He made into a woman, and He brought her to the man.
>
> And Adam said: "This is now bone of my bones and flesh of my flesh; she shall be called Woman, because she was taken out of Man."
>
> Therefore a man shall leave his father and mother and be joined to his wife, and they shall become one flesh.
>
> And they were both naked, the man and his wife, and were not ashamed (Genesis 2:18–25).

Let's look closely at this passage and note several key phrases that indicate God's intent for marriage to be monogamous — one man for one woman. First, God intended to make "a helper" for Adam, not several helpers. Second, from one rib God made one woman for Adam. Genesis 2:24 reveals the pattern of a man leaving his family to "be joined to his wife," not wives. This union is then described as becoming "one flesh."

Jesus confirmed this understanding of marriage when He was asked about divorce by the Pharisees. This is recorded in Mark 10:1–12 and

Matthew 19:1–12. In His response Jesus quoted from Genesis 2, confirming that His understanding of marriage was one man for one woman. Confirming the covenantal nature of marriage, Jesus said that divorce was only allowed because of the hardness of the hearts of man. God intended, from the beginning, for marriages to consist of one man and one woman for the duration of their lives. Divorce and polygamy were regulated in the laws given to Moses, but polygamy was recorded long before then.

Polygamy and the Bible

The first reference to polygamy is found in Genesis 4 in the lineage of Cain. Of Lamech, a descendant of Cain, we read:

> Then Lamech took for himself two wives: the name of one was Adah, and the name of the second was Zillah. And Adah bore Jabal. He was the father of those who dwell in tents and have livestock. His brother's name was Jubal. He was the father of all those who play the harp and flute. And as for Zillah, she also bore Tubal-Cain, an instructor of every craftsman in bronze and iron. And the sister of Tubal-Cain was Naamah.

> Then Lamech said to his wives:
> "Adah and Zillah, hear my voice;
> Wives of Lamech, listen to my speech!
> For I have killed a man for wounding me,
> Even a young man for hurting me.
> If Cain shall be avenged sevenfold,
> Then Lamech seventy-sevenfold." (Genesis 4:19–24)

Before the Flood, we have a clear distortion of what God had intended for marriage. To compound Lamech's sin, he brags of his murderous deeds. The Flood was brought upon the earth to judge the sinfulness of mankind, including the sins committed by Lamech.

After the Flood, there are many mentions of polygamous relationships — including among the patriarchs of Israel. Abraham, Jacob, David, and Solomon all had multiple wives. It is interesting to note that there are no passages in Scripture that clearly state, "No man should have more than one wife." However, polygamous relationships are never mentioned in a positive light, and, indeed, the problems of such relationships are presented.

Consider the consequences revealed in Scripture in each of the following cases: Abraham — led to bitterness between Sarah and her maid, Hagar, and the eventual dismissal of Hagar and Ishmael; Jacob — led to Rachel's jealousy of Leah and to Joseph being betrayed and sold by his half-brothers; David — led to the rape of one of his daughters (Tamar) by one of his sons (Tamar's half-brother Amnon) and Amnon's subsequent murder by Tamar's brother Absalom; Solomon — his many wives "turned away his heart" from the Lord and to the worship of false gods (1 Kings 11:1–8). Just because the Bible records polygamous relationships does not mean that God approves of such things.

The only direct command against polygamy is given to the kings that were to rule Israel, as they are told not to "multiply wives" to themselves (Deuteronomy 17:17). It is also interesting to note that polygamous relationships seem to be regulated in the commands Moses gave to the nation of Israel. Leviticus 18:18 instructs that a man should not marry sisters, and Deuteronomy 21:15 talks of assigning an heir to a man with two wives. Many commentators suggest that the passages do not endorse polygamy but rather prohibit it. Deuteronomy 21:15 may also be translated as "has had two wives" in succession rather than at the same time. The sisters in Leviticus 18:18 are understood by some to be any Israelite women. Regardless of the interpretation of these passages, the taking of multiple wives is not in accord with God's design from the beginning.

Moving to the New Testament, there are several passages that can be understood to speak against polygamous relationships. The first to come to the mind of many would be the qualifications for leaders in the Church given by the Apostle Paul to Timothy and Titus. In 1 Timothy 3:2 and 12 and Titus 1:6, we are told that leaders of the Church must be the "husband of one wife."

In 1 Corinthians 7:1–16 Paul answered questions that the Corinthian church had about marriage. In this passage Paul used the singular form of wife and husband throughout the passage. In fact, this is true of the New Testament writers in general.

Scripture compares the relationship of husband and wife to that of Christ and the Church. In Ephesians 5:25–33 Paul explained this relationship and referred back to Genesis 2:24. Once again, God's standard for marriage is defined as one man and one woman. Paul finished this analogy by stating, "Let each one of you in particular so love his own wife as himself, and let the wife see that she respects her husband" (Ephesians 5:33).

Polygamy in Other Religions

Other religions have promoted polygamy. For example, according to Sura 4:3 of the Koran, Islamic men are allowed to take up to four wives under certain circumstances. Muhammad was granted the privilege of many wives in Sura 33 and had many wives. Modern Muslims practice polygamy in various ways according to their cultural context.

Historically, members of the Latter-day Saints (LDS or Mormons) practiced polygamy, although the acceptance of the practice changed as new "revelation" was given to the prophets of the church. Initially, the *Book of Mormon* decried polygamy. Jacob 2:23–28 and 3:5–8 denounce the practice of polygamy as an abomination before God. Likewise, the *Doctrine and Covenants* (a supposed revelation given to Joseph Smith) state clearly that marriage should be one man for one woman (D&C 42:22). Later writings of Smith allow for unlimited plural marriage to virgins (D&C 132:51–66) and directly contradict what had been written earlier.[1]

Polygamy, more accurately polygyny, was practiced secretly by some Latter-day Saints from the 1830s until the 1850s, when the church admitted to the teaching after many previous denials. Eventually, they were pressured into denouncing polygamy after it was vigorously

---

1. The direct contradictions within the "revelations" given to Joseph Smith are evidence confirming they did not come from God. Consider the following passages:

> Verily, thus saith the Lord unto you my servant Joseph, that inasmuch as you have inquired of my hand to know and understand wherein I, the Lord, justified my servants Abraham, Isaac, and Jacob, as also Moses, David and Solomon, my servants, as touching the principle and doctrine of their having many wives and concubines. (*Doctrine and Covenants* 132:1)
>
> But the word of God burdens me because of your grosser crimes. For behold, thus saith the Lord: This people begin to wax in iniquity; they understand not the scriptures, for they seek to excuse themselves in committing whoredoms, because of the things which were written concerning David, and Solomon his son. Behold, David and Solomon truly had many wives and concubines, which thing was abominable before me, saith the Lord. (*Book of Mormon*, Jacob 2:23–24)

Also notice that Isaac is described as having many wives when he had only one — Rebekah. This is further evidence that God was not speaking through Joseph Smith since God would not make a mistake, let alone on such a simple matter.

prosecuted by the federal government. From the 1870s on, many LDS leaders encouraged rebellion against the laws, but in 1890, LDS president Wilford Woodruff encouraged members to obey the laws.[2] This caused a large split in the church, and new organizations were formed by those who continued the practice of polygamy and considered themselves as faithfully adhering to the commands of God over man's laws. Some secretly practiced polygamy while others abstained.[3] What has become the mainline LDS Church currently denounces polygamy and claims that anyone who practices it is not a true Mormon.[4] It is clear that, despite appeals to the patriarchs, the Bible was not the source of the Mormon doctrine of polygamy.

Conclusion

Despite these supposed additional revelations from God, the Bible makes it clear that He intends marriage to be between one man and one woman — as it was "from the beginning" (Matthew 19:8; Mark 10:6). Any challenge to this teaching stands in opposition to God's plan for His creation. This short chapter cannot exhaustively cover all of the issues related to polygamy, but we can look to the Bible as the standard for understanding the world we live in. As we face specific questions regarding plural marriage, let us prayerfully consider what God has revealed and apply the principles He has given us in Scripture.

---

2. It is worth noting that, as the president of the church, Woodruff had the authority to change official church doctrines. He could have amended the *Doctrine and Covenants*, but he simply advised members not to continue the practice. He later stated it was a command of God, but if that were so, it needed no vote of ratification. With the current tide of the redefinition of marriage, polygamous marriages may be legal in the near future. Once that prohibition is removed, it will be interesting to see how the members of the LDS Church respond. A recent case in Canada concerning the legality of plural marriages is being watched by fundamentalist Mormons who still hold to polygamy as a part of their religious practice. According to the D&C, plural marriages are acceptable.

3. Raymond D. Moore, *Mormonism Against Itself: A Handbook for Christian Workers* (United States: 1st Books Library, 2001), p. 279–294.

4. For the current LDS position, see "Polygamy: Latter Day Saints and Plural Marriage" at http://www.lds.org.

Chapter 15

Evolution and the Challenge of Morality

Jason Lisle

✿✿✿✿✿✿✿✿✿✿✿✿✿✿✿✿✿✿✿✿✿

Morality is a very difficult problem for the evolutionary worldview. This isn't to say that evolutionists are somehow less moral than anyone else. Most of them adhere to a code of behavior. Like the biblical creationist, they do believe in the concepts of *right* and *wrong*. The problem is that evolutionists have no logical reason to believe in right and wrong within their own worldview. Right and wrong are Christian concepts that go back to Genesis. By attempting to be moral, therefore, the evolutionist is being irrational; for he must borrow biblical concepts that are contrary to his worldview.

The Genesis of Morality

The Bible teaches that God is the Creator of all things:

In the beginning God created the heavens and the earth (Genesis 1:1).

In the beginning was the Word, and the Word was with God, and the Word was God. He was in the beginning with God. All things were made through Him, and without Him nothing was made that was made (John 1:3).

168 • How Do We Know the Bible Is True?

All things belong to God (Psalm 24:1) and thus, God has the right to make the rules. So an absolute moral code makes sense in a biblical creation worldview. But if the Bible were not true, if human beings were merely the outworking of millions of years of mindless chemical processes, then why should we hold to a universal code of behavior? Could there really be such concepts as right and wrong if evolution were true?

Evolutionary "Morality"

Some might respond, "Well, I believe in right and wrong, and I also believe in evolution, so obviously they can go together." But this does not follow. People can be irrational; they can profess to believe in things that are contrary to each other. The question is not about what people believe to be the case, but rather what actually is the case. Can the concepts of right and wrong really be meaningful apart from the biblical God? To put it another way, is morality *justified* in an evolutionary worldview?

In response to this, an evolutionist might say, "Of course. People can create their own moral code apart from God. They can adopt their own standards of right and wrong." However, this kind of thinking is arbitrary, and will lead to absurd consequences. If everyone can create his or her own morality, then no one could argue that what *other* people do is actually wrong, since other people can also invent their own personal moral code. For example, a person might choose for himself a moral code in which murder is perfectly acceptable. This might seem upsetting to us, but how could we argue that it is wrong *for others* to murder if morality is nothing but a personal standard? If morality is a subjective personal choice, then Hitler cannot be denounced for his actions, since he was acting in accord with his chosen standard. Clearly this is an unacceptable position.

Some evolutionists argue that there *is* an absolute standard; they say, "Right is what brings the most happiness to the most people." But this is also arbitrary. Why should *that* be the selected standard as opposed to some other view? Also, notice that this view borrows from the Christian position. In the Christian worldview, we should indeed be concerned about the happiness of others since they are made in God's image. The happiness of others, though important, is not the primary concern within the Christian worldview. To love and obey the God who has created and saved us should be our primary focus (Mark 12:30; Ecclesias

One aspect of this is that we should treat others with love a

(Matthew 7:12; Mark 12:31). But if other people are simply chei

dents, why should we care about their happiness at all? Concern about others does not make sense in an evolutionary universe.

Perhaps the evolutionist will claim that morality is what the majority decides it to be. But this view has the same defects as the others. It merely shifts an unjustified opinion from one person to a group of people. It is arbitrary and leads to absurd conclusions. Again, we find that we would not be able to denounce certain actions that we know to be wrong. After all, Hitler was able to convince a majority of his people that his actions were right, but that doesn't really make them right.

Without the biblical God, *right* and *wrong* are reduced to mere personal preferences. In an evolutionary universe, the statement "murder is wrong" is nothing more than a personal opinion on the same level as "blue is my favorite color." And if others have a different opinion, we would have no basis for arguing with them. Thus, when evolutionists talk about morality as if it is a real standard that other people should follow, they are being inconsistent with their own worldview.

Evolutionary Inconsistency

As one example, consider those evolutionists who are very concerned about children being taught creation. "This is wrong," they say, "because you're lying to children!" Now, obviously this begs the question, since the truth or falsity of creation is the concern at issue: we are convinced that creation is true, and evolution is the lie. But the truly absurd thing about such evolutionary arguments is that they are contrary to evolution! That is, in an evolutionary worldview why shouldn't we lie — particularly if it benefits our survival value?

Now certainly the Christian believes that it's wrong to lie, but then again, the Christian has a reason for this. God has indicated in His Word that lying is contrary to His nature (Numbers 23:19), and that we are not to engage in it (Exodus 20:16). But apart from the biblical worldview, why *should* we tell the truth? For that matter, why should we do anything at all? Words like *should* and *ought* only make sense if there is an absolute standard given by one who has authority over everyone.

If human beings are merely chemical accidents, why should we be so concerned about what they do? We wouldn't get mad at baking soda for reacting with vinegar; that's just what chemicals do. So why would an evolutionist be angry at anything one human being does to another, if we are all nothing more than complex chemical reactions? If we are simply evolved animals, why should we hold to a code of conduct in this "dog-eat-dog" world? After all, what one animal does to another is morally irrelevant. When evolutionists attempt to be moral, they are "borrowing" from the Christian worldview.

Evolutionists Must Borrow Morality from the Biblical Worldview

One humorous example of this happened at the opening of the Creation Museum. A group (The Campaign to Defend the Constitution, or "Defcon") opposing the museum had hired a plane to circle above with a trailing banner that read, "Defcon says: Thou shalt not lie." Of course, we couldn't agree more! After all, this is one of the Ten Commandments. In fact, the purpose of the Creation Museum is to present the truth about origins. So the evolutionists had to borrow from the biblical worldview in order to argue against it. In an evolutionary universe, Defcon's moral objection makes no sense (although we certainly appreciated the free advertising).

Making Sense of the Evolutionary Position

The Christian worldview not only accounts for morality, it also accounts for why evolutionists behave the way they do. Even those who have no basis for morality within their own professed worldview nonetheless hold to a moral code; this is because in their heart of hearts, they really do know the God of creation — despite their profession to the contrary. Scripture tells us that everyone knows the biblical God, but that they suppress the truth about God (Romans 1:18–21). Why would anyone do this?

We have inherited a sin nature (a tendency to rebel against God) from Adam (Romans 5:12), who rebelled against God in the Garden of Eden (Genesis 3). John 3:19 indicates that people would rather remain in spiritual darkness than have their evil deeds exposed:

And this is the condemnation, that the light has come into the world, and men loved darkness rather than light, because their deeds were evil.

Just as Adam tried to hide from God's presence (Genesis 3:8), so his descendents do the same. But the solution to sin is not suppression, it is confession and repentance (1 John 1:9; Luke 5:32). Christ is faithful to forgive anyone who calls on His name (Romans 10:13).

Conclusions

Nearly everyone believes that people ought to behave in a certain way — a moral code. Yet, in order for morality to be meaningful, biblical creation must be true. Since God created human beings, He determines what is to be considered *right* and *wrong*, and we are responsible to Him for our actions. We must therefore conclude that evolutionists are being irrational when they talk about right and wrong, for such concepts make no sense in an evolutionary universe.

Chapter 16

Three Days and
Three Nights

Bodie Hodge and Paul Taylor

❦❦❦❦❦❦❦❦❦❦❦❦❦❦❦❦❦❦❦

M ost Christians believe Jesus was crucified on a Friday and raised from the dead on the following Sunday. However, some believers have put forth arguments in support of Jesus being crucified on Wednesday or Thursday. Most agree that the Lord's Day, the first day of the week, was when Christ rose from the dead. This is based on Matthew 28:1, which states, "Now after the Sabbath, as the first day of the week began to dawn, Mary Magdalene and the other Mary came to see the tomb.

Difficulties arise because of the language used to describe the amount of time Jesus was in the grave.

> Then, as they were afraid and bowed their faces to the earth, they said to them, "Why do you seek the living among the dead? He is not here, but is risen! Remember how He spoke to you when He was still in Galilee, saying, 'The Son of Man must be delivered into the hands of sinful men, and be crucified, and the *third day* rise again' " (Luke 24:5–7, emphasis ours).

> They will scourge Him and kill Him. And the *third day* He will rise again (Luke 18:33; see also Acts 10:40, 1 Corinthians 15:4, Luke 24:46, etc., emphasis ours).

For as Jonah was three days and three nights in the belly of the great fish, so will the Son of Man be *three days and three nights in the heart of the earth* (Matthew 12:40, emphasis ours).

Since the Resurrection was on a Sunday (first day of the week) and this was the "third day," some hold that Jesus was actually crucified on a Thursday rather than a Friday in an effort to reconcile this with the prophetic statement about being in the belly of the whale for three days and three nights. But this introduces a different problem: Christ would be dead on a Thursday — 1, Friday — 2, Saturday — 3, and Sunday — 4 (again, Christ rose on a Sunday, Luke 24:21). Was this *on* the third day?

We need to look more closely at the days and how they are calculated. Several places in Scripture lead us to deduce that Jesus was crucified on a Friday. A solution that seems more convincing is that Jesus was indeed crucified on a Friday, but that the Jewish method of counting days was not the same as ours.

Counting Days in the Bible

The first clue is to understand how the Jews counted a day. The day began in the evening and ended the following evening. Unlike our modern days, where a day begins at midnight, their day basically began at sunset. So what we view as Thursday evening was actually the beginning of Friday to the Jews. And Friday night was actually the beginning of Saturday to the Jews.

In fact, many ancient cultures counted days this way, which goes back to creation ordinance. In Genesis 1, when God created it was dark, and when God created light, it was day. So the cycle was dark first, then light second to mark a day, that is, an evening and a morning.

In Esther 4:16 we find Esther exhorting Mordecai to persuade the Jews to fast. "Neither eat nor drink for three days, night or day." This was clearly in preparation for her highly risky attempt to see the king. Yet just two verses later, in Esther 5:1, we read, "Now it happened on the third day that Esther put on her royal robes and stood in the inner court of the king's palace." If three days and nights were counted in the same way as we count them today, then why would Esther see the king prior to the end of the fast, which would be on the fourth day? This is analogous to the situation with the Lord's Crucifixion and Resurrection.

For as Jonah was three days and three nights in the belly of the great fish, so will the Son of Man be three days and three nights in the heart of the earth (Matthew 12:40).

Saying, "Sir, we remember, while He was still alive, how that deceiver said, 'After three days I will rise' " (Matthew 27:63).

And He began to teach them that the Son of Man must suffer many things, and be rejected by the elders and chief priests and scribes, and be killed, and after three days rise again (Mark 8:31).

If the three days and nights were counted the way we count them, then Jesus would have to rise on the fourth day (being *after* three days). But, by comparing these passages, we can see that in the minds of people in Bible times, "the third day" *was equivalent to* "after three days."

In fact, the way they counted was this: part of a day would be counted as one day. The following table, reproduced from the Christian Apologetics and Research Ministry (CARM) website, shows how the counting works.[1]

Day One		Day Two		Day Three	
FRI starts at sundown on Thursday	FRI ends at sundown	SAT starts at sundown on Friday	SAT ends at sundown	SUN starts at sundown on Saturday	SUN ends at sundown
Night	Day	Night	Day	Night	Day
Crucifixion		Sabbath		Resurrection	

Analyzing this table, we can see how Jesus died on Good Friday; that was day one. In total, day one includes the day and the previous night, even though Jesus died in the day.[2] So, although only part of Friday was left, that was the first day and night to be counted. Saturday was day two. Jesus rose

---

1. Christian Apologetics and Research Ministry, "How Long Was Jesus Dead in the Tomb?" http://www.carm.org/diff/Matt12_40.htm.

2. Keep in mind that Jesus was arrested the night before the Crucifixion and endured false accusations, a crown of thorns, lashes, and so on. Mark 8:31 may add more understanding to the phrase "after three days." Perhaps this time period included the suffering and handing over of Christ to the elders and chief priests and scribes.

in the morning of the Sunday.[3] That was day three. Thus, by Jewish counting, we have three days and nights, yet Jesus rose *on* the third day.

It should not be a surprise to us that a different culture used a different method of counting days. As soon as we adopt this method of counting, the supposed biblical problems with counting the days disappear. But let's take a closer look.

A Closer Look at the Details

There are all sorts of difficulties with determining the date of the Crucifixion, and we would certainly not want to insist on the Crucifixion being on a Friday for traditional reasons — but rather, for biblical reasons. Our hope here is to explain this in more detail. However, we are not being dogmatic about such a stance either — just showing that is acceptable biblically.

Difficulties

Some have suggested alternative timings that place the Crucifixion on a Wednesday or Thursday rather than a Friday. The Bible does not explicitly state which day of the week Jesus died.

However, to have Jesus dying on a Wednesday requires the postulation of an *extra* Sabbath day on the Thursday, though nothing is mentioned for this instance.[4] And for those pushing for a Thursday crucifixion, it would require an extra Sabbath on a Friday. Again, nothing is mentioned for this.

The Wednesday and Thursday crucifixion views need to insert an extra Sabbath day during Christ's final week. In fact, for many years, one

---

3. Before or after the sun had risen? Does it matter? Since Sunday started at 6:00 P.M. Saturday (for them), Sunday would have been going for roughly 12 hours already by the time He had risen — if He rose at dawn. It seems that Mary Magdalene and the other women left while it was still dark (John 20:1) and arrived at the tomb right after the sun had risen (Mark 16:2). Matthew 28 says it was as that day began to dawn and Luke just states it was very early in the morning.

4. The closest we have are things like a special Sabbath-rest (*shabbathown*) such as Leviticus 23:24; 39, which was not necessarily a Sabbath day, but an extra celebratory day such as the first day of the seventh month (Tishri) or the Day of Atonement. On these days denoted as Sabbath-rest days, they were bound to the strict limitations of "no work," similar to the restrictions on a normal Sabbath day. But note that in Scripture, these days are specifically listed as Sabbath-rest days, not as Sabbaths. These mentioned Sabbath-rest special times in Leviticus were specifically for the Jewish month of Tishri not Nisan, which was the time of Passover when Christ was crucified.

of the writers of this chapter (Paul Taylor) held to the view of an extra Sabbath day based on the following verse:

> Therefore, because it was the Preparation Day, that the bodies should not remain on the cross on the Sabbath (for that Sabbath was a high day), the Jews asked Pilate that their legs might be broken, and that they might be taken away (John 19:31).

There is some dispute about the meaning of the term "high day." Some view it as the actual Sabbath day during the Passover week or one of the other Jewish festivals. Some believe the term refers to one of those special Jewish feast days described in Leviticus 23 — no matter which day of the week it happened to fall on. These holidays were sometimes identified as Sabbaths (Leviticus 23:24).

Jesus died on the Preparation Day, the day before the Sabbath (*Mark 15:42*). However, this could refer to the day to prepare for the weekly Sabbath or to "the Preparation Day of the Passover" (John 19:14). Jesus was placed in the tomb on the Preparation Day (*John 19:42*), but was this the weekly Preparation Day or a special one? It would seem the answer to this question is that it was the Preparation Day for the weekly Sabbath since Jesus and His disciples ate the Passover the previous evening, which would have been the start of the same day according to traditional Jewish reckoning (Luke 22:15).

However, it is more complicated than this. John 18:28 states, "Then they led Jesus from Caiaphas to the Praetorium, and it was early morning. But they themselves did not go into the Praetorium, lest they should be defiled, but that they might eat the Passover."

This verse seems to indicate that John viewed the day of the Crucifixion as the same day as the Preparation Day *prior* to the Passover. Is there any solution to this confusing difficulty? Actually it is rather easy to resolve; but first Dr. John MacArthur adds insight to this dilemma in his introduction to the Gospel of John.

> The chronological reckoning between John's gospel and the synoptics presents a challenge, especially in relation to the time of the Last Supper (13:2). While the synoptics portray the disciples and the Lord at the Last Supper as eating the Passover meal on Thursday evening (Nisan 14) and Jesus being crucified on Friday,

John's gospel states that the Jews did not enter into the Praetorium "lest they should be defiled, but that they might eat the Passover" (18:28). So, the disciples had eaten the Passover on Thursday evening, but the Jews had not. In fact, John (19:14) states that Jesus' trial and crucifixion were on the day of Preparation for the Passover and not after the eating of the Passover, so that with the trial and crucifixion on Friday Christ was actually sacrificed at the same time the Passover lambs were being slain (19:14). The question is, "Why did the disciples eat the Passover meal on Thursday?"

The answer lies in a difference among the Jews in the way they reckoned the beginning and ending of days. From Josephus, the Mishna, and other ancient Jewish sources we learn that the Jews in northern Palestine calculated days from sunrise to sunrise. That area included the region of Galilee, where Jesus and all the disciples, except Judas, had grown up. Apparently most, if not all, of the Pharisees used that system of reckoning. But Jews in the southern part, which centered in Jerusalem, calculated days from sunset to sunset. Because all the priests necessarily lived in or near Jerusalem, as did most of the Sadducees, those groups followed the southern scheme.

That variation doubtlessly caused confusion at times, but it also had some practical benefits. During Passover time, for instance, it allowed for the feast to be celebrated legitimately on two adjoining days, thereby permitting the temple sacrifices to be made over a total period of four hours rather than two. That separation of days may also have had the effect of reducing both regional and religious clashes between the two groups.

On that basis the seeming contradictions in the gospel accounts are easily explained. Being Galileans, Jesus and the disciples considered Passover day to have started at sunrise on Thursday and to end at sunrise on Friday. The Jewish leaders who arrested and tried Jesus, being mostly priests and Sadducees, considered Passover day to begin at sunset on Thursday and end at sunset on Friday. By that variation, predetermined by God's sovereign provision, Jesus could thereby legitimately celebrate the last Passover meal with His disciples and yet still be sacrificed on Passover day.[5]

Although MacArthur holds to a Friday Crucifixion, this two-fold approach to reckoning days does not really solve the problem of determining the day of the Crucifixion, but it does explain how Jews could celebrate the Passover on two successive days (depending on which part of Israel they came from). However, this may not be the best explanation of trying to deal with the Preparation Day of the Passover.

Dr. John Gill points out that the Preparation Day was a preparation day before the Sabbath that occurred on the Passover Week. So this day is not to be confused with a day of preparation before the Passover. He further points out that preparation for the Passover was not just *one day* before but for a number of days before (e.g., separating out the Passover lamb on 10th day of the month well before it was to be turned over for sacrifice on the 14th day, and so on). These things happened in preparation for the Passover, far sooner than one day before. Gill wrote:

> Ver. 14. And it was the preparation of the passover, &c.] So the Jews say, that Jesus suffered on the eve of the passover; and the author of the blasphemous account of his life says, it was the eve both of the passover and the sabbath; which account so far agrees with the evangelic history; but then this preparation of the passover was not of the passover lamb, for that had been prepared and eaten the night before. Nor do I find that there was any particular day which was called "the preparation of the passover" in such sense, and much less that this day was the day before the eating of the passover. According to the law in #Ex 12:3-6 the lamb for the passover was to be separated from the rest of the flock on the tenth day of the month, and to be kept up till the fourteenth; but this is never called the preparation of the passover; and was it so called, it cannot be intended here; the preparing and making ready the passover the evangelists speak of, were on the same day

5. John MacArthur, *The MacArthur Study Bible*, electronic ed. (Nashville, TN: Word Publishing, 1997). For a detailed description of how and why the days were reckoned differently, see http://www.biblicalperspectives.com/books/crucifixion/4.html, accessed April 13, 2011.

it was eaten, and design the getting ready a place to eat it in, and things convenient for that purpose, and the killing the lamb, and dressing it, and the like, #Mt 26:17,19 Mr 14:12,15,16 Lu 22:8,9,12,13 there is what the Jews call *xoph owrp*, which was a space of fifteen days before the passover, and began at the middle of the thirty days before the feast, in which they used to ask questions, and explain the traditions concerning the passover: but this is never called the preparation of the passover: and on the night of the fourteenth month they sought diligently, in every hole and corner of their houses, for leavened bread, in order to remove it; but this also never went by any such name: wherefore, if any respect is had to the preparation for the passover, it must either design the preparation of the "Chagigah," which was a grand festival, commonly kept on the fifteenth day, and which was sometimes called the passover; or else the preparation for the whole feast all the remaining days of it; see Gill on "Joh 18:28" but it seems best of all to understand it only of the preparation for the sabbath, which, because it was in the passover week, is called the passover preparation day: and it may be observed, that it is sometimes only called "the day of the preparation," and "the preparation," #Mt 27:62, Lu 23:54, Joh 19:31 and sometimes the "Jews' preparation day," #Joh 19:42 and it is explained by the Evangelist #Mr 15:42. "It was the preparation, that is, the day before the sabbath"; on which they both prepared themselves for the sabbath, and food to eat on that day; and this being the time of the passover likewise, the preparation was the greater: and therefore to distinguish this preparation day for the sabbath, from others, it is called the passover preparation; nor have I observed that any other day is called the preparation but that before the Sabbath.[6]

Various Views

So let's look at the strengths and weaknesses of the various views. A Wednesday Crucifixion solves some difficulties, but seems to introduce others. For example, Jesus would have been in the grave for three full

6. John Gill, *Exposition of the Bible*, Commentary Notes on John 19:14, as adapted in Online Bible by Larry Pierce.

daytime periods (along with a few hours on Wednesday afternoon), but this time frame also includes four full nights. So if one is trying to find a precisely literal fulfillment of the "three days and three nights" in Matthew 12:40, then a Wednesday Crucifixion does not meet that criteria. This would simply not make sense of Jesus rising on the third day, as many Scriptures reveal (Luke 18:33, see also Acts 10:40, 1 Corinthians 15:4, Luke 24:46, etc.). However, as will be demonstrated below, the "three days and three nights" does not necessarily need to be fulfilled by a 72-hour period.

The Wednesday also requires the postulation of an extra Sabbath day on Thursday, since the day of the Crucifixion was the Preparation Day and there was a rush to remove the bodies from the crosses before the Sabbath (the Passover on this view) started on the next day. This means the "high day" must be interpreted as the Passover, which is contested.

A Thursday Crucifixion also solves some of the difficulties. It is commonly believed that a portion of a day or evening would count as the entire day or evening, respectively. As such, a Thursday Crucifixion would give exactly three days and three nights. Jesus died at the ninth hour (Matthew 27:46), which corresponds to 3:00 P.M. (by our modern reckoning). So there would be three hours of daylight on Thursday, a full night and a full day for Friday, a full night and a full day for Saturday, and then a full night on Sunday. Jesus likely rose at dawn the following morning,[7] so a Thursday Crucifixion fits the "three days and three nights" concept very well.

The Thursday Crucifixion idea requires an extra Sabbath day on Friday and the "high day" must also be interpreted as the Passover. These are both debatable, as there would be *two* high Sabbaths that week, as the normal Sabbath would have been a high day as well since it fell *on* Passover week. Furthermore, the Bible lists no such days as Sabbath-rest days in the month of Nisan (the month that Passover is in). There is nothing in the text that leads us necessarily to suspect that the Sabbath was anything other than the regular *day seven* Sabbath.

The Thursday Resurrection scenario, while trying to make the prophetic statement by Jesus about being *in the heart of the earth for three*

---

7. By putting together the Gospel accounts of the Resurrection, we can conclude the women left for the tomb while it was still dark (John 20:1) and arrived as the day began to dawn (Mark 28:1; Mark 16:2; Luke 24:1), at which point Jesus had already risen.

182 • How Do We Know the Bible Is True?

days and three nights, neglects the clear statements that Jesus resurrected on the third day (Luke 18:33, see also Acts 10:40, 1 Corinthians 15:4, Luke 24:46, etc.). If it is a full three days and three nights Jesus is in the grave, then He would have been resurrected on the fourth day.

We want to emphasize that this is not a major point of doctrinal concern. The "special Sabbath" analysis is certainly a valid analysis to resolve the alleged contradiction, and it is maintained by people whose commitment to the authority of Scripture is sound. So please do not misunderstand us in this. We maintain that the Friday-Sunday time scale is scripturally sound — and we believe it is to be preferred, since it does not require adding extra assumptions to the text.

Some have tried to push for an extra Sabbath by appealing to John 18:28, saying the Jews were looking to celebrate the Passover after Jesus was crucified, the next day by Jewish reckoning. The Thursday crucifixion scenario encounters a major problem when we accept the view that the Jewish leaders wanted to eat the Passover the day after Christ's death — that would be saying that Jesus didn't eat the Passover on the correct day, since He ate the evening before (Luke 25:15), prior to his suffering, which took place soon after, beginning with the betrayal in Gethsemane.

It is true that they were planning on eating the Passover at a later time, but *not* the next day. John 18:28 indicates that they were wanting to eat later that day, which was *still the same day* Jesus ate; but Jesus ate at the beginning of the day (evening in the Jewish calendar), whereas the others wanted to eat later in the day (probably the afternoon prior to sunset) before the Passover was finished. Regarding John 18:28, Numbers 9:3–5 indicates that the Israelites were to eat the Passover at twilight when the Passover began — which is exactly when Jesus did it with the disciples. The others waited to eat well after the following morning after Christ was led to the Praetorium, indicating they were not being obedient to the Word of God.

Sir Robert Anderson, in *The Coming Prince*, calculated which days would have been Passovers for various years on the Jewish calendar.[8] For example, A.D. 30 was a Thursday, A.D. 31 was Tuesday, A.D. 32 was a Monday, A.D. 33 was a Friday, A.D. 34 was a Tuesday, A.D. 35 was a

---

8. As indicated in James Ussher, *The Annals of the World*, translated by Larry and Marion Pierce, second printing (Green Forest, AR: Master Books, 2003), p. 822.

Monday, and A.D. 36 was a Friday. For a Wednesday Passover, one would need to go to A.D. 27, as this is the closest year.

The Traditional View

One thing that is often overlooked is that John 2:20 establishes that Christ's first Passover while He was in public ministry (A.D. 30) was 46 years after Herod began building the Temple in 17 B.C. — assuming the date Ussher gives is accurate. Jesus celebrated at least two more Passovers (e.g., John 6:4) and the final recorded Passover was His Crucifixion, most likely A.D. 33, which occurred on a Friday.[9]

So the beginning of the Jewish Friday (which is Thursday evening for most of us today) is when Jesus ate the Passover — then was betrayed, beaten, put on trial, and ultimately crucified in the daylight hours that followed the same day. This occurred on the Preparation Day of the Sabbath, which was fell during the Passover that year and immediately before the Sabbath — a High Sabbath (High Day) because it fell *during* Passover week.

Furthermore, the Wednesday and Thursday views require the "Preparation Day" to be the day prior to a Passover rather than the normal Preparation Day before the weekly Sabbath. However, there is no known usage in Scripture or any other writing where the term "Preparation Day" refers to anything but the weekly Sabbath.

Significance of the Passover

God has always been very strict about the Passover. When the firstborn of Egypt were struck down, the Lord gave specific instructions in Exodus 12 that the Israelites were to follow to the letter. Throughout Israelite history, the Passover was among the most honored and sacred times of sacrifice. Recall that even Jesus, during His recorded years of ministry, diligently kept Passovers (John 2:13; John 6:4; John 13:1). Even Jesus' parents celebrated the Passover each year (Luke 2:41).

---

9. We simply do not know how many years Jesus did ministry. Many assume His ministry was three years long due to the recorded Passovers He celebrated in the Gospel accounts. Since He died during the third Passover celebration mentioned in John, His ministry may have been just over two years in length or it could have been several years, since the Bible may not have recorded each of the Passover celebrations during His ministry. John 5:1 references a Jewish feast at which Jesus went to Jerusalem. It is not specifically called Passover, but it may have been one.

It seems likely that Jesus, who is the ultimate sacrificial Lamb (John 1:29, 36), would be sacrificed on the Passover, especially considering that God was so strict with the Israelites about performing sacrifices on the Passover.

> Therefore purge out the old leaven, that you may be a new lump, since you truly are unleavened. For indeed Christ, our Passover, was sacrificed for us (1 Corinthians 5:7).

> You know that after two days is the Passover, and the Son of Man will be delivered up to be crucified (Matthew 26:2).

Such verses lead to the conclusion that Jesus was sacrificed later on the same day that He ate the Passover. The great scholar Archbishop James Ussher affirmed that Jesus *was* crucified on the Passover.[10]

In Detail: "Three Days and Three Nights" or "The Third Day"?

Let's return to the phrases "three days and three nights" and the "third day." If it can be shown that these two phrases are used interchangeably then there is little reason to abandon the Friday view of the Crucifixion.

We must use Scripture to interpret Scripture within the relative context and culture. Old Testament Jewish culture equates "three days and three nights" with "on the third day." The scriptural basis for this was already established. But to reiterate we want to explain it in detail and then look at other Scriptures to affirm this view. We have clear biblical evidence from the Book of Esther that the biblical method of counting was not necessarily the same as our Western method.

> Go, gather all the Jews who are present in Shushan, and fast for me; neither eat nor drink for three days, night or day. My maids and I will fast likewise. And so I will go to the king, which is against the law; and if I perish, I perish! (Esther 4:16).

Now, if the days and nights were counted in a Western way, this should result in Esther going to see the king on the fourth day. However, this is what we actually read:

> Now it happened on the third day that Esther put on her royal robes and stood in the inner court of the king's palace, across from

---

10. Ussher, *The Annals of the World*, , p. 815.

the king's house, while the king sat on his royal throne in the royal house, facing the entrance of the house (Esther 5:1).

So it seems that three days and three nights are virtually equated here. However, one could argue that Esther wanted everyone to fast and she does this *during* the fast. This is also possible. But let's consider another example in the New Testament culture.

> Saying, "Sir, we remember, while He was still alive, how that deceiver said, 'After three days I will rise.' Therefore command that the tomb be made secure until the third day, lest His disciples come by night and steal Him away, and say to the people, 'He has risen from the dead.' So the last deception will be worse than the first" (Matthew 27:63–64).

The above example is particularly relevant. If the chief priests and Pharisees had counted in the Western fashion, they would surely have wanted the tomb to be made secure until the beginning of the fourth day, especially since they referred to the danger of Jesus' body being stolen "by night."[11]

If you look up the many passages about Christ's death, you will find both instances of "three days and three nights" (Matthew 12:40) and "on the third day" (Luke 24:46), even in reference to raising the temple in three days (Mark 15:29; Luke 2:46).

Church Fathers Equate Three Days with Three Days and Three Nights

Ignatius (c. A.D. 100), a disciple of the Apostle John, equated three days with three days and three nights.

> He also rose again in three days, the Father raising Him up; and after spending forty days with the apostles, He was received up to the Father, and "sat down at His right hand, expecting till His enemies are placed under His feet." On the day of the preparation, then, at the third hour, He received the sentence from Pilate, the Father permitting that to happen; at the sixth hour

---

11. It is true that this was stated the following day after the Crucifixion, but the point is that the two phrases are being used almost interchangeably. We are not certain if this is in reference to the three days from when they say this or if they were looking back. Regardless, it was under guard when Christ arose.

He was crucified; at the ninth hour He gave up the ghost; and before sunset He was buried. During the Sabbath He continued under the earth in the tomb in which Joseph of Arimathaea had laid Him. At the dawning of the Lord's day He arose from the dead, according to what was spoken by Himself, "As Jonah was three days and three nights in the whale's belly, so shall the Son of man also be three days and three nights in the heart of the earth." The day of the preparation, then, comprises the passion; the Sabbath embraces the burial; the Lord's Day contains the resurrection.[12]

The early Church father Irenaeus (d. A.D. 202) also equated three days with three days and three nights.

And the Lord Himself says, "As Jonas remained three days and three nights in the whale's belly, so shall the Son of man be in the heart of the earth." Then also the apostle says, "But when He ascended, what is it but that He also descended into the lower parts of the earth?" This, too, David says when prophesying of Him, "And thou hast delivered my soul from the nethermost hell"; and on His rising again the third day, He said to Mary, who was the first to see and to worship Him, "Touch Me not, for I have not yet ascended to the Father; but go to the disciples, and say unto them, I ascend unto My Father, and unto your Father."[13]

These early writings are not Scripture, nor were they perfect, but they equated three days and three nights with being on the third day. So the practice was commonly used and should be used as the better explanation.

Conclusion

This is a complicated issue and since the date of the Crucifixion is not as vital as the fact that He died for our sins, we would not want to "start a

---

12. Ignatius, *The Epistle of Ignatius to the Trallians*, chapter 9, reference to the history of Christ, longer version.
13. Irenaeus, *Against Heresies*, Book 5, chapter 31. The preservation of our bodies is confirmed by the Resurrection and Ascension of Christ: the souls of the saints during the intermediate period are in a state of expectation of that time when they shall receive their perfect and consummated glory.

new church" over this issue. The Friday Crucifixion scenario has the strongest textual support and all objections to it can be handled. It has been the traditional view throughout Church history and represents a conservative evangelical interpretation of Scripture.

The other views have some merit, but seem to have more difficulties. Nevertheless, we want to encourage deeper study of the Scriptures. It is good to endeavor to be consistent in our use of counting the days, but due to Matthew 27:63–64 and other reasons outlined, we favor the Friday–Sunday view.

Chapter 17

Framework Hypothesis

Tim Chaffey and Bob McCabe

❧❀❀❀❀❀❀❀❀❀❀❀❀❀❀❀❀❀❀

Since the early 1800s, many Christians have accepted the idea that the earth is billions of years old. This notion contradicts a plain reading of the biblical text, so many have searched for a way to harmonize the early chapters of Genesis with the idea of long ages. Many theories have been proposed, such as the gap theory, the day-age theory, and progressive creationism. However, as these views were promoted, it became apparent that each view was based on arbitrary methods of interpretation and forced contradictions with the biblical text.[1]

In 1924, a new view, the framework hypothesis, was developed by Arie Noordtzij, which sought to eliminate these problems. Approximately 30 years later, Meredith Kline popularized the view in the United States while N.H. Ridderbos did the same in Europe. It is currently one of the most popular views of Genesis 1 being taught in seminaries. Despite its popularity in academia, people in our churches have not heard this view fully explained, though they have heard of some of its claims.

---

1. This chapter is an adaptation of Tim Chaffey's booklet *God Means What He Says: A Biblical Critique of the Framework Hypothesis* (Midwest Apologetics, 2008) and Robert V. McCabe's "A Critique of the Framework Interpretation," in Terry Mortenson and Thane H. Ury, editors, *Coming to Grips with Genesis: Biblical Authority and the Age of the Earth* (Green Forest, AR: Master Books, 2008), p. 211–249.

The framework hypothesis is essentially an attempt to reclassify the genre of Genesis 1 as being something other than historical narrative. Proponents have attempted to identify figurative language or semi-poetic devices in the text. Thinking they have successfully shown that the Bible's first chapter is not to be taken in its plain sense, they make the claim that Genesis 1 simply reveals that God created everything and that He made man in His own image, but it gives us no information about how or when He did this.

The leading promoter of the framework hypothesis pulled no punches when explaining his goal in promoting it. "To rebut the literalist interpretation of the Genesis creation week propounded by the young-earth theorists is a central concern of this article. . . . The conclusion is that as far as the time frame is concerned, with respect to both the duration and sequence of events, the scientist is *left free of biblical constraints* in hypothesizing about cosmic origins."[2] How can a biblical scholar like Meredith Kline, who held to the inerrancy of Scripture, claim that he desires that scientists be "free of biblical constraints"? In order to make this type of radical claim, a literal interpretation of the creation account must be replaced by a nonliteral view, such as the framework hypothesis. Further, what would motivate a biblical scholar to reinterpret the creation account in this way?

This chapter focuses on evaluating three major arguments that Kline and other framework advocates use to support their nonliteral interpretation of Genesis 1:1–2:3: two triad of "days," the unending nature of the seventh day, and ordinary providence. These three arguments will be followed by an evaluation of a key presupposition that undergirds the framework view.

Two Triads of "Days"

The two triad of "days" argument is a premise that all framework advocates agree with. Framework supporters claim that the two triads of "days" is a topical parallelism where the topics of days 1–3 are parallel with those of days 4–6. About the parallel nature of days 1 and 4, Mark Futato states, "Days 1 and 4 are two different perspectives on the same

---

2. Meredith G. Kline, "Space and Time in the Genesis Cosmogony," *Perspectives on Science and Christian Faith* 48 (March 1996): 2, italics added for emphasis.

creative work."[3] Returning to the overall topical arrangement of the entire creation account, Kline writes, "The successive members of the first triad of days [days 1–3] correspond to the successive days of the second [days 4–6]."[4] In other words, days 1 and 4 are simply two different ways of stating the same event, as are days 2 and 5, and days 3 and 6. The following chart is representative of that used by many framework advocates and reflects this topical parallelism.[5]

Day	Formation of the World (Items Created)	Day	Fillng of the World (Items Created)
1	darkness, light	4	heavenly light-bearers
2	heavens, water	5	birds of the air, water animals
3	seas, land, vegetation	6	land animals, man, provision of food

At first glance, it may seem as if these writers are on to something. However, a closer look reveals some problems with this argument. First, this supposed semi-poetic construction is inconsistent with the fact that Genesis 1 is a historical narrative. Hebrew scholar Stephen Boyd has clearly shown that Genesis 1 is written as historical narrative rather than poetry. Hebrew poetry commonly utilizes a high percentage of imperfect and perfect verbs. By contrast, Hebrew narrative is marked by a high frequency of waw-consecutive preterite verbs that indicate a sequence of events in past tense material. Comparing Judges 4 and 5 shows a good example of these differences. In Judges 4, the account of Deborah and Barak defeating the forces of Sisera is explained in historical narrative. The following chapter is a poetical song describing the same event. The difference in language is readily apparent even in English translations. The same is true with the historical narrative of Genesis 1 and poetic

3. Mark D. Futato, "Because It Had Rained: A Study of Gen 2:5–7 with Implications for Gen 2:4–25 and Gen 1:1–2:3," *Westminster Theological Journal* 60 (Spring 1998): 16.
4. Meredith G. Kline, "Because It Had Not Rained," *Westminster Theological Journal* 20 (May 1958): 148.
5. Willem VanGemeren, *The Progress of Redemption: The Story of Salvation from Creation to the New Jerusalem* (Grand Rapids, MI: Baker, 1988), p. 47.

descriptions of creation activities such as those found in Psalm 104. After studying and cataloging 522 texts, Boyd concluded that Genesis 1 can be classified as narrative with a probability of virtually one.[6]

Second, the above chart is inconsistent with the text of Genesis 1:1–2:3. Water was not created on the second day, but the first. Genesis 1:2 states, "The Spirit of God was hovering over the face of the waters." This occurred prior to the creation of light on the first day. So perhaps days 1 and 5 should be viewed as parallel. Another problem with this chart is that the "heavenly light-bearers" of day 4 were placed in the "heavens" of day 2 (Genesis 1:14). This is problematic for the framework advocate who believes days 1 and 4 are the same event viewed from different perspectives, because this must have occurred prior to the event described in days 2 and 5. How could the stars be placed in something that did not exist yet?

Third, the order of events is crucial here. The framework proposes that the days are not chronological, but theological. However, if one rearranges the chronology, then it breaks down into absurdity. The waters of day 1 must exist for them to be separated on day 2. On day 3, the dry land appeared from these waters. The sun, moon, and stars of day 4 were placed in the heavens (expanse, firmament) of day 2. The birds of day 5 flew on the face of the firmament of day 2 and multiplied on the land of day 3. Finally, mankind was made to rule over all of creation (Genesis 1:28). Any attempt to rearrange days of the creation week forces impossibilities into the text.

In the final analysis, the framework's reinterpretation of Genesis 1:1–2:3 as a topical account of two triad of days is an illegitimate approach that fails to accurately interpret the creation account.

The Unending Nature of the Seventh Day

The second argument supporting the framework position is that the seventh day of the creation week is an unending (or at least long and still continuing) period.[7] This premise is a standard argument for framework advocates since it reputedly proves that the first Sabbath is ongoing, and, therefore, implies that the other six days are each metaphors for extended

---

6. Boyd's research is described in Don DeYoung, *Thousands . . . Not Billions* (Green Forest, AR: Master Books, 2005), p. 158–70.
7. Kline, "Because It Had Not Rained," 156; also Lee Irons, "The Framework Interpretation: An Exegetical Summary," *Ordained Servant* 9 (January 2000): 9–10.

temporal periods.[8] Two items are alleged to support the unending nature of day 7. First, while each of the six days of the creation week are concluded by the evening-morning formula, the description of day 7 in Genesis 2:1–3 omits the evening-morning formula, implying that it is an ongoing period. Second, Hebrews 4 confirms this understanding of day 7 with the motif of an eternal Sabbath rest.

In response to this argument, it is necessary to notice how "evening" and "morning" are used in the creation account. The clauses "there was evening" and "there was morning" have a function in the creation narrative of marking a transition from one day of creation to the next. This is to say, an "evening" denotes the conclusion of a period of light when God suspends His creative activity of one day and the "morning" marks the renewal of light when God resumes His work. Just as the fiat ("let there be" or an equivalent) and fulfillment ("it was so" or "there was") expressions used on each day of creation are not needed on day 7 because God's creative activities are finished, so there is no need to use the evening-morning conclusion because God's work of creation is concluded. Thus, the omission of the evening-morning formula on day 7 neither proves nor implies that this day was unending.

In addition, Hebrews 4 provides no substantive evidence indicating that day 7 is an eternal day. The eternal rest presented in Hebrews 4 is based on an analogy with God's creative rest in Genesis 2:1–3. Based upon the Mosaic omission of the evening-morning conclusion, the author of Hebrews is able to use the first Sabbath as a type patterned after God's eternal rest. We should further note that the actual kind of rest in Genesis 2:2–3 is completely different than the rest in Hebrews 4:3–11. The rest of Genesis 2:2–3 is a cessation from divine creative activity. Only the Creator can cease from that activity. It is absolutely impossible for the creature to

---

8. Henri Blocher, *In the Beginning*, trans. David G. Preston (Downers Grove, IL: InterVarsity Press, 1984), p. 56; R. Kent Hughes, *Genesis: Beginning and Blessing, Preaching the Word* (Wheaton, IL: Crossway, 2004), p. 26; Mark Ross, "The Framework Hypothesis: An Interpretation of Genesis 1:1–2:3," in *Did God Create in Six Days?* ed. Joseph A. Pipa Jr., and David W. Hall (Taylors, SC: Southern Presbyterian Press, 1999), p. 121–122. Though the vast majority of framework advocates use the unending nature of the seventh day as a primary argument, Kline has integrated it as supporting argument into his unnecessary "Two Register Cosmology" explanation ("Space and Time," 10). According to Kline's framework disciple Robert Godfrey, the two-register cosmology is not "a helpful key with reference to the literal days of Genesis 1," Robert Godfrey, *God's Pattern for Creation* (Phillipsburg, NJ: Presbyterian & Reformed, 2003), p. 53.

experience that cessation. However, the Sabbath-rest of Hebrews 4:3–11 is a rest that the people of God actually experience. Therefore, the "rest" in both contexts cannot be identical. The framework position assumes that the "rest" of Genesis 2 is identical with Hebrews 4. However, instead of assuming that the "rests" of Genesis 2 and Hebrews 4 are identical, framework advocates need to demonstrate this identity.

Moreover, notice that Hebrews 4 never states that day 7 is continuing. It says that God's rest is ongoing. He started His cessation from divine creative activity on that day, but the day itself has not continued. Imagine that a person leaves for week-long vacation on a Friday. On Tuesday, he could say that He is still resting from work, but that does not mean that Friday is continuing.

Finally, this argument actually proves too much, or at least would, if it could be shown day 7 is unending. If day 7 is ongoing because it lacks the evening and morning phrase, then this seems to be an unintentional admission that the first six days are normal-length days because they do have "evening and morning."

Ordinary Providence

Meredith Kline called the ordinary providence argument "the most decisive argument against the traditional interpretation."[9] According to Kline, Genesis 2:5–6 describes the earth on the third "day" of creation. He believed that the reason there were not any plants of the field or herbs of the field was because God had not caused it to rain yet. He saw this as evidence that God was not creating via miraculous means but through the same natural processes we observe today. He wrote:

> Embedded in Gen. 2:5 ff. is the principle that the modus operandi of the divine providence was the same during the creation period as that of ordinary providence at the present time. It is not to be demonstrated that those who adopt the traditional approaches cannot successfully integrate this revelation with Genesis 1 as they interpret it. In contradiction to Gen. 2:5, the twenty-four-hour day theory must presuppose that God employed other than the ordinary secondary means in executing his works of providence. To take just one example, it was the work of the

---

9. Kline, "Because It Had Not Rained," p. 148.

"third day" that the waters should be gathered together into seas and that the dry land should appear and be covered with vegetation (Gen. 1:9-13). All this according to the theory in question transpired within twenty-four hours. But continents just emerged from under the sea do not become thirsty land as fast as that by the ordinary process of evaporation. And yet according to the principle revealed in Gen. 2:5 the process of evaporation at that time was the ordinary one.[10]

Once again, there are numerous problems with Kline's argument. First, Genesis 2:5–6 does not refer to the third day, but to the sixth day just prior to the creation of man. These verses use two specific Hebrew terms to refer to the "plant of the field" (*siah hassadeh*) and "herb of the field" (*eseb hassadeh*). These Hebrew terms are different than the ones used on the third day when God made the "grass," the "herb that yields seed," and the "tree that yields fruit" (Genesis 1:11–12). Ironically, Futato, who also promoted this view, describes the "plant of the field" as the wild shrubs of the steppe, which contain thorns and thistles, and the "herb of the field" as cultivated grain. [11] It should be fairly obvious why the thorny plants and cultivated grains did not exist yet. Man had not been created yet to till the ground and he had not sinned yet bringing about the Curse on the earth of which thorny plants were one of the results (Gen 3:18).

Second, the concept of ordinary providence, as promoted by framework advocates, is no different than uniformitarianism. This unbiblical philosophy undergirds every old-earth view. Essentially, it states that the way things occur in the world today is the way they have always happened. Since scientists do not observe miracles today, then they have never happened. As such, slow and gradual processes must be used to explain the events of the past. The Apostle Peter warned that men holding this philosophy would come and use it to deny the creation, the Flood, and to mock Christ's return (2 Peter 3:3–6).

Third, God demonstrates His power to man in at least two ways. Through ordinary providence, God upholds all things by the word of His power (Hebrews 1:3). Since this is the "natural" order of things, men often

---

10. Ibid., p. 151–52.
11. Futato, "Because It Had Rained," 4. He believed these terms are examples of a merism, a literary device in which two items are named to refer to the entire class of items.

fail to credit God for preserving His creation. Through miracles, God temporarily suspends or overrides the "natural" order of things to perform His work. When this occurs, it is immediately clear that something extraordinary has occurred. We may call this the "principle of immediacy."

A classic example of this is found when Jesus said to the recently deceased daughter of Jairus, "Little girl, I say to you, arise." Mark states, "Immediately the girl arose and walked" (Mark 5:42–43). The reason immediacy is so important is that if Jesus spoke these words and the girl rose a few days later, few would attribute the incredible turn of events to Jesus. The same is true in Mark 10:52 when a blind man "immediately" received his sight when Jesus healed him. Once again, if the blind man did not receive his sight immediately, but slowly gained sight over the next few years, many would fail to attribute the miracle to Jesus.

Psalm 33:8–9 makes some interesting statements regarding creation that are highly relevant to this discussion. "Let all the earth fear the Lord; Let all the inhabitants of the world stand in awe of Him. For He spoke, and it was done; He commanded, and it stood fast." When God brought something into existence during the creation week, "He spoke, and it was done." There is no indication of a lengthy process of time in which creation unfolded through some developmental process. Contrary to Kline's statement, God did not create via ordinary providence during the creation week.

There are two particular Old Testament miracles that must be cited here. Exodus 14:21–22 reveals that when God parted the Red Sea, the Israelites were able to cross on "dry ground." Joshua 3 describes the entrance of the Israelites into the Promised Land and the crossing of the Jordan River. Verse 15 describes how the water immediately stopped as the priests who bore the ark of the covenant stepped into the water. Verse 17 states that these priests "stood firm on dry ground in the midst of the Jordan." Since God miraculously caused the land to appear on the third day, perhaps a continent freshly emerged from the sea could indeed be "thirsty ground."

Finally, there is a logical flaw in this argument. If God used millions of years of ordinary providence to bring the land from the ocean and to grow vegetation on the land, then why wasn't there any rain for that amount of time? After all, if God merely used natural processes, then the hydrologic cycle must have been in full swing at the time, too. The ordinary providence argument contradicts itself at this point.

The Importance of Presuppositions

While there are other problems with the framework that could be addressed, we will address the issue of a presupposition that undergirds the framework hypothesis. Since the literal day interpretation has been the dominant view of Christian interpreters from the Church fathers until Charles Lyell in the mid-1800s, what *a priori* would motivate framework defenders to reinterpret the creation account? What has primarily changed since Lyell's time is the way man defines and uses science. Modern scientific opinion has seemingly been elevated to the status of being equal or superior to biblical revelation. Many nonliteral interpreters refer to "science's" opinion as general revelation. And with its elevation, "scientific opinion" has become a presupposition that influences many evangelicals to jettison the literal interpretation of Genesis 1:1–2:3 in favor of a nonliteral view, such as the framework.

The "scientific opinion" of our world has a major impact on framework advocates. For example, this is true of Kline as our opening quote of him reflects: "To rebut the literalist interpretation of the Genesis creation week propounded by the young-earth theorists is a central concern of this article. . . . The conclusion is that as far as the time frame is concerned, with respect to both the duration and sequence of events, the scientist is left free of biblical constraints in hypothesizing about cosmic origins." How does Kline propose to free scientists from any "biblical constraints" about the age of the earth? In short, by rebutting those who interpret the creation account literally. Besides indicating his rejection of the historical interpretation of the creation narrative, does this not also reflect Kline's presuppositional commitment that modern science should have an impact on biblical interpretation?

Another framework advocate, Bruce Waltke, shares this commitment to the scientific majority. According to him, "The days of creation may also pose difficulties for a strict historical account. Contemporary scientists almost unanimously discount the possibility of creation in one week, and we cannot summarily discount the evidence of the earth sciences. General revelation in creation, as well as the special revelation of Scripture is also the voice of God. We live in a 'universe,' and all truth speaks with one voice."[12] Does it not sound like the "earth sciences," as interpreted by "contemporary scientists," communicates "general revelation"? If this is correct, does this not imply that the "general revelation" communicated by "contemporary scientists" is something other than what the Bible calls general revelation since it was unavailable from the time of creation until the modern era? Further, this confuses general revelation with scientific opinion and implies that general revelation has the same propositional force as special revelation. It is the propositional revelation of Scripture (Psalm 19:1–6; Ecclesiastes 3:11; Acts 14:17; 17:23–31; Romans 1:18–25; 2:14–15; 10:18) that defines general revelation. And, Scripture defines general revelation as a constant knowledge about God that is available to all men.[13] Consequently, it is biblically inadequate to equate scientific opinion with general revelation.

In light of these statements by Kline and Waltke, we should ask ourselves this question: If we did not live in our current age, would this type of statement have been made and, furthermore, would the framework or any other reinterpretations of Genesis 1:1–2:3 even be valid options for evangelicals? It seems that the spirit of our age has created a modern mindset conducive to a reinterpretation of the creation account. However, many of the influences that shape such reinterpretations are external to Scripture, rather than being derived from a consistent biblical theology. In the final analysis, there is no biblical reason to reinterpret Genesis 1:1–2:3.

Conclusion

The framework hypothesis is an ingenious attempt to reinterpret Genesis 1. Using sophisticated arguments, its promoters have convinced many that the plain words of Genesis 1 should be reclassified as something other than straightforward, historical narrative. As such, the words dealing with the *how* and *when* of creation are ignored.

This brief survey has shown the erroneous arguments posed by its supporters. This view may be more dangerous than any harmonistic view

---

12. Bruce K. Waltke with Cathi J. Fredricks, *Genesis: A Commentary* (Grand Rapids, MI: Zondervan, 2001), p. 77.
13. See Richard Mayhue, "Is Nature the 67th Book of the Bible," in Mortenson and Ury, *Coming to Grips with Genesis*, p. 111–115.

since it encourages believers to ignore the text, essentially turning it into a divine Aesop's fable. Does it really matter if a slow but persistent tortoise ever really raced a speedy hare and won? Of course not, as long as you understand the moral of the story — persistence pays off. In a similar way, framework proponents minimize the force of the many textual details of the creation account as long as one believes God is the Creator and that He made man in His image. It is simply the latest in a long line of failed attempts to reinterpret the unchanging Word of God to fit man's ever-changing opinions and should be rejected by all Bible-believing Christians.

Chapter 18

Laminin and
the Cross

Georgia Purdom

❁❁❁❁❁❁❁❁❁❁❁❁❁❁❁❁❁❁

One of the most popular questions I receive concerns a popular Christian icon — the protein laminin. Laminin, interestingly, is in the shape of a cross.[1] In fact, a quick Internet search turns up multiple websites selling T-shirts, mouse pads, stickers, coffee mugs, and a host of other items with a picture of the laminin protein.[2] These items usually include a catch phrase, such as "Great designers always leave their mark" or "Fingerprint of the Creator." As a molecular biologist, I can certainly appreciate excitement concerning a protein (which really shows what a science nerd I am!), but should this protein really be viewed as an icon of Christianity?

What Is Laminin?

Laminin is a protein that is part of the extracellular matrix in humans and animals. The extracellular matrix (ECM) lies outside of cells and provides support and attachment for cells inside organs (along with its many other functions). Laminin has "arms" that associate with other

---

1. Sigma-Aldrich, Laminin, http://www.sigmaaldrich.com/life-science/metabolomics/ enzyme-explorer/learning-center/structural-proteins/laminin.html.
2. This site is an example. Soul Harvest, http://www.virtuousplanet.com/cottonglow/ c000000003291.

laminin molecules to form sheets and bind to cells. Laminin and other ECM proteins essentially "glue" the cells (such as those lining the stomach and intestines) to a foundation of connective tissue. This keeps the cells in place and allows them to function properly. The structure of laminin is very important for its function (as is true for all proteins). One type of congenital muscular dystrophy results from defects in laminin.

How Has Laminin Become an Icon of Christianity?

An argument that has become quite common in modern Christianity is relating the structure and function of laminin to biblical truths. This little, practically unknown protein became popular after it was used as an illustration in a sermon by Louie Giglio.[3] The topic of laminin quickly appeared in many emails and blogs. Here is one such email:

> Thousands of years before the world knew anything about laminin, Paul penned those words [Colossians 1:15–17]. And now we see that from a very LITERAL standpoint, we are held together . . . one cell to another . . . by the cross.
>
> You would never in a quadrillion years convince me that is anything other than a mark of a Creator who knew EXACTLY what laminin "glue" would look like long before Adam even breathed his first breath!![4]

According to the person who wrote this email, the shape of laminin is absolute proof of God's existence. Mr. Giglio in his sermon stated:

> God is making a promise to us tonight. He's saying I am a universe maker and I am a heart former, but I'm also big enough to be intimately acquainted with all the circumstances of every one of your lives, and I promise you no matter what comes in this lifetime, no matter how difficult the road or how dark the night, I will hold on to you, and I will literally hold you together and carry you through any and every circumstance that ever comes your way any moment on this planet. That's the promise of God. So you say, well man, that sounds good, but how do I know that's

3. Louie Giglio, Laminin, http://www.youtube.com/watch?v=_e4zgJXPpI4.
4. Snopes.com, Laminin, http://www.snopes.com/glurge/laminin.asp.

true in my life right now? That's really what we want to know. And *I'll tell you how you can know tonight that God will always hold you together, no matter what. It's by looking a little deeper into the human body, and it's a little protein molecule called laminin* (emphasis mine).[5]

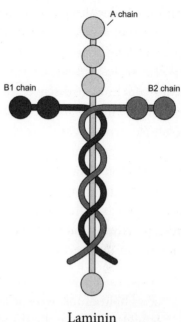

Laminin

Mr. Giglio then discussed the function of laminin (as glue) and its structure (a cross) in the body. He related this to Colossians 1:17, which states, "He [Christ] is before all things, and in Him all things hold together" (NASB). His argument is basically that God designed laminin in the shape of a cross and gave it the particular function of "glue" in the body so that we can know the truth that Christ holds all things together.

What Is the Problem with This Type of Argument?

While I appreciate Mr. Giglio's passion for the Word, I would suggest that this type of argument is not a good one to use. The main problem is that this type of argument asserts that something outside of Scripture (in this case, laminin) is vital to know the truthfulness of the Bible. Laminin is used to prove a biblical truth. However, we should never use our fallible, finite understanding of the world to judge the infallible Word of God. What we observe in the world can certainly be used to confirm God's Word (and it does), but our finite observations are not in a position to evaluate the infinite things of God. Only if we start with the Bible as our ultimate standard can we have a worldview that is rational and makes sense of the evidence.[6]

5. Louie Giglio, Laminin, http://www.youtube.com/watch?v=_e4zgJXPpI4.
6. Jason Lisle, "Atheism: An Irrational Worldview," October 10, 2007, answersingenesis. org, http://www.answersingenesis.org/articles/aid/v2/n1/atheism-irrational; Jason Lisle, "Evolution: the Anti-science," February 13, 2008, answersingenesis.org, http://www. answersingenesis.org/articles/aid/v3/n1/evolution-anti-science.

204 • How Do We Know the Bible Is True?

The structure of laminin was not made popular until 2008, yet I have no doubt that many Christians before that time have trusted the truth presented in Colossians 1:17 because it is God's Word. Would Colossians 1:17 be any less true if laminin were not in the shape of a cross? No. If five years from now we discover that the laminin protein actually has a different shape (in fact, some electron micrographs of the protein do not resemble a cross at all[7]), would that change the truth found in Colossians 1:17? No, because our belief in the truth that Christ holds all things together should start and end with God's Word alone!

Many Christians have told me how wonderful they think it is that laminin is in the shape of a cross and that it is confirmation of the truths in God's Word. One Christian blogger commented:

> This is a glorious reminder to me [the shape of laminin in a cross] that when the rough times comes, and the storm of life takes hold of me, what is holding my physical body together is a cellular protein in the shape of a cross!!! We truly are wonderfully made.[8]

As a molecular biologist, I can honestly say that when the storms of life come it isn't the shape of a protein that comes first to my mind. I don't turn to my fallible mind to give meaning to a sin-cursed world. Rather, I look to God's perfect, infallible, inerrant Word. The verses I've memorized over the years spring to life, reminding me of God's care and goodness.

Looking for Signs

Unfortunately, this type of argument — which effectively treats our fallible, finite knowledge of the evidence as superior to God's Word — is very popular in today's society, especially among young people. One blogger commented:

> I cried out from my insides, "How did I get here? Where did you go, God? Why does it seem like I am way off track, here? I feel like my life is so fractured . . . etc." Then, like I mentioned, I

7. Konrad Beck, Irene Hunter, and Jurgen Engel, "Structure and Function of Laminin: Anatomy of a Multidomainglycoprotein," *The FASEB Journal*, 4 (1990):148–160.

8. Sandy, "So how does laminin hold you together through those tough times?" September 9, 2007, Jesus and Dark Chocolate, http://samismom22.wordpress.com/2007/09/09/156/.

checked my email to open this clip that someone had sent to me, not knowing what it was. The clip [of the sermon by Mr. Giglio talking about laminin] was a powerful reminder of hope. The timing was perfect: a message to me that God heard me at that very moment when I was screaming from my inmost being. It was Him reminding me that He would never leave me. He would be holding me together during this time.[9]

Certainly, God can use people and circumstances to confirm the truths in His Word, but it seems like people today spend more time "looking for signs" than they do actually reading and studying God's Word, praying for guidance, and trusting the Creator.

As a former Christian college professor, I have a lot of experience with college students. I lost track of the number of times students came into my office and told me they were going to switch majors or date someone or decide to do something because God had given them a "sign." I always posed a series of questions to them after hearing about their "sign." Had they been praying and asking for God's guidance? Had they been studying the Bible? Had they been talking with spiritually mature mentors? Usually this was met with a half-hearted "Yes," and then it was back to telling me about the amazing "sign."

God did use signs to reveal things, and that is evident from Scripture. In Luke 2:12 an angel tells the shepherds, "And this will be the sign to you: You will find a Babe wrapped in swaddling cloths, lying in a manger." However, Jesus also admonished those who improperly sought signs (Matthew 16:4). In today's "fast food" society, many people prefer the "drive-thru" when it comes to knowing God's truths. A sign is much quicker than studying and reasoning from the Scriptures, taking the time to pray, and discussing God's Word with other believers.

Young Christians have started doubting God's Word (especially the Book of Genesis) because this is what is drummed into them from the secular world through much of the media and most public schools. Many desperately want to accept the claims of Scripture but have been taught to improperly think that the unaided mind is the ultimate standard for

---

9. Kristen, response to "So how does laminin hold you together through those tough times?" September 9, 2007, Jesus and Dark Chocolate, http://samismom22.wordpress.com/2007/09/09/156/.

acquiring knowledge. That is why the type of argument used with the laminin protein likely resonates with them and many other Christians as well. As one blogger said, "I Believe God Is Sending Us A Message Saying Im [*sic*] Here And Im [*sic*] Holding You Together."[10] Yet Proverbs 1:7 tells us, "The *fear of the* LORD is the beginning of knowledge" (emphasis added; see also Colossians 2:3).

Consider what happens when people try to prove the Resurrection of Christ (a biblical truth) using unaided reasoning. We can observe that dead people do not come back to life. Consequently, many scientists believe the Bible to be in error about the Resurrection. Does that prove that Jesus did not rise from the dead? Of course not! Science and human reasoning are not the limits of what is possible; God is the limit. Scripture should be our ultimate standard to understand this miraculous event. It's also important to realize that the fact we don't see people coming back to life in modern times has no bearing on whether or not Jesus rose from the dead in the first century A.D.

Starting with unaided reasoning and reading our own ideas into the Bible can lead us to all sorts of absurd conclusions. For example, the Ebola virus, which causes a horrific form of hemorrhagic fever that usually results in death, happens to have the structure of what is commonly referred to as a shepherd's crook. The Bible tells us that Jesus is the Good Shepherd (John 10:14). If the shape of laminin supports the biblical truth that Christ holds all things together, then what would we conclude about the Good Shepherd from the shape of the Ebola virus? And if laminin can represent a cross, then why not a sword (Ephesians 6:17; Hebrews 4:12)? A skeptic wrote the following in response to a blog post by a Christian about laminin:

> While it may be neat that this protein molecule, when dia-
> grammed, is in the shape of a cross, that's really all it is: neat. What
> it is not is some kind of innate proof of the existence of a god, the
> God of the Bible or Jesus.

If a researcher found a molecule in the shape of a sleigh, would it be proof of the existence of Santa Claus? Would they go head-over-heels about it? No. It would go something like this:

---

10. Editorial response to "The Supremacy of Christ over Biology," April 29, 2008, Jonathan Chambers, http://gospelife.wordpress.com/2008/04/29/the-supremacy-of-christ-over-biology/.

"Wow, that kind of looks like a sleigh."

And then they would move onto something of importance.

Please remember that critical thinking is what strengthens ideas.[11]

I agree! We need to think critically as Christians and not allow our fallible, finite interpretations to supersede the Word of God.

Conclusion

Romans 1:20 makes it clear that we can know about God through what He has made. God certainly designed the laminin protein and gave it a structure that allows it to perform the function He designated for it. In fact, one of the early papers on the structure and function of laminin said this: "Globular and rodlike domains are arranged in an extended four-armed, *cruciform shape that is well suited for mediating between distant sites on cells and other components of the extracellular matrix*" (emphasis mine).[12] Whether the shape of laminin was purposefully designed by God to illustrate the cross is unknown.

Colossians 1:15–20, highlighting the supremacy of Christ, is probably one of my favorite Scripture passages. Paul began by writing about Christ as Creator and moved to Christ as Redeemer. We know this is true, not because it appeals to our unaided reasoning, but because it is revealed in God's Word.

---

11. Joshua, response to "So how does laminin hold you together through those tough times?" September 9, 2007, Jesus and Dark Chocolate, http://samismom22.wordpress.com/2007/09/09/156/.

12. Ibid., ref. 6.

Chapter 19

How Can We Stand on Scripture in an Evolution-Pushing Culture?

Jim Gardner

Today, many Christians think the creation versus evolution controversy is not that important. They think we should not let this issue divide the Church. By thinking that way, they misunderstand the foundational nature of this issue. Recently, I spoke on the importance of creation. As he introduced me the pastor stated, "I'm just an old country boy from Kentucky. God said He created it, and I believe it. Period. But," the pastor continued, "we not only need to believe it, we need to understand it, and then we need to be able to defend it." That pastor had a true understanding of how critical this issue of creation versus evolution really is.

A Foundational Issue

I believe the creation versus evolution debate is the most foundational issue facing the Church today. A large number of people who go to church are being overwhelmed by the so-called "scientific evidence" that supports evolution. Many are accepting these secular humanistic explanations because they think, *The scientists are the ones with the PhDs, and they say they have proven the earth is billions of years old with radiometric dating, so it must be true.*

The battle is raging between Satan, the usurper, and Jesus Christ, the Creator. The prizes in this battle are the hearts and minds (and ultimately the eternal souls) of our children and grandchildren. Yet few understand the nature or manner in which the battle is being waged.

One can visit church after church, regardless of denomination, and notice few have a vibrant, growing number of young people. There also seems to be a lack of young families with kids. It is only natural to wonder why such a large percentage of the people going to church today have gray hair.

Most Christians would agree that many of our churches are dying. Some are slipping down a slow decline, and others are facing a much quicker demise. I recently spoke in a church to about 90 people in a Sunday morning service where not a single person was under the age of 60. When I asked the pastor where the young people were, he said there weren't any. I asked him why he thought that was. He responded, "I really don't know." Sadly, his response is representative of many pastors.

Ken Ham clearly identified the problem nearly 25 years ago. He wrote, "There is a war going on in society — a very real battle. The war is Christianity versus humanism, but we must wake up to the fact that, at the foundational level, it's really creation versus evolution."[1]

We are losing entire generations of church kids to a faith-based belief system called evolutionary humanism. Further, many church leaders do not understand why this is happening. Young people are abandoning the Church in droves when they leave home. As demonstrated in the recent book, *Already Gone* by Ken Ham and Britt Beemer, many of the young people sitting in the pews are "already gone" before they ever leave home.

Authority of Scripture

This war is really about the authority of Scripture. Either God meant exactly what He said and said exactly what He meant regarding the creation account, or He didn't.

In this battle of ideas between creation and evolution, one of the central defining issues is the age of the earth. Many battles have been fought over the interpretation of the scientific evidence as well as the interpretation of the Bible itself regarding this issue. Because we are not teaching

---

1. Ken Ham, *The Lie: Evolution* (Green Forest, AR: Master Books, 1987), p. 97.

science to our children from the biblical worldview, our children are succumbing to science teaching from the secular humanist worldview.

In its creation account and genealogies, the Bible clearly reveals the earth is about 6,000 years old, but evolutionary humanists and even some Christians claim it is billions of years old. Although many people believe naturalistic evolution would be possible over the course of several billion years, it is not. Life forms do not become more complicated without the input of intelligence. You see, our children and young people have figured it out. If you cannot trust the Bible about the creation account in Genesis, how can you trust the Bible about the things that are hard to understand?

Personal Experience

I experienced this battle firsthand. When I was two years old, my parents became missionaries to the country of Thailand. I was raised on the mission field for about ten years. Twice a year, I was sent to a missionary boarding school in Vietnam. All I was ever taught about the origin of the universe was "In the beginning God created the heavens and the earth" (Genesis 1:1). At age 12, we came back to the United States where my father served as a pastor in churches for 50 years. I entered the public education system in junior high where I first began to hear about evolution. When my classmates would ask me what I thought about evolution, I would simply respond, "The Bible says, 'In the beginning God created the heavens and the earth,' and that's good enough for me." Then in my twenties the scientists started raving about carbon-14 dating and how that proved the earth was millions of years old. When asked about this alleged proof, I simply responded, "The Bible says, 'In the beginning God created the heavens and the earth,' and if He took a million years to do it, that's still okay with me."

What I didn't realize is that I was beginning to take the words of scientists — who do not know everything, who have less than perfect brains, and who were not there at the beginning — and add or substitute their words for the Word of the God who does know everything, who has a perfect brain, who was there at the beginning, and who told us how He did it. Genesis reveals who the Creator was (God), when He created (in the beginning), what He created (heavens and earth), and even how He created (in many cases, He spoke things into existence).

I now realize something else. I wanted to believe in evolution. Yes, without even realizing it I wanted evolution to be true because evolution taught that I was the top of the food chain, that I could live any way I wanted to, that I made up the rules for my life, and that I determined what truth was for myself. In other words, I was the "god" in control of my own life. Further, when I died, that was the end of the story. They would put my body in the grave and plant flowers on it and that would be the end of me — no heaven and no hell. If there were no accountability to a Creator, I could do whatever I wanted. Besides, secular humanist scientists made the alleged evidence for evolution sound so convincing.

Competing Worldviews

The Bible teaches something very different. It teaches that God created everything. If true, then God makes the rules, He set penalties for breaking the rules, and He has the power to execute the penalty. As evolutionary ideas crept into my thinking, I slowly abandoned my biblical upbringing. I began a downward slide spiritually and morally that did not end for 20 years.

Today, many of the youth in our churches are caught in the same net, the same seductive lie. Evolutionary humanism and its millions of years are perhaps Satan's most effective lie ever, and Christians are not immune to it. Belief in this lie of evolution continues to have devastating consequences on us individually, our families, our churches, our communities, and our nation.

People need to understand that evolution is a worldview teaching that man got here without God being involved. Creation is a worldview about how man got here through the Creator God. Both are ideas about origins going in opposite directions. These ideas have consequences because a person's worldview influences every decision he makes. When comparing these two worldviews and the behavior that results from them, a stark contrast emerges. Evolution is the foundation of humanism. Genesis is the foundational book of God's Word, the Bible. When people believe there is no accountability for their actions, they tend to act quite differently from those who believe there are consequences for their actions (we admit that all of us, including Christians, often fail to live up to God's standards).

Let's consider the issue of alcohol from the perspective of these two worldviews. From the secular humanist point of view, there is no absolute

standard of right and wrong. The humanist believes he can decide for himself what is right and what is wrong or that society gets to decide these things. Either way, man is the authority and right and wrong are subject to change.

The humanist can decide that drinking alcohol is a perfectly acceptable activity, especially after a tough week at work. Let's say that a secular humanist has a bad week at work and on Friday loses his job. Why not go out and get drunk? It is his right to drink, isn't it? Now if millions of Americans do that (and millions of Americans do), why would we be surprised if some of them get in their cars and drive drunk? They might wander across the median and slam head-on into a van carrying a whole family, killing half of them and putting the other half in the hospital. Medical costs go up, legal costs go up, and insurance costs go up, not to mention the cost in pain and suffering.

On the other hand, if you believe God created the heavens and the earth, then you believe He owns it all. He makes the rules and sets the penalties for breaking those rules. Since His Word commands us to not get drunk, then to break the rule is sinful. The Bible states that the penalty for sin is death (Romans 6:23). If people had a biblical worldview, then the amount of drunk driving would be drastically reduced.

This isn't to claim that all humanists get drunk and that all Christians remain sober. However, drunkenness is a perfectly acceptable behavior for a secular humanist and is consistent with their worldview. In fact, taking the life of another person through vehicular manslaughter (or any other method) isn't really wrong from a humanist perspective because there is no absolute standard of right and wrong. Of course, many humanists believe it is wrong to harm other people, but their worldview can provide no basis for such a view. On the other hand, drunkenness is entirely inconsistent with a biblical worldview and therefore unacceptable for a Christian.

People think believing in evolution is no big deal, but it leads to all manner of destructive behavior to an individual, the family, the Church, and the culture.

Finding Answers to Some Evolutionary Questions

Evolutionary humanists often emphatically state, "No real scientist with a degree from a real university believes in creation. All the real scientists know evolution is a fact." However, thousands of scientists (and I have met many) believe that special creation by God as described in the Bible makes better sense of the scientific evidence. So what about this evidence that allegedly "proves" evolution to be a fact? Let's briefly look at three.

The assertion: radiometric dating proves the earth is billions of years old, so evolution has plenty of time to work.

Radiometric dating does nothing of the kind because it is based on a number of unprovable assumptions. The concept of radiometric dating is not too complicated. Scientists are able to measure very small amounts of chemicals and the decay rates of radioactive elements. They know what a radioactive element decays into and what particles it gives off as it decays. Dr. Alan White says:

> The radiometric dating method is done by measuring the ratio of parent to daughter products in radioactive decay chains, like potassium (^{40}K) to argon (^{40}Ar) or uranium (^{238}U) to lead (^{206}Pb). Unlike carbon-14 dating, radiometric dating with these elements is used for the estimation of longer times. This technique applies to igneous rocks from their time of solidification. Isotope concentrations can be measured very accurately today.[2]

The dates derived from radiometric dating are based on these untested and unprovable assumptions:

1. We must assume the beginning concentration of the parent and daughter elements. Question: How do you know how much of each element was there at the beginning?
2. We must assume the decay rates for parent to daughter have remained constant. Question: How do you know if the decay rate has remained constant for even a few thousand years, let alone remained constant for billions of years?
3. We must assume that no parent or daughters were gained or lost. Question: How do you know none of the elements were leached into or out of the rock during those billions of years?

Today, scientists assume natural processes have always been the same as they are now (uniformitarianism). They cannot know this since they were not there observing for billions of years. However, we know that uniformitarian assumptions are wrong. The Bible reveals that God flooded the entire world in judgment. This fact is ignored by uniformitarian scientists but would have had a drastic impact on our world. So what

---

2. Alan White Ph.D., in a Canopy Ministries lecture, "The Age of the Earth."

does all this mean? It means that if the assumptions are incorrect, then the conclusions based on them will be false.[3]

The assertion: the fossil record proves that evolution occurred.

The fossil record does not prove evolution. Instead, it demonstrates mass destruction on a global scale. In Genesis 6–8 we are told about Noah's Flood, an event that killed all people and air-breathing land animals not on board the ark, ripped up plants and vegetation, and buried much of the remains in and under layers that became sedimentary rock.

In those layers of rock, we find the fossilized remains of those animals buried in the Flood. We also find the remains of massive amounts of vegetation. This is the likely source of the coal, natural gas, and oil deposits that we use to heat our homes and power our automobiles today.

Dr. Duane Gish, in a book titled *The Fossils Say No*,[4] and in a follow-up book, *The Fossils Still Say No*, makes an iron-clad case that the fossil record is inconsistent with evolution but is entirely consistent with special creation and a worldwide Flood. He rightly points out that if evolution were true, then there should be billions of transitional fossils indicating incremental changes between kinds. So where are they? This is no small question for evolutionists because, of the many billions that should be found, they have only produced a handful of highly questionable examples. This exposes evolution for what it is: a faith-based belief system.

Of course, there are no true transitional forms in the fossil record. Darwin wrote, "The number of intermediate varieties, which have formerly existed, [must] be truly enormous," but added that the lack of these fossils was the most obvious and serious objection to his theory,[5] and if they were not found, his theory would be invalid. For more than 150 years, scientists have been looking for the "missing link," and it is still missing. Not one indisputable transitional form has ever been discovered.

---

3. In a groundbreaking book and DVD called *Thousands Not Billions*, the Institute for Creation Research (ICR) published eight years of research on this very question. The DVD in particular is for the average person and makes it easy to understand why radiometric dating is inherently unreliable and, in many cases, fraudulent. If the world is not billions of years old, then few would believe evolution is a viable explanation for origins.

4. Duane Gish, Ph.D., *The Fossils Still Say No* (Green Forest, AR: Master Books, 1995).

5. Charles Darwin, *On the Origin of Species*, a facsimile of the first edition (Cambridge, MA: Harvard University Press, 1964, 1859), p. 280.

In the first chapters of Genesis, God states ten times that everything was created "after its kind" and would only reproduce "after its kind." That series of proclamations clearly indicates that evolution, in the molecules-to-man sense, would not, could not, and will never happen. These verses stop the idea of evolution in its tracks. They also refute "theistic evolution," the idea that God somehow used evolution as part of His creative process.

The assertion: special creation is only a religion, but evolution is real science.

Secular humanists have been effective at ripping science away from the Bible. We have let them define the debate between creation and evolution as being between religion and science. The implication is clear. Religion is a fairy tale, something you must believe in, something that requires "faith." Science is based on proof or "facts." You can believe in whatever religion you want, but evolution is scientific.

However, when examined closely, both creationism and evolutionism are shown to be faith-based belief systems. Therefore, the debate needs to be redefined as a faith-based belief system against an opposing faith-based belief system. Evolutionists cannot prove evolution happened any more than creationists can prove God created. They both require faith. Evolutionists have known and understood this for decades.

Dr. Harrison Matthews was asked to write the 1971 foreword to a massive reprint of Darwin's book, *On the Origin of Species*. In it, he stated:

> The fact of evolution is the backbone of biology.... [B]iology is thus in the peculiar position of being a science founded on an unproved theory — is it then a science or a faith? ... belief in the theory of evolution is thus exactly parallel to the belief in special creation. Both are concepts which believers know to be true but neither, up to the present, has been capable of proof.[6]

His first statement shows him to be a strong evolutionist, but he admits the faith-based nature of his position. Remember, this is an evolutionist saying this. I would agree with him that his position is faith-based. Clearly, evolutionists have been aware of the religious nature of their

---

6. Charles Darwin, *The Origin of Species,* reprint (London: J.M. Dent & Sons, Ltd., 1971), L.H. Matthews, Introduction to Charles Darwin, p. XI.

beliefs for a long time. Yet they continue to deceive our children by teaching them that evolution has been proven to be a scientific fact.

Today, we are seeing the consequences of evolutionary teaching. When you teach generation after generation of children they are nothing more than evolved animals, why should it surprise us when they begin to act like animals? When we teach there is no accountability, we should not be surprised to see large increases in school violence, lawlessness, homosexual behavior, pornography, abortion, and many other destructive behaviors.

We must begin to take responsibility for the education of our own children. If the public schools (and even many Christian schools and colleges) continue to teach our children a false belief system called evolution, then we must begin to teach them true science ourselves. We must first educate ourselves and then our children. Even though secular humanists have been effective at ripping science apart from the Bible, God has not left us defenseless.

Dr. Henry Morris was particularly effective in showing the scientific accuracy of the Bible.[7] The author of dozens of books, Dr. Morris was mightily used by God to stand against the onslaught of evolutionary humanism. Yet the body of material to help us only begins there. God has raised up organizations like Answers in Genesis to help us teach the truth about science to our children.

Of course, one cannot scientifically prove special creation. Dr. Henry Morris III stated, "The central message (of the Bible) cannot be tested in a laboratory by scientific analysis or verified by archaeological research. The foundation of truth begins in Genesis."[8] It takes faith to believe in special creation. However, it is not the blind faith, or better called credulity, required to believe in evolution.

Yes, God said that He created, when He created, and how He created. That settles the matter. I have learned how to understand creation science and how to defend it. I encourage you, too, to learn how to understand and then defend it. Then start teaching the truth of God's spectacular creation to the next generation.

---

7. Henry M. Morris, *The Genesis Record* (Grand Rapids, MI: Baker, 1976) and Henry M. Morris, The New Defenders Study Bible (Nashville, TN: Nelson, 2004).
8. Henry M. Morris III, *The Big Three: Major Events that Changed History Forever* (Green Forest, AR: Master Books 2009), p. 81.

Chapter 20

Is the Perpetual Virginity of Mary a Biblical View?

Bodie Hodge

✿✿✿✿✿✿✿✿✿✿✿✿✿✿✿✿✿✿✿✿

Mary, the mother of Jesus, was an incredible woman. In fact, precious few women's names could even be mentioned to give her a "run for her money," and God honored Mary in a way that all other women could only dream about. The Lord favored her for an event that had been long awaited since the Genesis 3:15 prophecy of the Seed of a woman (i.e., the Virgin Birth). Luke 1 describes it:

> And having come in, the angel said to her, "Rejoice, highly favored one, the Lord is with you; blessed are you among women!"
> But when she saw him, she was troubled at his saying, and considered what manner of greeting this was. Then the angel said to her, "Do not be afraid, Mary, for you have found favor with God. And behold, you will conceive in your womb and bring forth a Son, and shall call His name JESUS. He will be great, and will be called the Son of the Highest; and the Lord God will give Him the throne of His father David. And He will reign over the house of Jacob forever, and of His kingdom there will be no end."
> Then Mary said to the angel, "How can this be, since I do not know a man?"

And the angel answered and said to her, "The Holy Spirit will come upon you, and the power of the Highest will overshadow you; therefore, also, that Holy One who is to be born will be called the Son of God" (Luke 1:28–35).

Mary was a virgin who was to conceive by being overshadowed by the Holy Spirit and give birth to the Son of God. Few in Christian realms would deny Mary was a virgin *and* remained a virgin through pregnancy and the birth of Christ. This was the ultimate fulfillment of a prophecy from Isaiah:

Therefore the Lord Himself will give you a sign: Behold, the *virgin shall conceive and bear a Son*, and shall call His name Immanuel (Isaiah 7:14, emphasis added).

However, Mary's virginity after the birth of Christ can become a heated debate in some circles. Though some may think this is a Roman Catholic versus Protestant view, it is not. Many Protestants, including people like Martin Luther and John Calvin, have held to Mary remaining a virgin for the duration of her life. Let's look at the issues in a little more detail.

What Does the Bible State?

Two different Gospels accounts state Mary had other sons and daughters.[1] These accounts even give the names of the sons.

"Is this not the carpenter's son? Is not His mother called Mary? And His brothers James, Joses, Simon, and Judas? And His sisters, are they not all with us? Where then did this Man get all these things?" (Matthew 13:55–56).

"Is this not the carpenter, the Son of Mary, and brother of James, Joses, Judas, and Simon? And are not His sisters here with us?" So they were offended at Him (Mark 6:3).

---

1. Some have suggested that Joseph may have died before fathering children with Mary so that these sons and daughters were the children of Mary and another husband. However, it seems unlikely that Jesus would have been called "the carpenter's son" if His earthly father had died some 20–30 years earlier. Furthermore, even the people in Capernaum (roughly 20 miles from Nazareth) recognized Him as "the son of Joseph" and claimed to "know" (present tense) His father and mother (John 6:42). Although the Bible does not record Joseph's death, it likely happened prior to the Lord's Crucifixion since Jesus entrusted John with the care of His mother (John 19:27).

Some have suggested these brothers and sisters were cousins or more distant relations. If true, why didn't the writers use the Greek term for cousins (*anepsios*)? The Greek word did exist and was used in Scripture (Colossians 4:10). If they were more distant relatives, then why not use a Greek word that meant relatives (*suggenes*), such as the one describing Mary and Elizabeth's relational status in Luke 1:36? Why did Matthew and Mark use the words most commonly translated as brothers (*adelphos*) and sisters (*adelphē*)? In any other context no one would have questioned this meaning.

A logical point concerning this passage was brought up by expositor Adam Clarke in his commentary:

> Why should the children of another family be brought in here to share a reproach which it is evident was designed for Joseph the carpenter, Mary his wife, Jesus their son, and their other children? Prejudice apart, would not any person of plain common sense suppose, from this account, that these were the children of Joseph and Mary, and the brothers and sisters of our Lord, according to the flesh?[2]

It seems rather obvious that these Gospel accounts refer to Joseph's and Mary's children. Why would these people criticize Jesus by mentioning his father (as they presumed) and mother and then seemingly switch to distant relatives?

The Apostle Paul also claimed that Jesus had at least one brother. Concerning his first trip to Jerusalem after his conversion, Paul wrote, "But I saw none of the other apostles except James, the Lord's brother" (Galatians 1:19).

The first chapter of Acts tells how the disciples met to select a replacement for Judas. Luke specifically singled out Mary and the brothers of Jesus.

> Then they returned to Jerusalem from the mount called Olivet, which is near Jerusalem, a Sabbath day's journey. And when they had entered, they went up into the upper room where they were staying: Peter, James, John, and Andrew; Philip and

---

2. Adam Clarke, *Clarke's Commentary*, electronic edition (New York: Carlton & Phillips, 1853), Matthew 13:55.

Thomas; Bartholomew and Matthew; James the son of Alphaeus and Simon the Zealot; and Judas the son of James. These all continued with one accord in prayer and supplication, with the women and Mary the mother of Jesus, and with His brothers. (Acts 1:12–14)

To claim Mary was a perpetual virgin even after Christ was born is to deny the words of the Apostle Matthew, who wrote, "Then Joseph, being aroused from sleep, did as the angel of the Lord commanded him and took to him his wife, and did not know her *till* she had brought forth her firstborn Son. And he called His name JESUS" (Matthew 1:24–25, emphasis added).

"Knew" was a modest way of describing sexual relations in ancient times. For example, Adam knew Eve, and she conceived Cain, and he knew her again, and she bore Seth (Genesis 4:1, 25). Cain knew his wife, and she bore Enoch (Genesis 4:17). If Joseph never knew Mary at all, the phrase "till she had brought forth her firstborn Son" is pointless. Obviously, Joseph did not sleep with Mary until after she gave birth to Jesus, fulfilling both parts of the prophecy (virginal conception and Virgin Birth, as Isaiah 7:14 states, "the virgin shall conceive *and* bear a Son," emphasis added). But this means Joseph did know her after she gave birth to Jesus, so she was no longer a virgin.

In fact, sex within marriage is not a sin but is a creation ordinance within marriage that existed *prior* to sin and the Curse. Jesus quoted Genesis 2:24 in Matthew 19:5–6, reiterating "the two shall be one flesh."

Consider that God commanded people to be fruitful and multiply in Genesis 1:28 and twice in Genesis 9 (verses 1 and 7). Malachi 2:14–15 indicates one reason for marriage is to have godly offspring. Why would Mary be disobedient to God? Since she was truly a godly woman, she would have respected His commands and honor them. Having at least two daughters and five sons would indeed be fulfilling God's commands to be fruitful and multiply.

The following Gospel account provides more evidence Jesus had siblings:

While He was still talking to the multitudes, behold, His mother and brothers stood outside, seeking to speak with Him.

Then one said to Him, "Look, Your mother and Your brothers are standing outside, seeking to speak with You."

But He answered and said to the one who told Him, "Who is My mother and who are My brothers?" And He stretched out His hand toward His disciples and said, "Here are My mother and My brothers! For whoever does the will of My Father in heaven is My brother and sister and mother" (Matthew 12:46–50).

This event is also described in Mark 3:32–35 and Luke 8:19–21. Here Christ indicated a distinction between His fleshly brothers and mother and His spiritual brothers and mother. This account also further corroborates the idea that Jesus had brothers.

When Did the Idea of Mary Being a "Virgin Forever" Begin?

The idea of the perpetual virginity of Mary comes from a dubious apocryphal book written well after the New Testament. The book is called the *Infancy Gospel of James, The Protoevangelium of James*, or sometimes simply *Protoevangelium*, and it is estimated to have been written in the middle part of the second century.

Authoritative works were those written or approved by the Apostles. A host of false teachings and books came out after the canonical books. Some were written by well-intentioned Christians, some by Gnostics (thinking they had secret knowledge of God), and others by pagans of the day. Some of these books challenged New Testament teachings while others tried to fill in information.

Often, people tried to associate a particular writing with one of the Apostles to give it a little more credibility. However, the Church usually recognized easily what the Apostles had written. But this didn't stop the controversies, nor did it prevent some Christians from being led astray. Even today people are often led astray, even Christians, by things they read concerning the Bible.

The Protoevangelium of James is like other forgeries trying to capitalize on an Apostle. James, the half-brother of Jesus, was elevated to an Apostle after he saw the resurrected Savior (Galatians 1:19; 1 Corinthians 15:7). So some people thought using his name would give some much-needed credibility to the book. However, the Church rightly recognized this book was not from the Apostle James. The early Church father Origen wrote a commentary on Matthew in which he rejected the *Protoevangelium of James* as spurious and affirmed Mary had other children.[3]

The concept of Mary's perpetual virginity is conveniently explained in *The Protoevangelium of James* since James is viewed as an older step-brother of Jesus being a child of Joseph and his first wife, *prior* to his marriage to Mary. However, there are a number of mistakes in this book and statements that contradict the Bible that an Apostle writing under the inspiration of the Holy Spirit would not make.

The following is a table of some contradictions between *The Protoevangelium of James*[4] and the Bible:

	Protoevangelium of James	The Bible
1	Gabriel is called an archangel (chapter 9:22), which was a common designation for Gabriel in apocryphal literature written after the first century. (For example, see *Revelation of Paul, The Book of John Concerning the Falling Asleep of Mary*, and *The Apocalypse of the Holy Mother of God*.)	The Bible never identifies Gabriel as an archangel, but Michael is described as an archangel in Jude 1:9. The idea of Gabriel as an archangel seems to be a misconception that began in the second century.

---

3. *Origen's Commentary on Matthew in Ante-Nicene Fathers,* Volume IX, http://www.ccel. org/ccel/schaff/anf09.xvi.ii.iii.xvii.html.
4. Quotations are from *The Protoevangelium of James*, translated by Alexander Walker, Esq., in Alexander Roberts and James Donaldson, *The Ante-Nicene Fathers*, electronic edition (Garland, TX: Galaxie Software, 2000).

   Another translation of this work is available at http://ministries.tliquest.net/ theology/apocryphas/nt/protevan.htm. Mary's reply is rendered differently in this version, in which she replied, "What! By the living God, shall I conceive and bring forth as all other women do?" The angel responded, "Not so, O Mary, but the Holy Spirit will come upon you, and the power of the Most High will overshadow you." This version makes better sense, since the angel corrects her thinking that this would occur via natural means. Walker's translation (cited in the table) makes little sense. Mary assumes it would be a supernatural conception, and then the angel "corrects" her by telling her it would be supernatural. However, both versions of *The Protoevangelium of James* have Mary knowing more at this point than she does in the biblical account. In the Bible, Mary wonders how she could become pregnant since she was a virgin. In *The Protoevangelium of James*, she seems to guess right away that this would be a supernatural event.

2	Mary's response to the angel is different than what is recorded in Scripture. "What! Shall I conceive by the living God, and bring forth as all other women do?" (chapter 9:12).2	Luke 1:34 states, "Then Mary said to the angel, 'How can this be, since I do not know a man?' "
3	Elizabeth fled the Bethlehem region with her son John (the Baptist) to the mountains because of Herod's wrath when he decided to kill all the baby boys around and in Bethlehem (chapter 16:3).	Concerning John the Baptist, Luke 1:80 states, "So the child grew and became strong in spirit, and was in the deserts till the day of his manifestation to Israel." It was Joseph, Mary, and Jesus who fled from Bethlehem because of Herod (Matthew 2:13–15).
4	Jesus was born in a cave outside the city of Bethlehem (chapters 12:11–14:31).	Jesus was born in Bethlehem, the town of David, according to Luke 2:4, 11 and Matthew 2:1.
5	The angel of the Lord, when speaking to Joseph in a dream, said to take Mary but does not mention having her as a wife. The priest chastised Joseph and accused him for taking Mary as a wife secretly by the priest. Joseph takes her home but is reluctant to call her his wife when they go to Bethlehem (chapters 10:17–18, 11:14, 12:2–3).	Matthew 1:19 reveals that Joseph was already Mary's husband (they were betrothed) before the angel visited him in a dream. Matthew 1:24 points out that after the angel visited Joseph, he kept her as his wife.
6	Mary wrapped Jesus in swaddling cloths and hid him in a manger at the inn to keep him from the massacre by Herod's men (chapter 16:2).	Mary and Joseph were warned of Herod's plot by an angel, and they fled to Egypt (Matthew 2:13–14).
7	Wise men came to Bethlehem and inquired of Herod where the Child was born (chapter 21:1–2).	Wise men came to Jerusalem to inquire where the child king was (Matthew 2:1).

Conclusion

The Protoevangelium of James contains the first known mention of Mary's continual virginity. This book likely influenced subsequent people to write of the perpetual virginity of Mary. But the book was not the work of the Apostle James, the brother of Christ. The work's demotion by the early Church, especially its non-inclusion with other books of the canon due to its numerous errors, is further verification it was not authentic.

Keep in mind that no passage of Scripture states Mary perpetually remained a virgin and many state the opposite. So to make a case for the perpetual virginity of Mary, one must use ideas that come from *outside* the Bible and then reinterpret Scripture with some wild hermeneutical gymnastics. This would be appealing to fallible, sinful ideas that originate in the minds of mankind — not God. Why not trust God when He speaks? After all, it would not be a sin for Mary to have sexual relations with her husband Joseph, but it would have been sinful for her to withhold herself from him throughout their marriage (1 Corinthians 7:3–5). There is no biblical or logical reason why Mary would have needed to remain a virgin following the birth of Christ.

The issue is quite simple: should we trust the imperfect sources and traditions that come from outside of Scripture and contradict it or should we trust God's Word?

Chapter 21

Why Should We Believe in the Inerrancy of Scripture?

Brian Edwards

༒༒༒༒༒༒༒༒༒༒༒༒༒༒༒༒༒

"Y ou don't really believe the Bible is true, do you?" The shock expressed by those who discover someone who actually believes the Bible to be without error is often quite amusing. Inevitably, their next question takes us right back to Genesis. But what does the Christian mean by "without error," and why are we so sure?

Inspiring or Expiring?

Let's start by understanding what we mean when we talk about the Bible as "inspired" because that word may mislead us. The term is an attempt to translate a word that occurs only once in the New Testament, and it's not the best translation, even though William Tyndale introduced it back in 1526. The word is found in 2 Timothy 3:16, and the Greek is *theopneustos*. This term is made from two words, one being the word for God (*theos*, as in theology) and the other referring to breath or wind (*pneustos*, as in pneumonia and pneumatic). It is significant that the word is used in 2 Timothy 3:16 passively. In other words, God did not "breathe into" (inspire) all Scripture, but it was "breathed out" by God (expired). Thus, 2 Timothy 3:16 is not about how the Bible came to us but where it came from. The Scriptures are "God-breathed."

To know how the Bible came to us, we can turn to 2 Peter 1:21 where we discover that "holy men of God spoke as they were moved by the Holy Spirit." The Greek word used here is *pherō*, which means "to bear" or "to carry." It was a familiar word that Luke used of the sailing ship carried along by the wind (Acts 27:15, 17). The human writers of the Bible certainly used their minds, but the Holy Spirit carried them along in their thinking so that only His God-breathed words were recorded. The Apostle Paul set the matter plainly in 1 Corinthians 2:13: "These things we also speak, not in words which man's wisdom teaches but which the Holy Spirit teaches."

The word "inspiration" is so embedded in our Christian language that we will continue to use it, though we now know what it really means. God breathed out His Word, and the Holy Spirit guided the writers. The Bible has one Author and many (around 40) writers.

With these two acts of God — breathing out His Word and carrying the writers along by the Spirit — we can come to a definition of inspiration:

> The Holy Spirit moved men to write. He allowed them to use their own styles, cultures, gifts, and character. He allowed them to use the results of their own study and research, write of their own experiences, and express what was in their minds. At the same time, the Holy Spirit did not allow error to influence their writings. He overruled in the expression of thought and in the choice of words. Thus, they recorded accurately all God wanted them to say and exactly how He wanted them to say it in their own character, styles, and languages.

The inspiration of Scripture is a harmony of the active mind of the writer and the sovereign direction of the Holy Spirit to produce God's inerrant and infallible Word for the human race. Two errors are to be avoided here. First, some think inspiration is nothing more than a generally heightened sensitivity to wisdom on the part of the writer, just as we talk of an inspired idea or invention. Second, some believe the writer was merely a mechanical dictation machine, writing out the words he heard from God. Both errors fail to adequately account for the active role played by the Holy Spirit and the human writer.

How Much Is Inerrant?

If "inspired" really means "God-breathed," then the claim of 2 Timothy 3:16 is that all Scripture, being God-breathed, is without error and therefore can be trusted completely. Since God cannot lie (Hebrews 6:18), He would cease to be God if He breathed out errors and contradictions, even in the smallest part. So long as we give *theopneustos* its real meaning, we shall not find it hard to understand the full inerrancy of the Bible.

Two words are sometimes used to explain the extent of biblical inerrancy: plenary and verbal. "Plenary" comes from the Latin *plenus,* which means "full," and refers to the fact that the whole of Scripture in every part is God-given. "Verbal" comes from the Latin *verbum,* which means "word," and emphasizes that even the words of Scripture are God-given. Plenary and verbal inspiration means the Bible is God-given (and therefore without error) in every part (doctrine, history, geography, dates, names) and in every single word.

When we talk about inerrancy, we refer to the original writings of Scripture. We do not have any of the original "autographs," as they are called, but only copies, including many copies of each book. There are small differences here and there, but in reality they are amazingly similar. One 18th-century New Testament scholar claimed that not one thousandth part of the text was affected by these differences.[1] Now that we know what inerrancy means, let's cover what it doesn't mean.

- Inerrancy doesn't mean everything in the Bible is true. We have the record of men lying (e.g., Joshua 9) and even the words of the devil himself. But we can be sure these are accurate records of what took place.
- Inerrancy doesn't mean apparent contradictions are not in the text, but these can be resolved. At times different words may be used in recounting what appears to be the same incident. For example, Matthew 3:11 refers to John the Baptist *carrying* the sandals of the Messiah, whereas John 1:27 refers to him *untying* them. John preached over a period of time, and he would repeat himself; like any preacher he would use different ways of expressing the same thing.

---

1. Bishop Brook Foss Westcott, *The New Testament in the Original Greek* (London, MacMillan, 1881), 2.

- Inerrancy doesn't mean every extant copy is inerrant. It is important to understand that the doctrine of inerrancy only applies to the original manuscripts.

Inerrancy does mean it is incorrect to claim the Bible is only "reasonably accurate," as some do.[2] That would leave us uncertain as to where we could trust God's Word.

What Does the Bible Claim?

Is it true, as John Goldingay stated, that this view of inerrancy "is not directly asserted by Christ or within Scripture itself"?[3] Let's look at what the Bible says about itself.

The View of the Old Testament Writers

The Old Testament writers saw their message as God-breathed and therefore utterly reliable. God promised Moses He would eventually send another prophet (Jesus Christ) who would also speak God's words like Moses had done. "I will raise up for them a Prophet *like you* from among their brethren, and will put My words in His mouth, and He shall speak to them all that I command Him" (Deuteronomy 18:18). Jeremiah was told at the beginning of his ministry that he would speak for God. "Then the LORD put forth His hand and touched my mouth, and the LORD said to me: 'Behold, I have put My words in your mouth' " (Jeremiah 1:9).

The Hebrew word for prophet means "a spokesman," and the prophet's message was on God's behalf: "This is what the LORD says." As a result they frequently so identified themselves with God that they spoke as though God Himself were actually speaking. Isaiah 5 reveals this clearly. In verses 1–2 the prophet speaks of God in the third person (*He*), but in verses 3–6 Isaiah changes to speak in the first person (*I*). Isaiah was speaking the very words of God. No wonder King David could speak of the Word of the Lord as "flawless" (2 Samuel 22:31; see also Proverbs 30:5, NIV).

The New Testament Agrees with the Old Testament

Peter and John saw the words of David in Psalm 2, not merely as the opinion of a king of Israel, but as the voice of God. They introduced a

2. John Goldingay, *Models for Scripture* (Toronto: Clements Publishing, 2004), 282.
3. Ibid., 273.

quotation from that psalm in a prayer to God by saying, "who by the mouth of Your servant David have said: 'Why did the nations rage, and the people plot vain things?' " (Acts 4:25).

Similarly, Paul accepted Isaiah's words as God Himself speaking to men: "The Holy Spirit spoke rightly through Isaiah the prophet to our fathers" (Acts 28:25).

So convinced were the writers of the New Testament that all the words of the Old Testament Scripture were the actual words of God that they even claimed, "Scripture says," when the words quoted came directly from God. Two examples are Romans 9:17, which states, "For the Scripture says to Pharaoh," and Galatians 3:8, in which Paul wrote, "the Scripture, foreseeing that God would justify the Gentiles by faith, preached the gospel to Abraham beforehand. . . ." In Hebrews 1 many of the Old Testament passages quoted were actually addressed to God by the Psalmist, yet the writer to the Hebrews refers to them as the words of God.

Jesus Believed in Verbal Inspiration

In John 10:34 Jesus quoted from Psalm 82:6 and based His teaching upon a phrase: "I said, 'You are gods.' " In other words, Jesus proclaimed that the words of this psalm were the words of God. Similarly, in Matthew 22:31–32 He claimed the words of Exodus 3:6 were given to them by God. In Matthew 22:43–44 our Lord quoted from Psalm 110:1 and pointed out that David wrote these words "in the Spirit," meaning he was actually writing the words of God.

Paul Believed in Verbal Inspiration

Paul based an argument upon the fact that a particular word in the Old Testament is singular and not plural. Writing to the Galatians, Paul claimed that in God's promises to Abraham, "He does not say, 'And to seeds,' as of many, but as of one, 'And to your Seed,' who is Christ" (Galatians 3:16). Paul quoted from Genesis 12:7; 13:15; and 24:7. In each of these verses, our translators used the word "descendants," but the Hebrew word is singular. The same word is translated "seed" in Genesis 22:18. Paul's argument here is that God was not *primarily* referring to Israel as the offspring of Abraham, but to Christ.

What is significant is the way Paul drew attention to the fact that the Hebrew word in Genesis is singular. This demonstrates a belief in verbal inspiration because it mattered to Paul whether God used a singular or plural in these passages of the Old Testament. It is therefore not surprising Paul wrote that one of the advantages of being a Jew was the fact that "they have been entrusted with the very words of God" (Romans 3:2; NIV). Even many critics of the Bible agree that the Scriptures clearly teach a doctrine of verbal inerrancy.

Self-authentication

To say the Bible is the Word of God and is therefore without error because the Bible itself makes this claim is seen by many as circular reasoning. It is rather like saying, "That prisoner must be innocent because he says he is." Are we justified in appealing to the Bible's own claim in settling this matter of its authority and inerrancy?

Actually, we use "self-authentication" every day. Whenever we say, "I think" or "I believe" or "I dreamed," we are making a statement no one can verify. If people were reliable, witness to oneself would always be enough. In John 5:31–32 Jesus said that self-witness is normally insufficient. Later, when Jesus claimed, "I am the light of the world" (John 8:12), the Pharisees attempted to correct Him by stating, "Here you are, appearing as your own witness; your testimony is not valid" (John 8:13; NIV). In defense, the Lord showed that in His case, because He is the Son of God, self-witness is reliable: "Even if I bear witness of Myself, My witness is true . . ." (John 8:14). Self-witness is reliable where sin does not interfere. Because Jesus is God and therefore guiltless (a fact confirmed by His critics in John 8:46), His words can be trusted. In a similar manner, since the Bible is God's Word, we must listen to its own claims about itself.

Much of the Bible's story is such that unless God had revealed it we could never have known it. Many scientific theories propose how the world came into being. Some of these theories differ only slightly from each other, but others are contradictory. This shows no one can really be sure about such matters because no scientist was there when it all happened. Unless the God who was there has revealed it, we could never know for certain. The same is true for all the great Bible doctrines. How can we be sure of God's anger against sin, His love for sinners, or His plan to choose a people for Himself, unless God Himself has told us? Hilary of Poitiers, a fourth-century theologian, once claimed, "Only God is a fit witness to himself" — and no one can improve upon that.

Who Believes This?

The belief that the Bible is without error is not new. Clement of Rome in the first century wrote, "Look carefully into the Scriptures, which are the true utterances of the Holy Spirit. Observe that nothing of an unjust or counterfeit character is written in them."[4] A century later, Irenaeus concluded, "The Scriptures are indeed perfect, since they were spoken by the Word of God and his Spirit."[5]

This was the view of the early Church leaders, and it has been the consistent view of evangelicals from the ancient Vaudois people of the Piedmont Valley to the 16th-century Protestant Reformers across Europe and up to the present day. Not all used the terms "infallibility" or "inerrancy," but many expressed the concepts, and there is no doubt they believed it. It is liberalism that has taken a new approach. Professor Kirsopp Lake at Harvard University admitted, "It is we [the liberals] who have departed from the tradition."[6]

Does It Matter?

Is the debate about whether or not the Bible can be trusted merely a theological quibble? Certainly not! The question of ultimate authority is of tremendous importance for the Christian.

Inerrancy Governs Our Confidence in the Truth of the Gospel

If the Scripture is unreliable, can we offer the world a reliable gospel? How can we be sure of truth on any issue if we are suspicious of errors anywhere in the Bible? A pilot will ground his aircraft even on suspicion of the most minor fault, because he is aware that one fault destroys confidence in the complete machine. If the history contained in the Bible is wrong, how can we be sure the doctrine or moral teaching is correct?

4. Clement of Rome First letter to the Corinthians XLV.
5. Irenaeus, Against Heresies, XVII.2.
6. Kirsopp Lake, *The Religion of Yesterday and Tomorrow* (Boston, MA: Houghton, Mifflin Co., 1926), p. 62.

The heart of the Christian message is history. The Incarnation (God becoming a man) was demonstrated by the Virgin Birth of Christ. Redemption (the price paid for our rebellion) was obtained by the death of Christ on the Cross. Reconciliation (the privilege of the sinner becoming a friend of God) was gained through the Resurrection and Ascension of Christ. If these recorded events are not true, how do we know the theology behind them is true?

Inerrancy Governs Our Faith in the Value of Christ

We cannot have a reliable Savior without a reliable Scripture. If, as many suggest, the stories in the Gospels are not historically true and the recorded words of Christ are only occasionally His, how do we know what we can trust about Christ? Must we rely upon the conflicting interpretations of a host of critical scholars before we know what Christ was like or what He taught? If the Gospel stories are merely the result of the wishful thinking of the Church in the second or third centuries, or even the personal views of the Gospel writers, then our faith no longer rests upon Jesus but upon the opinions of men. Who would trust an unreliable Savior for their eternal salvation?

Inerrancy Governs Our Response to the Conclusions of Science

If we believe the Bible contains errors, then we will be quick to accept scientific theories that appear to prove the Bible wrong. In other words, we will allow the conclusions of science to dictate the accuracy of the Word of God. When we doubt the Bible's inerrancy, we have to invent new principles for interpreting Scripture that for convenience turn history into poetry and facts into myths. This means people must ask how reliable a given passage is when they turn to it. Only then will they be able to decide what to make of it. On the other hand, if we believe in inerrancy, we will test by Scripture the hasty theories that often come to us in the name of science.

Inerrancy Governs Our Attitude to the Preaching of Scripture

A denial of biblical inerrancy always leads to a loss of confidence in Scripture both in the pulpit and in the pew. It was not the growth of education and science that emptied churches, nor was it the result of two world wars. Instead, it was the cold deadness of theological liberalism. If the Bible's history is doubtful and its words are open to dispute, then people understandably lose confidence in it. People want authority. They want to know what God has said.

Inerrancy Governs Our Belief in the Trustworthy Character of God

Almost all theologians agree Scripture is in some measure God's revelation to the human race. But to allow that it contains error implies God has mishandled inspiration and has allowed His people to be deceived for centuries until modern scholars disentangled the confusion. In short, the Maker muddled the instructions.

Conclusion

A church without the authority of Scripture is like a crocodile without teeth; it can open its mouth as wide and as often as it likes — but who cares? Thankfully, God has given us His inspired, inerrant, and infallible Word. His people can speak with authority and boldness, and we can be confident we have His instructions for our lives.

Chapter 22

Are There Contradictions in the Bible?

Jason Lisle

❧❧❧❧❧❧❧❧❧❧❧❧❧❧❧❧❧❧

Y ou can't trust the Bible! It's full of contradictions!" It is a popular view
these days. Many people have the impression that the Bible is simply
an outdated book of fairy tales and contradictions. We are told that biblical stories are fine for children, and perhaps they even contain some
moral value. "But, surely" says the critic, "such stories cannot be taken
seriously in our modern age of science and technology."

After all, the Bible speaks of floating ax-heads, the sun apparently
going backward, a universe created in six days, an earth that has pillars
and corners, people walking on water, light before the sun, a talking
snake, a talking donkey, dragons, and a senior citizen taking two of every
animal on a big boat! On the surface, these things may seem absurd, particularly to those unfamiliar with the Christian worldview. But to make
matters even worse, it is alleged that the Bible contains *contradictions*.
That is, the Bible seems to say one thing in one place, and then the opposite in another. Which are we to believe? Obviously, two contradictory
statements cannot both be true.

While we might come to accept many of the peculiar claims of
Scripture, a genuine contradiction cannot be true *even in principle*. It is
not possible to have a sunny night, a married bachelor, dry water, a true

238 • How Do We Know the Bible Is True?

falsehood, and so on. Thus, the claim that the Bible contains contradictions is a serious challenge indeed. For if the Bible has even one real contradiction, then it cannot be completely true. Yet the Christian asserts that the Bible is the Word of God and without error. The claim of contradictions is a serious allegation against the Christian worldview, and we must be prepared to defend the Bible against such claims.

Logical vs. Psychological Problems

Aside from the claim of contradictions, most objections to the Bible are not actually problems at all from a logical perspective. For example, suppose that someone claims, "The Bible can't be trusted because it contains accounts of miracles, and miracles are clearly impossible." This argument is not rationally sound because it *begs the question*. Clearly, an all-powerful God as described in the Bible would be capable of doing miracles. Thus, by merely assuming that miracles are impossible, the critic has already dismissed the possibility that the Bible is true. His argument is circular. The critic is essentially arguing that the Bible is false because the Bible is false.

But if the Bible is true, then certainly it is not a problem for an all-powerful God to make the sun go backward, to walk on water, to make a donkey talk, or to raise the dead. These things may seem counter-intuitive, but they are not *illogical*. They are merely a *psychological* problem for some. So someone may subjectively feel that it is impossible for the sun to go backward as suggested in 2 Kings 20:11, but there is nothing illogical about an all-powerful God doing just that. To argue that something is impossible because it "seems" counter-intuitive is not rational. Just imagine a lawyer arguing that his client is innocent by saying, "Your Honor, I just really, really believe in my heart that he is innocent. I just don't feel that he could have done it." This is nothing more than a mere opinion; it is not evidence at all and would be a silly argument.

Yet people apply this same kind of thinking to the Bible. They essentially argue that the Bible cannot be true because it doesn't "feel" right to them. Whenever someone asserts that miracles are impossible or that some biblical claim doesn't "seem" plausible to him, he is essentially just assuming that the Bible is false. These kinds of assertions need no refutation because they are not *logical* objections, merely psychological opinions. They simply tell us about the emotional state of the critic rather than presenting a genuine challenge to the Christian worldview.

The Challenge of Contradictions

But contradictions are different. If the Bible asserts a particular claim and also asserts a contrary claim, clearly they cannot both be true at the same time. If the Bible contains genuinely contradictory information, then it cannot really be completely true, since one of the two claims would have to be false. Thus, unlike mere subjective opinions about what is plausible, the claim that the Bible contains contradictions is a real challenge — one that Christians should take seriously.

But what constitutes a contradiction? Most alleged biblical contradictions are not even "apparent" contradictions because there is no necessary conflict between the two propositions. For example, the statements, "Jesus is descended from Adam" and "Jesus is descended from Noah" are not contradictory since both are true. A contradiction is a proposition and its negation (symbolically written, "**A** and not **A**") at the same time and in the same relationship. The law of non-contradiction states that a contradiction cannot be true: "It is impossible to have **A** and not **A** at the same time and in the same relationship." The last part of this definition is crucially important. Obviously, **A** and not **A** could each be true at *different* times. And this resolves a number of alleged biblical contradictions. They could even be true at the same time if the relationship is different.

Difference of Sense or Relationship

Since words can be used in different senses, it is possible to have **A** and not **A** at the same time as long as the relationship or sense of the word is different. A man can be a bachelor and also married, in the sense that he is "married to his job." This does not conflict with the fact that the bachelor is unmarried in the sense of not having a wife. There is no contradiction if the sense of the word differs. Some of the alleged Bible contradictions fall under this category. For example, it is claimed that James contradicts Romans on the topic of justification:

Romans 4:2–3 teaches that Abraham was justified by faith alone, not by works. However, James 2:21, 24 teaches that Abraham was justified by works and not by faith alone. Do we have a contradiction here? We do have A and not A at the same time, but the relationship differs. Romans 4 is teaching about justification before God; by faith alone Abraham was considered righteous *before God*. But James 2 is teaching about justification *before men* (James 2:18); by works (as a result of faith) Abraham was considered righteous before men. There is no contradiction here.

Along the same lines, the Trinity is sometimes alleged to be a contradictory concept: "How can God be both one and three?" But upon inspection we can see that there is no contradiction because the relationship differs. The Bible teaches that God is one in one sense, and three in a *different* sense. Specifically, there is one God (Isaiah 45:5–6, 18, 22), and yet there are three persons who are God: the Father (Galatians 1:1), the Son (John 20:31), and the Holy Spirit (Acts 5:3–4). It may seem counterintuitive that God is one in nature and three in persons, but there is no *contradiction* here. The Trinity may be a psychological problem for some people, but it is not a logical problem.

False Dilemma

Some alleged contradictions of the Bible are presented as a dilemma: "Was the Bible given by inspiration of God as indicated in 2 Timothy 3:16 or was it written by men as indicated in other passages (Luke 1:3; John 21:24)?" The implication is that only one of these can be true, and so, the Bible must contain errors. But this is the *fallacy of the false dilemma* because there is no reason why the Bible cannot be both inspired by God and also written by men. God used men to write His Word (2 Peter 1:21). Another example of a false dilemma is when two words or names are synonymous: Is Reuben the son of Jacob (Genesis 35:22–23) or the son of Israel (Genesis 46:8)? Both are true because Israel is Jacob.

Contextual Considerations

Some examples of alleged contradictions commit the fallacy of *taking the text out of context*. For example, Genesis 1:1 indicates that God exists and has made everything. Suppose someone argued that this contradicts Psalm 14:1 in which we read "there is no God." But to suppose that this is a contradiction would be absurd, since the excerpt from the Psalms is out of context. In context, Psalm 14:1 teaches that "The fool has said in his heart, 'There is no God.'" When the context is considered, there is no contradiction at all. We must remember that the Bible records statements and events that it does not endorse.

Clearly, we must endeavor to honor the author's intentions whenever we study any work of literature. The Bible is no exception. Historical narrations should be taken in the normal (literal) way. Poetic passages in the Bible should not be pressed beyond their intention. Prophetic sections that use a lot of verbal imagery should be taken as such. Figures of speech in the Bible should not be taken as anything other than figures of speech. No, the earth does not *literally* have pillars, or corners, but it does *figuratively*. Even today a person may be considered a "pillar of the community," and we still sometimes use the "four corners of the earth" as a reference to the cardinal directions. To suggest that such passages are teaching a flat earth is unwarranted, and commits the fallacy of taking the text out of context.

There are places where the Bible uses language of appearance, where something is described as it appears from a human perspective. Obvious examples are where the Bible mentions sunrise and sunset. When we examine the context of such verses it is clear that the authors are not advancing an astronomical model; they are talking about sunrise and sunset (or the direction thereof: east and west respectively) in the same sense that we do today. It would be fallacious to pull such verses out of context to argue that the Bible is teaching that the sun goes around the earth in a Newtonian physics sense.

Fallacy of Sweeping Generalization

There are a number of places where the Bible speaks in terms of generalizations — things that are usually (but not universally) true. The Book of Proverbs contains many of these. It is not a contradiction to have some instances where the general rule does not apply. Therefore, we must be careful not to commit the fallacy of a *sweeping generalization* — applying a general principle as if it were a universal rule. The Proverbs are not intended to be taken as universal rules, but rather as general principles that work most of the time.

Moreover, the Bible also contains things that are indeed rules, but that have acceptable exemptions. Clearly, the Bible teaches that it is wrong to kill, and yet understandably makes exceptions for self-defense, punishment for certain extreme crimes, and during battle. Exceptions to a general principle or exemptions to a rule are not contradictions and thus pose no challenge to the Christian worldview.

Translational Issues

Another difficulty arises due to the fact that most of us read the Bible in a different language than the original. This allows for the possibility of translational issues. One example of confusion that can arise due to translation is found in John 21:15–17. Here Jesus asks Peter three times, "Do you love me?" Peter replies three times that he does love Jesus. In English translations, one word is used for *love* in all instances, and so, the conversation seems strange. However, in Greek, two words for *love* are used. The first and second times Jesus asked Peter if he loved Him, He used the word *agape* — intending a selfless, godly love. However, when Peter answered he used the word *phileo* — intending brotherly love. Although *love* is a perfectly correct way to translate both of these words, some of the subtlety of the original is lost in English versions.

In some instances the correct English translation of a word is disputed. In such cases, it is often helpful to consult several different versions of the Bible to see the range of possible interpretations, or to consult a Hebrew/Greek lexicon. Recall that we should always attempt to honor the intentions of the author, and in many cases this entails a careful study of the word or phrase in question. It would be disingenuous to accuse the Bible of a contradiction in an English translation when there is no contradiction in the original language.

Additionally, there are very slight variations in ancient manuscripts of the Bible. Although none of the ancient variants differ in any essential way, some do contain differences of numbers, spelling, and an occasional word or phrase. In most cases, it is easy to tell from context which variant is the original. Variations in ancient manuscripts that are clearly copyist errors should not be taken as the intention of the author, since the author is not responsible for transmission errors. The informed Christian does not claim that a miscopying of Scripture contains no errors — only that the original manuscripts contained none, since they were divinely inspired. Therefore, an alleged contradiction can be dismissed if the ancient manuscripts do not contain the error.

Contradictions of Inference

Nor are *contradictions of inference* a genuine problem for the Christian worldview. A contradiction of inference is where we merely *infer* a contradiction that the text does not actually state. As one example, we might ask, "Where did Mary and Joseph take Jesus after Bethlehem?" Matthew 2:13–15 indicates that they went to Egypt to be safe from King Herod. However, Luke 2:22, 39 indicates that they took the child to Jerusalem (only a few miles from Bethlehem) and then to Nazareth after that. There is no mention of Egypt in Luke's account. Is this a contradiction?

Although we might *infer* that both Matthew and Luke are describing the same time period and the same visit to the Bethlehem region, the text does not actually state this. Perhaps Matthew is describing a second journey to Bethlehem (or possibly one of the surrounding regions); in fact the visit of the wise men may have been as much as two years after the birth of Christ according to Matthew 2:16. So, it may be that Joseph and his family went to Nazareth a few months after the birth of Christ in Bethlehem and then to Egypt after their second trip to the Bethlehem region. Although this is only one possibility, the point is that there is no necessary contradiction between Matthew 2 and Luke 2. Any apparent conflict exists only in the mind, not in the text.

Another contradiction of inference is what we might call the *X and only X fallacy*. This occurs when a reader erroneously assumes that a number stated in the Bible (**X**) indicates *only X* and not more. As an example, consider the account of the demon-possessed man recorded in Mark 5:2–16 and Luke 8:26–37. According to Matthew 8:28–34, there were two men who were demon-possessed. Does this conflict with Mark and Luke? We might be inclined to *infer* from Mark and Luke that there was *only* one man, but the text does not actually say this.

So to call this a contradiction is to commit the *X and only X fallacy*. After all, if there were two men, then it must also be true that there was one man (as well as one other man)! The fact that Mark and Luke do not mention the other man is interesting. Perhaps one man was much more violent or otherwise noteworthy than the other; we can only speculate. In any case, Mark and Luke do not say that there was *only* one man; therefore, there is no contradiction here.

Contradictions of inference tell us that we have incorrectly imagined the details that were not provided by the text. They are not problems with the Bible because such contradictions exist only in our speculations, not in the biblical text. We must always be careful about drawing dogmatic conclusions from things the Bible does not actually state.

Factual Contradictions and Begging the Question

Another type of criticism might be called an *apparent factual contradiction*. In this case, rather than claiming that the Bible contradicts itself, the critic alleges that the Bible contradicts a well-established fact. There are two types of alleged factual contradictions, and both turn out to be fallacious. The first type comes from a misreading of the text. This could stem from any of the fallacies already listed. A word could be taken in the wrong sense; a verse could be taken out of context; there could be a translational or manuscript dispute; or something could be assumed to be a teaching of Scripture when in fact it is only an inference by the reader.

An example of this type of alleged factual contradiction is the claim that the Bible teaches that the earth is stationary, which contradicts the fact that the earth moves around the sun. In this case, the biblical passages (such as Psalm 93:1, 96:10) have been taken out of context. These are poetic passages indicating the world has been established by God and will not deviate from His plan. These poems are not attempting to develop an astronomical model, and say nothing about physical motion. In fact, the Psalmist also says, "I shall not be moved" (Psalm 16:8). Clearly the author does not intend that he will be physically stationary — rather he means that he will not deviate from the path God has created for him.

In the second kind of alleged factual contradiction, the critic has understood the biblical text properly, but is confused about what the external facts actually are. In this case, secular beliefs are assumed to be facts that are beyond question. Examples include: the big bang, evolution, a billions-of-years time scale, naturalism, and the secular order of events. The Bible does indeed contradict all of these things, but the critic merely assumes that it is the Bible that is wrong. He then argues that since the Bible contradicts these "facts," it must be wrong. But this is the fallacy of *begging the question*. The critic has simply assumed that the Bible is wrong (by assuming the secular claims are true), and then uses this to argue that the Bible is wrong. This is nothing more than a vicious circular argument.

The Law of Non-contradiction — a Problem for the Non-Christian

The critic asserts that the Bible is false because it contains contradictions. Perhaps the most intriguing aspect of this claim is that it actually backfires on the critic. The reason is this: *only if the Bible is true, would contradictions be unacceptable*! Most people simply assume the law of non-contradiction; they take it for granted that a contradiction cannot be true. But have you ever stopped to think about why a contradiction cannot be true?

According to the Bible, all truth is in God (Colossians 2:3; Proverbs 1:7), and God cannot deny (go against) Himself (2 Timothy 2:13). So, it makes sense that truth cannot go against itself. Since the sovereign, eternal God is constantly upholding the entire universe by His power (Hebrews 1:3), the Christian expects that no contradiction could possibly happen anywhere in the universe at any time. The universal, unchanging law of non-contradiction stems from God's self-consistent nature.

But, apart from the Bible, how could we know that contradictions are *always* false? We could only say that they have been false in our experience. But our experiences are very limited, and no one has experienced the future. So if someone claimed that he or she has finally discovered a true contradiction, the non-Christian has no basis for dismissing such a claim. Only in a biblical worldview can we know that contradictions are always false; only the Christian has a basis for the *law* of non-contradiction.

The Bible tells us that all knowledge comes from God (Colossians 2:3), and when we reject biblical principles, we are reduced to foolishness (Proverbs 1:7). We see this demonstrated in the critic who tries to use God's laws of logic to disprove the Bible. Such an attempt can only fail. The law of non-contradiction is a *biblical principle*. Therefore, whenever anyone uses that law as a basis for what is possible, they are tacitly assuming that the Bible is true. The critic of the Bible must use biblical principles in order to argue against the Bible. In order for his argument to be meaningful, it would have to be wrong.

Conclusion

In this chapter, we've seen that many criticisms of the Bible are not even alleged contradictions, but mere opinions about what is possible.

These are not logical problems for the Bible; they are simply psychological problems for the critic. A contradiction would be "**A** and not **A** at the same time and in the same relationship." Many alleged biblical contradictions have been asserted. But, in most cases, we find that **A** and not **A** are *not* at the same time, or are used in a *different* sense or relationship and are thus not contradictions at all. The critic sometimes presents a pair of biblical principles as if they were two mutually exclusive options, when, in fact, this is not the case — a *false dilemma*.

In other instances, we find that the words or phrases have been taken *out of context*: poetic passages taken hyper-literally, figures of speech not taken as such, or language of appearance taken as Newtonian physics. Sometimes critics commit the fallacy of *sweeping generalization*: taking a general principle as if it were universally true, or taking a rule as if it had no exceptions. Some alleged contradictions are nothing more than a *translational or manuscript issue*; the original text contains no contradiction at all.

Additionally, a number of contradictions are merely erroneous *inferences*: they exist only in the mind of the critic, not in the biblical text. One in particular that occurs frequently is when the critic assumes that a number (**X**) means "only **X**" when the Bible does not state this. Also, the Bible is sometimes alleged to conflict with an external "fact." A number of these claims stem from a misreading of Scripture. In other cases, the critic has simply assumed that the Bible is in error when it contradicts a particular belief. In doing so, the critic has committed the fallacy of *begging the question*.

Perhaps most significantly, we have shown that any claim of alleged contradiction actually *confirms* that the Bible is true. This is because the law of non-contradiction is based on the biblical worldview. When the critic accepts that a contradiction cannot possibly be true, he has implicitly presumed that the Bible must be true.

So when someone alleges that the Bible cannot be trusted because it contains contradictions, we might turn the question around and simply ask him, "If the Bible is not true, then why would contradictions be *wrong*?" If the Bible were not true, there would be no basis for saying that contradictions are always false; thus, the critic could not argue that the Bible must be false for allegedly containing them. But if the Bible is true, then it cannot have contradictions. Thus, alleged contradictions really cannot possibly be a problem for the Bible — even in principle.

Nonetheless, it is appropriate to be aware of some of the most frequently cited claims of contradictions and to understand the details of why such claims fail when we understand the context. This will serve to confirm that the Bible does not contain contradictions; it is true in its entirety. Alleged contradictions turn out to be nothing more than fallacious reasoning of the critic. Essentially, all of the claims addressed here fall under one of the categories listed above; but it is helpful to see each one fleshed-out, lest we be accused of skirting the hard questions.

The Bible tells us "but sanctify Christ as Lord in your hearts, always being ready to make a defense to everyone who asks you to give an account for the hope that is in you, yet with gentleness and reverence" (1 Peter 3:15; NASB). In this spirit, we offer this study. We trust it will affirm the faith of Christians and challenge the beliefs of non-Christians. We pray this series will glorify our Lord Jesus, "in whom are hidden all the treasures of wisdom and knowledge" (Colossians 2:3).

Chapter 23

Is There Purpose and Meaning in Life?

Ken Ham

❀❀❀❀❀❀❀❀❀❀❀❀❀❀❀❀❀❀❀❀

The only compilation of books in the world that gives a detailed history that enables us to fully comprehend the purpose and meaning of life is God's Word, the Bible. Over three thousand times the Bible claims to be the revealed Word of the God who created the universe and all life, and who has made Himself known to man. If this book really is God's Word, then it should explain the meaning of the universe and life — and it does. Not only that, but observational science continues to confirm the Bible's history as true.

Genesis (which basically means "origins"), the first book of the Bible, gives an account of the origin of life and the universe. It tells of the origin of matter, light, earth, sun, moon, stars, plants, animals, humans, marriage, clothing, death, languages, nations, and so on.

In Genesis 1:27 and 2:7, we read of the creation of the first man called "Adam." Interestingly, in 1 Corinthians 15:45, the one born in Bethlehem is called "the last Adam." To understand the reason for the "last Adam," you have to understand what happened to the "first Adam."

The First Adam

The Bible records that on the sixth day of creation, God made the first man and woman:

So God created man in His own image; in the image of God
He created him; male and female He created them (Genesis 1:27).

We read more of the details concerning the creation of the first man
in Genesis 2:7:

And the LORD God formed man [Adam] of the dust of the
ground, and breathed into his nostrils the breath of life; and man
became a living being.

We are later told in Genesis 2:21–23 that God created the first woman
from the first Adam's side. From elsewhere in the Bible, we learn that all
humans who have ever lived descended from these two people (Genesis
3:20; Acts 17:26; etc.). Therefore, all humans today are related because we
have the same first ancestors.

God's Instruction

When God created Adam, He didn't make him to be a puppet; Adam
had the ability to choose and make decisions. God gave Adam an instruction to obey in Genesis 2.

Then the LORD God took the man and put him in the Garden
of Eden to tend and keep it. And the LORD God commanded the
man, saying, "Of every tree of the garden you may freely eat; but of
the tree of the knowledge of good and evil you shall not eat, for in
the day that you eat of it you shall surely die" (Genesis 2:15–17).

Adam's Fall

Adam, however, chose to disobey God by eating the fruit of the one
tree God had told him not to eat from (Genesis 3:6). Because Adam was
the first or "head" of the human race and all humans ultimately have
come from this first man, what Adam did affected all of humanity. When
Adam disobeyed his Creator's instruction (resulting in his "fall" from his
state of perfection), that was the first sin. And just as God had warned, the
punishment for Adam's sin was death — not only for Adam, but for all his
descendants (including you and me) as well:

Therefore, just as through one man sin entered the world, and
death through sin, and thus death spread to all men, because all
sinned (Romans 5:12).

Why are we punished for what Adam did? As the head of the human race, Adam represented each of us and because we all come from Adam, we inherited his nature from him. He sinned (disobeyed God), so we sin (disobey God). If it had been any of us faced with the decision to eat or not eat from the forbidden tree instead of Adam, the result would have been the same.

Oh! The Nakedness

After Adam and Eve sinned, Genesis 3:7 states that "they knew that they were naked; and they sewed fig leaves together and made themselves coverings." In sewing fig coverings, it wasn't just that they recognized that they had no outer clothing — they also saw that they were destitute of righteousness. Their innocence was lost. Adam and Eve were no longer perfect but were now polluted creatures in their hearts and their flesh. They were naked before the justice of God's law, and the fig leaves were attempts to cover what they had done.

However, no man or woman can hide his or her sinfulness from the sight of a holy God by their own doings. God sees us in all our nakedness and knows our impure, sinful, rebellious hearts. The Bible says our attempts at covering ourselves (our "righteousness") are but "filthy rags" to the Creator (Isaiah 64:6). No ceremonies, rites, or attempts at keeping the law can change this. Our works cannot take away our sin because our hearts are impure (Jeremiah 17:9). We cannot make ourselves acceptable before a holy, pure God because of the gross imperfection of our very nature — just as Adam and Eve's fig-leaf coverings could not help them.

How can we ever be reconciled with a holy God? This is an important question since we are made in the image of God (Genesis 1:27), and as such, even though our bodies die because of sin, our soul (the "real us" that inhabits our bodies) lives forever. As sinners, we can't live with a holy and righteous God, nor can we make it to heaven by our own works — we would be separated from God forever and live in our evil, sinful states for eternity. What a horrible existence that would be.

As the Apostle Paul says in Romans 7:24, "O wretched man that I am! Who will deliver me from this body of death?"

The Promise of the "Last Adam"

In Genesis 3:15, God made a statement that actually sums up the message of the entire Bible and provided hope to Adam and Eve and their descendants (us!) that there was a way to be saved from the effects of sin. This declaration summarizes what Christ's earthly ministry was all about; in fact, it is the whole meaning of why many celebrate "Christmas":

> And I will put enmity between you and the woman, and between your seed and her Seed; He shall bruise your head, and you shall bruise His heel (Genesis 3:15).

What does this mean? Genesis 22:18 gives us further clues about the identity of the promised "Seed" of the woman who will bruise the head of the serpent:

> In your *seed* all the nations of the earth shall be blessed; because you have obeyed My voice (Genesis 22:18, emphasis added).

And Paul clarifies things in Galatians 3:16:

> Now to Abraham and his *Seed* were the promises made. He does not say, "And to seeds," as of many, but as of one, "And to your Seed," who is Christ (emphasis added).

Paul builds upon the use of the singular "seed" in Genesis 22:18. Here we see the extent of the infallibility of Scripture, down to the use of singular and plural words. The words "her seed" are actually a prophecy concerning the One who, conceived by God Himself, would be born of a woman (actually a "virgin"): the baby who was born in Bethlehem over 2,000 years ago — the last Adam.

The "Head" and the "Heel" of Genesis 3:15

It is a great mystery to fallible, created human beings like us that the Creator God (Colossians 1:16) became flesh (John 1:14) so that as a perfect Man, He could become "sin for us" (2 Corinthians 5:21) by dying on a cross to suffer the penalty for sin (the meaning of "bruise his heel"). But because He is the infinite Creator, He has ultimate power, and thus He rose from the dead, overcoming the Curse.

"Bruising the serpent's head" speaks of the mortal wound Satan received through Christ's victory over him at Calvary. He is a defeated foe. His operation now is like the pockets of Japanese soldiers of World War II fighting after the surrender in August 1945 — they could still instill casualties and do much harm, but they could not win the war.

Jesus came to take away sin and conquer the power of the grave — death.

Clothed by God

God illustrated what needed to be done to Adam and Eve by a particular act. In Genesis 3:21 we read:

> Also for Adam and his wife the LORD God made tunics of skin, and clothed them.

God killed at least one animal — the first blood sacrifice — to provide the garments as a covering for their sin. It was a picture of what was to come in Jesus, who is the "Lamb of God who takes away the sin of the world!" (John 1:29).

It is only the covering provided by God that can cover man's "filthy rags." The righteousness that enables a sinner to stand "just" in the sight of God is from God. No human being can put on the righteousness of Christ, for this can only be done by God (1 Corinthians 1:30). We can't rely on our good works (our "aprons of fig leaves") or on sacraments (e.g., communion, baptism) to stand just before God. It is only what God does for us that enables us to be clean before our Creator.

How Can We Be Clothed?

Now, if it is only God who is able to clothe us in righteousness, how can we obtain that clothing?

The Bible makes it very clear in Romans 10:9:

> . . . that if you confess with your mouth the Lord Jesus and believe in your heart that God has raised Him from the dead, you will be saved.

When we acknowledge that we are sinners before God, repent of our sin and confess the Lord Jesus, acknowledging that He died and rose from the dead, we receive the free gift of salvation from our Creator and will spend eternity with Him.

The Two Adams

The first Adam gave life to all his descendants. The last Adam, Jesus Christ, communicates "life" and "light" to all men, and gives eternal life to those who receive Him and believe on His name — giving them "the right to become children of God" (see John 1:1–14).

The first Adam experienced the judgment of God. He eventually died and his body turned to dust. Because of his sin, death came upon all men, "for all have sinned and fall short of the glory of God" (Romans 3:23).

The last Adam, Jesus Christ, also experienced the judgment of God — not for His own sins (He lived a perfect life), but for the sins of mankind. He died on the Cross to atone for sin (Isaiah 53:5; 1 Peter 3:18; Hebrews 2:9). But He did not stay dead, nor did His body "see corruption" (Acts 2:27, 13:35–37). On the third day, He rose again, thereby overcoming the devil and the power of death for all people who believe in Him (Hebrews 2:14), and bringing resurrection from the dead (1 Corinthians 15:22–23).

This is the message of the Babe born in Bethlehem. It starts with the creation of a perfect world, and then, because of our sin in Adam, leads to our need of a Savior — which is why Jesus stepped into history to become flesh 2,000 years ago.

What Is Happening to Today's Culture?

Throughout the world, generations of young people are being educated in schools, colleges, and by the media with evolutionary ideas about our origins. Sadly, they are being brainwashed into believing that the history in Genesis concerning the first Adam and the entrance of sin is not true. Logically then, they begin rejecting the truth of the last Adam, Jesus Christ.

If the history in Genesis concerning our origins is not true, and if there really is no absolute authority, then there is no ultimate purpose and meaning in life. The erosion of Christianity in society is directly linked to the attack on the history of Genesis and the increasing indoctrination in a false history that has permeated the culture: that man is a result of millions of years of evolutionary processes.

The message of the two Adams is what life is all about. But if we want people to understand this message, we need to ensure that we show them clearly that the history in Genesis is true, for otherwise, they will not fully understand or listen to the Christian message.

Chapter 24

Evolution — the Anti-Science?

Jason Lisle

⟨❄❄❄❄❄❄❄❄❄❄❄❄❄❄❄❄❄❄❄❄❄⟩

Some evolutionists have argued that science isn't possible without evolution. They teach that science and technology actually require the
principles of molecules-to-man evolution in order to work. They claim
that those who hold to a biblical creation worldview are in danger of not
being able to understand science![1]

Critical thinkers will realize that these kinds of arguments are quite
ironic because evolution is actually *contrary* to the principles of science.
That is, if evolution were true, the concept of science would not make
sense. Science actually requires a biblical creation framework in order to
be possible. Here's why.

---

1. Theodosius Dobzhansky wrote, "Nothing in biology makes sense except in the light of
   evolution." This was also the title of his 1973 essay first published in the *American Biology
   Teacher*, Vol. 35, p. 125–129. The National Academy of Sciences issued a book called
   Science, Evolution, and Creationism which stated that evolution is a "critical foundation
   of the biomedical and life sciences. . . ." and that evolutionary concepts "are fundamental
   to a high-quality science education." The National Academy of Sciences also published
   a document called "Teaching About Evolution and the Nature of Science" (1998) with
   a similar theme. In the preface (p. viii) the authors indicate that biological evolution is
   "the most important concept in modern biology, a concept essential to understanding
   key aspects of living things." They chose to publish the document in part "because of the
   importance of evolution as a central concept in understanding our planet."

The Preconditions of Science

Science presupposes that the universe is logical and orderly and that it obeys mathematical laws that are consistent over time and space. Even though conditions in different regions of space and eras of time are quite diverse, there is nonetheless an underlying uniformity.[2]

Because there is such regularity in the universe, there are many instances where scientists are able to make successful predictions about the future. For example, astronomers can successfully compute the positions of the planets, moons, and asteroids far into the future. Without uniformity in nature, such predictions would be impossible, and science could not exist. The problem for evolutionism is that such regularity only makes sense in a biblical creation worldview.

Science Requires a Biblical Worldview

The biblical creationist expects there to be order in the universe because God made all things, "All things were made through Him, and without Him nothing was made that was made" (*John 1:3*), and has imposed order on the universe. Since the Bible teaches that God upholds all things by His power (*Hebrews 1:3*), the creationist expects that the universe would function in a logical, orderly, law-like fashion (e.g., "ordinances of heaven and earth" in Jeremiah 33:25). Furthermore, God is consistent (1 Samuel 15:29, Numbers 23:19) and omnipresent (Psalm 139:7-8). Thus, the creationist expects that all regions of the universe will obey the same laws, even in regions where the physical conditions are quite different. The entire field of astronomy requires this important biblical principle.

Moreover, God is beyond time (*2 Peter 3:8*) and has chosen to uphold the universe in a consistent fashion throughout time for our benefit. So even though conditions in the past may be quite different than those in the present and future, the way God upholds the universe (what we would call the "laws of nature") will not arbitrarily change.[3] God has told us that

---

2. Uniformity should not be confused with "uniformitarianism." Uniformity simply insists that the laws of nature are consistent and do not arbitrarily change with time or space, though specific conditions and processes may change. Uniformitarianism is the (unbiblical) belief that present processes are the same as past processes; it asserts a consistency of conditions and rates over time and is summed up in the phrase, "The present is the key to the past."

3. Granted, God can use unusual and extraordinary means on occasion to accomplish an

there are certain things we can count on to be true in the future — the seasons, the diurnal cycle, and so on (*Genesis 8:22*). Therefore, under a given set of conditions, the consistent Christian has the right to expect a given outcome because he or she relies upon the Lord to uphold the universe in a consistent way.

These Christian principles are absolutely essential to science. When we perform a controlled experiment using the same preset starting conditions, we expect to get the same result every time. The "future reflects the past" in this sense. Scientists are able to make predictions only because there is uniformity as a result of God's sovereign and consistent power. Scientific experimentation would be pointless without uniformity; we would get a different result every time we performed an identical experiment, destroying the very possibility of scientific knowledge.

Can an Evolutionist Do Science?

Since science requires the biblical principle of uniformity (as well as a number of other biblical creation principles), it is rather amazing that one could be a scientist and also an evolutionist. And yet there are scientists who profess to believe in evolution. How is this possible?

The answer is that evolutionists are able to do science only because they are inconsistent. They accept biblical principles such as uniformity, while simultaneously denying the Bible from which those principles are derived. Such inconsistency is common in secular thinking; secular scientists claim that the universe is not designed, but they do science as if the universe *is* designed and upheld by God in a uniform way. Evolutionists can do science only if they rely on biblical creation assumptions (such as uniformity) that are contrary to their professed belief in evolution.[4]

How Would an Evolutionist Respond?

The consistent Christian can use past experience as a guide for what is likely to happen in the future because God has promised us that (in

---

extraordinary purpose — what we might call a "miracle." But these are (by definition) exceptional; natural law could be defined as the ordinary way that God upholds the universe and accomplishes His will.

4. Why would someone who professes to believe in evolution also accept creation-based concepts? Although they may deny it, evolutionists are also made in the image of God (Genesis 1:26–27). In their heart-of-hearts, they know the biblical God (Romans 1:19–20), but they have deceived themselves (James 1:22–24). They have forgotten that the principles of science come from the Christian worldview.

certain ways) the future will reflect the past (Genesis 8:22). But how can those who reject Genesis explain why there should be uniformity of nature? How might an evolutionist respond if asked, "Why will the future reflect the past?"

One of the most common responses is: "Well, it always has. So I expect it always will." But this is circular reasoning. I'll grant that in the past there has been uniformity.[5] But how do I know that in the future there will be uniformity — unless I already assumed that the future reflects the past (i.e., uniformity)? Whenever we use past experience as a basis for what is likely to happen in the future, we are assuming uniformity. So when an evolutionist says that he believes there will be uniformity in the future since there has been uniformity in the past, he's trying to justify uniformity by simply assuming uniformity — a circular argument.

An evolutionist might argue that the nature of matter is such that it behaves in a regular fashion;[6] in other words, uniformity is just a property of the universe. This answer also fails. First, it doesn't really answer the question. Perhaps uniformity is one aspect of the universe, but the question is why? What would be the basis for such a property in an evolutionary worldview? Second, we might ask how an evolutionist could possibly know that uniformity is a property of the universe. At best, he or she can only say that the universe — in the past — seems to have had some uniformity.[7] But how do we know that will continue into the future unless we already knew about uniformity some other way? Many things in this universe change; how do we know that the laws of nature will not?

Some evolutionists might try a more pragmatic response: "Well, I can't really explain why. But uniformity seems to work, so we use it." This answer also fails for two reasons. First, we can only argue that uniformity

---

5. In granting this assumption, I'm actually being very generous to the evolutionist. I could have been very thorough and asked, "How do we really know that even in the past nature has been uniform?" One might argue that we remember that the past was uniform. But since the memory portions of our brain require that the laws of chemistry and physics are constant over time, you would have to assume that the past is uniform in order to argue that we correctly remember that the past is uniform! Any non-Christian response would be necessarily circular.

6. The atheist Dr. Gordon Stein used essentially this response in the famous 1985 debate with Christian philosopher Dr. Greg Bahnsen on the existence of God.

7. Again, I'm being generous here. Even this response is begging the question, since the evolutionist would have to assume uniformity in the past in order to argue that his memories of the past are accurate.

seems to have worked in the *past*; there's no guarantee it will continue to work in the future unless you already have a reason to assume uniformity (which only the Christian does). Yet, evolutionists do assume that uniformity will be true in the future. Second, the answer admits that uniformity is without justification in the evolutionary worldview — which is exactly the point. No one is denying that there is uniformity in nature; the point is that only a biblical creation worldview can make sense of it. Evolutionists can only do science if they are inconsistent: that is, if they assume biblical creationist concepts while denying biblical creation.

Objection: "I cannot reconcile this article with the rigor required in academia, and wonder how you do? The logical leap required between 'science requires uniformity' to 'science requires a biblical worldview' is enormous. Where might I find information on the missing line of argument here?"

Response: The deduction is actually formally very simple; let me fill in the missing line:

1. Science requires uniformity.
2. Uniformity requires a biblical worldview
3. Therefore, science requires a biblical worldview.

The bulk of the article was in defense of the second premise. Uniformity really cannot be justified apart from the biblical worldview; thus, science requires the biblical worldview since it requires uniformity.

This is not to say that a scientist necessarily must have a fully biblical worldview, but rather, the biblical worldview must be true in order for science to be possible. (Obviously, scientists can be inconsistent: relying on the biblical worldview while simultaneously professing a secular worldview.)

In particular, the notion that the future will (under certain conditions) reflect the past is discussed at length; this is a crucial aspect of uniformity and is essential to science. The Christian worldview gives us a reason to expect uniformity: a God who is beyond time, who upholds the universe in a consistent fashion, and who has told us so. But without the biblical worldview, there would be no basis for such uniformity.

If you would like a more detailed treatment of this topic, a number of technical articles are available. Christian Philosophers Dr. Cornelius Van

Til and Dr. Greg Bahnsen wrote on the topic. David Hume wrote on the problem (from his secular point of view) of uniformity (or "induction").

Theistic Evolution Won't Save the Day

Some evolutionists might argue that they can account for uniformity just as the Christian does — by appealing to a god who upholds the universe in a law-like fashion.[8] But rather than believing in Genesis creation, they believe that this god created over millions of years of evolution. However, theistic evolution will not resolve the problem. A theistic evolutionist does not believe that Genesis is literally true. But if Genesis is not literally true, then there is no reason to believe that *Genesis 8:22* is literally true. This verse is where God promises that we can count on a certain degree of uniformity in the future. Without biblical creation, the rational basis for uniformity is lost.

> While the earth remains, seedtime and harvest, cold and heat, winter and summer, and day and night shall not cease (Genesis 8:22).

It's not just any god that is required in order to make sense of uniformity; it is the Christian God as revealed in the Bible. Only a God who is beyond time, consistent, faithful, all powerful, omnipresent, and who has revealed Himself to mankind can guarantee that there will be uniformity throughout space and time. Therefore, only biblical creationists can account for the uniformity in nature.

Evolution Is Irrational

In fact, if evolution were true, there wouldn't be any rational reason to believe it! If life is the result of evolution, then it means that an evolutionist's brain is simply the outworking of millions of years of random-chance processes. The brain would simply be a collection of chemical reactions that have been preserved because they had some sort of survival value in the past. If evolution were true, then all the evolutionist's thoughts are

---

8. A "day-age" creationist might also try to use this argument. But it also fails for the same reason. Day-age creationists do not believe that Genesis really means what it says (that God literally created in six ordinary days). So, how could we trust that Genesis 8:22 really means what it says? And if Genesis 8:22 does not mean what it says, then there is no reason to believe in uniformity. Therefore, the day-age creationist has the same problem as the evolutionist. Neither can account for science and technology within his own worldview.

merely the necessary result of chemistry acting over time. Therefore, an evolutionist must think and say that "evolution is true" not for rational reasons, but as a necessary consequence of blind chemistry.

Scholarly analysis presupposes that the human mind is *not just chemistry*. Rationality presupposes that we have the freedom to consciously consider the various options and choose the best. Evolutionism undermines the preconditions necessary for rational thought, thereby destroying the very possibility of knowledge and science.

Conclusions

Evolution is anti-science and anti-knowledge. If evolution were true, science would not be possible because there would be no reason to accept the uniformity of nature upon which all science and technology depend. Nor would there be any reason to think that rational analysis would be possible since the thoughts of our mind would be nothing more than the inevitable result of mindless chemical reactions. Evolutionists are able to do science and gain knowledge only because they are inconsistent; professing to believe in evolution while accepting the principles of biblical creation.

Chapter 25

What Is Wrong with Atheism?

Jason Lisle

❧❧❧❧❧❧❧❧❧❧❧❧❧❧❧❧❧❧❧❧❧

A theists are "coming out of the closet" and becoming more vocal about their message that "there is no God." Professor Richard Dawkins (Britain's leading atheist) is encouraging those who share his views to express their opinion. Author of *The God Delusion*, Dawkins says he wants to "free children from being indoctrinated with the religion of their parents or their community."[1] Will Christians be prepared to "give an answer" to the atheists' claims?[2]

Materialistic atheism is one of the easiest worldviews to refute. A materialistic atheist believes that nature is all that there is. He believes that there is no transcendent God who oversees and maintains creation. Many atheists believe that their worldview is rational — and scientific. However, by embracing materialism, the atheist has destroyed the possibility of knowledge, as well as science and technology. In other words, if atheism were true, it would be impossible to prove anything!

1. "Atheists Arise: Dawkins Spreads the A-word among America's Unbelievers" *The Guardian*, October 1st, 2007, http://www.guardian.co.uk/usa/story/0,,2180901,00.html.
2. Christian philosopher Dr. Greg Bahnsen often used this analogy. Dr. Bahnsen was known as the "man atheists most feared."

Here's Why

Reasoning involves using the laws of logic. These include the law of non-contradiction, which says that you can't have **A** and **not-A** at the same time and in the same relationship. For example, the statement "My car is in the parking lot, and it is not the case that my car is in the parking lot" is necessarily false by the law of non-contradiction. Any rational person would accept this law. But why is this law true? Why should there be a law of non-contradiction, or for that matter, any laws of reasoning? The Christian can answer this question. For the Christian there is an absolute standard for reasoning; we are to pattern our thoughts after God's. The laws of logic are a reflection of the way God thinks. The law of non-contradiction is not simply one person's opinion of how we ought to think, rather it stems from God's self-consistent nature. God cannot deny Himself (2 Timothy 2:13), and so the way God upholds the universe will necessarily be non-contradictory.

Laws of logic are God's standard for thinking. Since God is an unchanging, sovereign, immaterial Being, the laws of logic are abstract, universal, invariant entities. In other words, they are not made of matter — they apply everywhere and at all times. Laws of logic are contingent upon God's unchanging nature. And they are necessary for logical reasoning. Thus, rational reasoning would be impossible without the biblical God.

The materialistic atheist can't have laws of logic. He believes that everything that exists is material — part of the physical world. But laws of logic are not physical. You can't stub your toe on a law of logic. Laws of logic cannot exist in the atheist's world, yet he uses them to try to reason. This is inconsistent. He is borrowing from the Christian worldview to argue against the Christian worldview. The atheist's view cannot be rational because he uses things (laws of logic) that cannot exist according to his profession.

The debate over the existence of God is a bit like a debate over the existence of air.[3] Can you imagine someone arguing that air doesn't actually exist? He would offer seemingly excellent "proofs" against the existence of air, while simultaneously breathing air and expecting that we can hear his words as the sound is transmitted through the air. In order for us to hear and understand his claim, it would have to be wrong.

Likewise, the atheist, in arguing that God does not exist, must use laws of logic that only make sense if God does exist. In order for his argument to make sense, it would have to be wrong.

How Can the Atheist Respond?

The atheist might say, "Well, I can reason just fine, and I don't believe in God." But this is no different than the critic of air saying, "Well, I can breathe just fine, and I don't believe in air." This isn't a rational response. Breathing requires air, not a profession of belief in air. Likewise, logical reasoning requires God, not a profession of belief in Him. Of course the atheist can reason; it's because God has made his mind and given him access to the laws of logic — and that's the point. It's because God exists that reasoning is possible. The atheist can reason, but within his own worldview he cannot account for his ability to reason.

The atheist might respond, "Laws of logic are conventions made up by man." But conventions are (by definition) conventional. That is, we all agree to them and so they work — like driving on the right side of the road. But if laws of logic were conventional, then different cultures could adopt different laws of logic (like driving on the left side of the road). So in some cultures it might be perfectly fine to contradict yourself. In some societies truth could be self-contradictory. Clearly, that wouldn't do. If laws of logic are just conventions, then they are not universal laws. Rational debate would be impossible if laws of logic were conventional, because the two opponents could simply pick different standards for reasoning. Each would be right according to his own arbitrary standard.

The atheist might respond, "Laws of logic are material — they are made of electro-chemical connections in the brain." But then the laws of logic are not universal; they would not extend beyond the brain. In other words, we couldn't argue that contradictions cannot occur on Mars, since no one's brain is on Mars. In fact, if the laws of logic are just electro-chemical connections in the brain, then they would differ somewhat from person to person because everyone has different connections in their brain.

Sometimes an atheist will attempt to answer with a more pragmatic response: "We use the laws of logic because they work." Unfortunately for him, that isn't the question. We all agree the laws of logic work; they work because they're true. The question is why do they exist in the first place? How can the atheist account for absolute standards of reasoning like the laws of logic? How can non-material things like laws exist if the universe is material only?

As a last resort, the atheist may give up a strictly materialistic view and agree that there are immaterial, universal laws. This is a huge concession; after all, if a person is willing to concede that immaterial, universal, unchanging entities can exist, then he must consider the possibility that God exists. But this concession does not save the atheist's position. He must still justify the laws of logic. Why do they exist? And what is the point of contact between the material physical world and the immaterial world of logic? In other words, why does the material universe feel compelled to obey immaterial laws? The atheist cannot answer these questions. His worldview cannot be justified; it is arbitrary and thus irrational.

Objection: "The laws of logic (and causality, mathematics, etc.) are a necessary extension of the (macroscopic) laws of nature in this universe, and humankind has evolved enough to recognize and utilize these laws of logic."

Response: The argument is that laws of logic are a reflection of the thinking of the biblical God as revealed in the Scriptures, and that any alternative view really doesn't make sense. The hypothetical response that you have posed is essentially the conjecture that laws of logic are a reflection of the way the universe works. This position is also very easy to refute for a number of reasons.

First, it would be hard to support the notion that laws of logic are a reflection or extension of the physical universe because they do not describe the physical universe (as laws of nature do). Rather, laws of logic pertain more to the reasoning process; they describe the correct "chain of reasoning" from premises to conclusions. For example, the law of non-contradiction (**A** and **not-A** cannot both be true at the same time and in the same relationship) deals with concepts — not with nature, per se. Laws of logic connect conceptual relationships rather than describing specific conditions or processes in the physical universe.

More importantly, if laws of logic were a reflection of the universe (rather than of God's thoughts), then they would be contingent upon the universe. And that leads to some rather absurd consequences. If laws of logic were contingent on the universe, then we would expect that different parts of the universe would have different laws of logic. After all, the conditions in the core of the sun are quite different than conditions on the surface of earth. If laws of logic describe the universe, then they would be different from place to place, since different parts of the universe are described differently.

Moreover, if laws of logic were contingent upon the universe, then we would expect them to change with time, since the universe changes with time. Yet we all presume that laws of logic are invariant — the same yesterday, today, and tomorrow. This, of course, makes sense in the Christian worldview, since God is beyond time, and, thus, His thoughts are as well. If laws of logic were merely an extension of the physical universe, then we would have no basis for arguing that they must apply in unknown regions of the universe or in the future, since no one has experienced these things. It does no good to counter that laws of logic do work in known regions and have always worked in the past. This is irrelevant to unknown regions and the future unless we already presupposed an underlying uniformity, which only the consistent Christian has a right to expect.

Mathematics is similar, reflecting the thinking of an infinite God. Mathematics is not an extension of the physical universe, even though natural laws can often be expressed in terms of mathematical principles. Mathematicians frequently entertain concepts that have no corresponding physical reality whatsoever. We could consider a 38-dimensional space and compute the hyper-volumes of hyper-spheres and other shapes in such mathematical realms. Such concepts would be perfectly meaningful, even though such things do not and cannot exist physically in our three-dimensional space.

By the way, laws of logic (and mathematics) are not violated even at the quantum scale or at relativistic velocities. Energy and mass are not contraries, and so there is no problem with an equivalence relationship. Even wave-particle duality is not truly contradictory; objects behave wavelike in some ways at some times, and particle-like at other times and in other ways. When the time or sense is different, there is no contradiction.

Objection: "One of the arguments went as, 'The uniformity of the universe is a property of the universe.' This is obviously an assumption as you also said. Why do we have to account for this uniformity?"

Response: The answer is this: in order to be rational. The mark of rationality is to have a good reason for what we believe. And remember, it is biblical to have a reason for what we believe (1 Peter 3:15). The two key forms of irrationality are inconsistency and arbitrariness (not having a reason). You can imagine that when an evolutionist asked why I believe in creation if I replied, "Oh, there's no reason — it's just true," then he would rightly point out that this is arbitrary and irrational. And yet evolutionists do not have a good reason (on their own professed worldview) for their belief in uniformity — or for laws of logic. They are, therefore, being irrational. Biblical creation is the only rational position because it alone provides a reason for those things we take for granted — like uniformity and laws of logic.

It is fine to pose a hypothetical universe with stability and laws of logic. But those things would still need to be justified. How could we possibly know that the laws of logic are invariant (do not change with time), and not that they simply have not changed so far? And why does the material universe feel compelled to obey immaterial laws? How would we know that the laws are truly universal (applying everywhere) and invariant? The biblical creationist can answer these questions by pointing to God's special revelation, but these questions are simply not answerable apart from a biblical worldview. So the evolutionist is still left without a good reason for why he believes in laws of logic, why they have the properties they do, and why the physical universe does not violate them. He is indeed "borrowing" from Christianity.

The Christian worldview is not a mere assumption. It is the worldview that makes knowledge possible (Proverbs 1:7; Colossians 2:3). It alone provides the justification for those things we need for reasoning — such as laws of logic and uniformity. And that is a pretty good reason to believe in Christianity. Even presuppositions require a reason; it's just that the reason is provided after the fact in the case of a presupposition. In summary, a good reason to believe in the Christian worldview is that without it we couldn't reason at all.

Conclusions

Clearly, atheism is not a rational worldview. It is self-refuting because the atheist must first assume the opposite of what he is trying to prove in order to be able to prove anything. As Dr. Cornelius Van Til put it, "[A] theism presupposes theism." Laws of logic require the existence of God — and not just any god, but the Christian God. Only the God of the Bible can be the foundation for knowledge (Proverbs 1:7; Colossians 2:3). Since the God of Scripture is immaterial, sovereign, and beyond time, it makes sense to have laws of logic that are immaterial, universal, and unchanging. Since God has revealed Himself to man, we are able to know and use logic. Since God made the universe and since God made our minds, it makes sense that our minds would have an ability to study and understand the universe. But if the brain is simply the result of mindless evolutionary processes that conveyed some sort of survival value in the past, why should we trust its conclusions? If the universe and our minds are simply the results of time and chance, as the atheist contends, why would we expect that the mind could make sense of the universe? How could science and technology be possible?

Rational thinking, science, and technology make sense in a Christian worldview. The Christian has a basis for these things; the atheist does not. This is not to say that atheists cannot be rational about some things. They can because they too are made in God's image and have access to God's laws of logic. But they have no rational basis for rationality within their own worldview. Likewise, atheists can be moral, but they have no basis for that morality according to what they claim to believe. An atheist is a walking bundle of contradictions. He reasons and does science, yet he denies the very God that makes reasoning and science possible. On the other hand, the Christian worldview is consistent and makes sense of human reasoning and experience.

Chapter 26

Other Religious Writings: Can They Be from God, Too?

Bodie Hodge

T he answer seems too simple: other alleged divine writings are not from God because they are not among the 66 books of the Bible and, in fact, they contradict the Bible.

A Presuppositional Approach

This is a "presuppositional" approach, which means to presuppose that God exists and that His Word, the Bible, is the truth. In fact, this is the only starting point that makes knowledge possible. Any alternative would make knowledge impossible. In essence, it is the only book that has the preconditions for knowledge/logic (i.e. intelligibility). All other worldviews must *borrow* from the Bible for the world to make sense. Science, morality, and logic all stem from the Bible being true. So to reiterate, if the Bible were not true, then knowledge would be impossible. In other words, *if the Bible were not true, nothing would make sense — good or bad . . . everything would be meaningless and pointless.*

With this, God never tried to prove His existence or prove that His Word is superior to other writings. God simply opens the Bible with a statement of His existence and says His Word is flawless (Genesis 1:1; Proverbs 30:5). The Bible bluntly claims to be the truth (Psalm 119:160), and Christ repeated this claim (John 17:17).

If God had tried to prove that He existed or that His Word was flawless, then any "evidence" or "proof" would be greater than God and His Word, as God and His Word would be subject to those things. But God is indeed greater and there is no greater authority than God (Hebrews 6:13). But God knows that nothing is greater than His Word, and therefore He doesn't stoop to our carnal desires for such proofs. One must appeal to God and His Word to even make a case for (or against), which shows that God does exist (it is like pulling the rug out from underneath those arguing against God and His Word).

The Bible also teaches us to have faith that God exists and that having faith pleases Him (Hebrews 11:6). Accordingly, we are on the right track if we start with God's Word. So how do we know that other religious writings are not from God?

God Will Not Contradict Himself

In the Bible, we read that God cannot lie (Titus 1:2; Hebrews 6:18). This is significant because it means that God's Word will never have contradictions. Though skeptics have alleged that there are contradictions in the Bible, every such claim has been refuted (usually rather easily).[1] This is what we would expect if God's Word were perfect.

Yet the world is filled with other "religious writings" that claim divine origin or that have been treated as equal to or higher than the Bible on matters of truth or guidelines for living. In other words, these writings are treated as a final authority *over* the Bible.

Any religious writing that claims divine inspiration or authority equal to the Bible can't be from God if it is not part of the Bible and can be tested by contradictions: contradictions with the Bible, contradictions within itself, or contradictions with reality.

Examples of Contradictions in Religious Writings

A religious writing can be tested by comparing what it says to the Bible (1 Thessalonians 5:21). God will never disagree with Himself

---

1. To get started in this debate, see Ken Ham, editor, *Demolishing Supposed Bible Contradictions*, Volume 1 (Green Forest, AR: Master Books, 2010).

because God cannot lie (2 Timothy 2:13). When the Bible was being written and Paul was preaching to the Bereans (Acts 17:11), he commended them for checking his words against the Scriptures that were already written. If someone claims that a book is of divine origin, then we need to be like the Bereans and test it to confirm whether it disagrees with the 66 books of the Bible. Paul's writings, of course, were Scripture (2 Peter 3:16).

Religious books, such as Islam's Koran, Mormonism's Book of Mormon, and Hinduism's Vedas, Jehovah's Witnesses' Watchtower publications, and so on contradict the Bible; and so they cannot be Scripture. For example, the Koran in two chapters (Sura 4:171 and 23:91) says God had no son, but the Bible is clear that Jesus is the only begotten Son of God (Matthew 26:63–64).

The Book of Mormon says in Moroni 8:8 that children are not sinners, but the Bible teaches that children are sinful, even from birth (Psalm 51:5). Few would dispute that the Vedas and other writings in Hinduism are starkly different from the Bible. Jehovah's Witness literature has Jesus created, whereas Jesus is the creator according to John 1, Colossians 1, and Hebrews 1.

Also, such religious writings contain contradictions within themselves that are unanswerable without gymnastics of logic. In the Koran, one passage says Jesus will be with God in paradise (Sura 3:45) and another inadvertently states that He will be in hell for being worshiped by Christians (Sura 21:98).

The Book of Mormon, prior to the 1981 change, says that American Indians will turn white when they convert to Mormonism (2 Nephi 30:6). If such writings were truly from God, such discrepancies couldn't exist (Mormons have made numerous changes to the Book of Mormon over the years to correct errors, but the best option would be to discard it entirely in favor of the Bible).

Since such alleged holy books are not from the perfect God, who are they from? They are from deceived, imperfect mankind. Mankind's fallible reason is not the absolute authority. God and His Word are. Other books may have tremendous value, such as historical insight, but they are not the infallible Word of God.

Quick Comparison of the Bible with Islam and Mormonism

	Bible	Islamic Scriptures	Mormon Scriptures
View of Origins	God created all things in six, 24-hour days, about 6,000 years ago. All creatures, including man, were created after their own kinds. Sin, disease, sickness, and death were not part of this creation. They came as a result of the Fall.	The Koran teaches that Allah created all things, but it contradicts itself of the number of days. It also teaches that the first man and woman were created in Paradise but were later banished to earth after the fall into sin.	God created man physically after He created the earth. However, we had a pre-earth life, in which we existed as God's "spirit children." God did not create the universe ex- nihilo (from nothing) but merely used or manipulated some matter that already existed in the universe.
View of Christ	Jesus is the only begotten Son of God, who became man to live a perfect life, to be mankind's substitute on the Cross, and to rise from the dead, defeating death.	Allah (God) created Jesus and appointed him to be a messenger to the Jewish people. The Koran does teach that Jesus was sinless but He was not God.	Jesus is the spirit-brother to every man, and even Satan. Jesus is one of an endless number of gods and is a being separate from the Heavenly Father
Sin and Salvation	Every person has sinned and fallen short of the glory of God. Salvation is by grace through faith in Christ and His redeeming work on the Cross.	Salvation is possible after adherence to the Koran, as well as performing the five pillars of the Islamic faith. But even then, salvation is not guaranteed.	Sin was part of God's plan because without it mankind could not progress to become like God, know joy, or have children. Salvation is a combination of faith and works.

| Life After Death | Mankind will live forever, either in heaven or in hell. The only way for us to get to heaven is through faith in Christ as Christ endured the infinite punishment from an infinite God that we deserve, being the infinite Son of God. | Allah sends both righteous and unrighteous to hell unless they die in a holy war. But if their good works outweigh their bad, they should be admitted into Paradise. Paradise is only guaranteed to those who die in jihad (holy war). | Even after death, everyone has an opportunity to respond to the gospel. Heaven has three levels, and those who attain the highest level become gods, ruling and populating their own universe. |

Conclusion

The Bible warns that false philosophies will be used to turn people from the Bible (Colossians 2:8). So people need to stand firm on the Bible and not be swayed (1 Corinthians 15:58; 2 Thessalonians 2:15).

So there are two options: place our faith in the perfect, all-knowing God who has always been there, or trust in imperfect, fallible mankind and his philosophies. The Bible, God's Holy Word, is superior to all other alleged holy books. God will never be wrong or contradict Himself. So start with the Bible and build your faith on its teachings so that you please Him.

Chapter 27

How to Properly View Evidence

Ken Ham

❧❧❧❧❧❧❧❧❧❧❧❧❧❧❧❧❧❧❧❧

In 1986 a number of leading creationist researchers decided that the evidence of supposedly human and dinosaur footprints, found together at the Paluxy River in Texas, had serious problems.[1] They decided that, pending further research to establish the correct interpretation of the prints, they could no longer be safely used as evidence supporting the fact (based on the biblical account of creation) that man and dinosaur lived at the same time.

Regardless of what the correct interpretation really is, I want to discuss a related phenomenon that is rife throughout the church. I believe it is one of the reasons so many Christians believe in millions of years, and do not accept the days of creation as ordinary-length days. It is also why so many creationists are not able to successfully argue with evolutionists in a convincing way.

In 1993 an article about the popular "moon dust" argument supporting a young universe was unveiled and challenged in creationist literature.[2] The idea was that the thickness of dust on the moon when the astronauts

---

1. For example see John Morris, "The Paluxy River Mystery," ICR Website, http://www.icr.org/article/paluxy-river-mystery/.
2. A.A. Snelling and D. Rush, "Moon Dust and the Age of the Solar System," *CEN Tech. J.* 7(1):2–42, 1993.

landed was only enough to account for a few thousand years' worth of accumulation, given the amount that was presently pouring into the earth/moon system. But the authors of the article concluded that this argument should no longer be used, because new *measurements* showed that the influx of meteoric dust was much less than evolutionists had previously thought.

Later, a published article concerning the supposed plesiosaur carcass netted by a Japanese fishing trawler in 1977 came out.[3] These reported on research that substantiated that this carcass could not be of a plesiosaur, and was consistent with that of a basking shark. (They included photos of an actual decomposing basking shark.) This was despite our having previously given favorable publicity to the "plesiosaur" interpretation in our literature.

After this "plesiosaur" article, a person approached me at a creation seminar, and, obviously upset, stated, "First you take away the Paluxy prints, then the moondust, and now you've destroyed the 1977 plesiosaur argument. If you keep going, we won't have any great evidence left at all to counteract the evolutionists."

---

3. P.G. Jerlström, "Live Plesiosaurs: Weighing the Evidence," *CEN Tech. J.* 12(3):339–346, 1998; P.G. Jerlström and B. Elliott, "Letting Rotting Sharks Lie: Further Evidence for Shark Identity of the Zuiyo-maru Carcass," CEN Tech. J. 13(2):83–87, 1999.

In November 2001, Answers in Genesis published an article on its website about arguments we think creationists should not use.[4] This covered a substantial number of widely used arguments opposing evolution. It was meant to inform Christians why we felt these arguments were either factually incorrect or were very dubious and unsafe, even counterproductive, to use.

Again, some people became upset, expressing their dismay through phone calls, emails, and the like. Once more I had people complain to me at conferences. One man said, "Evolutionists have so much evidence; if you people at Answers in Genesis keep destroying some of the greatest evidence we've had, there'll be none left for creationists. You're helping the evolutionists win!"

Quite apart from the strange implication that we should not inform people of the truth about things that are believed to be in error, I've noticed that many people do not really understand the nature of "evidence." So they think that to oppose evolution or disprove an old earth, one has to come up with totally different or unique "evidence." I think this is a major reason why a number of Christians are drawn to what I call "flaky evidence" in the hope that this will counteract evolution. For instance, such things as:

- a supposed boat-like structure in the Ararat region as evidence of Noah's ark
- a "human hand print" (with virtually no documentation or credible research) supposedly from "dinosaur age" rock
- supposed "human hand fossils" from rock dated as millions of years old (but to date no credible substantiation of the claim); and many other dubious and/or unsubstantiated arguments

Most well-meaning creationists would agree in principle that things that are not carefully documented and researched should not be used. But in practice, many of them are very quick to accept the sorts of evidences mentioned here, without asking too many questions. Why this seeming urge to find a startling, exciting "magic bullet"?

I think it is because probably the majority of Christians believe that the "evidence" overwhelmingly supports an old (millions of years) earth.[5]

4. http://www.answersingenesis.org/get-answers/topic/arguments-we-dont-use.
5. Ken Ham, editor, *New Answers Book 3*, "How Old Does the Earth Look?" (Green Forest, AR: Master Book, 2010), chapter 15.

For many, it causes them to reject what the Bible makes so plain about history, to the great detriment of the gospel founded on that history.

But even those who keenly support Genesis still tend to see it as if there is a "mountain" of "their" facts/evidences lined up "against our side." This is, I believe, why they are less cautious than they might otherwise be, because they are so keen to have "our" facts/evidences to counter "theirs."

That is, both of the above groups suffer from the *same* basic problem. They really don't understand that it is not a matter of their evidence *versus* ours. *All* evidence is actually interpreted, and *all* scientists actually have the *same* observations — the same data — available to them in principle.

I have often debated evolutionists, or Christians who believe in millions of years, on various radio programs. A typical interview might go like this:

> "Well, today we have a creationist who believes he has evidence for creation, and on the other side is an evolutionist who believes he has evidence to support evolution."

> I then stop the interviewer and state, "I want to get something straight here, I actually have the same evidence the evolutionist

Too many people think it's a battle of sorting out **DIFFERENT** evidences.

has — the battle is not about the evidence or facts, as they are all the same. We live on the same earth, in the same universe, with the same plants and animals, the same fossils. The facts are all the same."

Then the evolutionist says, "But you're on about the Bible — this is religion. As an evolutionist I'm involved in real science."

I then respond, "Actually, as a creationist, I have no problem with your science; it's the same science I understand and trust. The argument is not about science or about facts — ultimately, the argument is about how you *interpret* the facts — and this depends upon your belief about history. The real difference is that we have different "histories" (accounts about what happened in the past), which we use to interpret the science and facts of the present."

I then give an example. "Let's consider the science of genetics and natural selection. Evolutionists believe in natural selection — that is real science, as you observe it happening. Well, creationists also believe in natural selection. Evolutionists accept the science of genetics — well, so do creationists.

"However, here is the difference: Evolutionists believe that, over millions of years, one kind of animal has changed into a totally different kind. However, creationists, based on the Bible's account of origins, believe that God created separate kinds of animals and plants to reproduce their own kind — therefore one kind will not turn into a totally different kind.

"Now this can be tested in the present. The scientific observations support the creationist interpretation that the changes we see are not creating new information. The changes are all within the originally created pool of information of that kind; sorting, shuffling, or degrading it. The creationist account of history, based on the Bible, provides the correct basis to interpret the evidence of the present — and real science confirms the interpretation."

My point is that if we Christians really understood that all evidence is actually interpreted on the basis of certain presuppositions, then we wouldn't be in the least bit intimidated by the evolutionists' supposed "evidence." We should instead be looking at the evolutionist's (or old-earther's) *interpretation* of the evidence, and how the same evidence could be interpreted within a biblical framework and be confirmed by testable and repeatable science.

I believe if more creationists did this, they would be less likely to jump at "flaky" evidence that seems startling, but in reality may be being interpreted incorrectly by the creationists themselves in their rush to find the magic-bullet, knock-down, drag-'em-out convincing "evidence" against evolution that they think they desperately need.

The same is true of dating methods. All dating methods suffer, in principle, from the same limitations — whether they are those used to support a young world or an old world. Even the famous moondust argument, back when it still seemed that this was an excellent one to use (given the information available), needed to involve assumptions — *uniformitarian* assumptions, just like radiometric dating does. Even before the error in the measurement of moondust influx was pointed out, evolutionists could rightly counter — how do you know that the dust has always been coming in at the same rate?

Of course, such creationist arguments have always been justified in that they are merely turning their own uniformitarian assumptions

against them. Creationists can rightly challenge radiometric dating on this same sort of basis, too. Once one understands the assumptions/presuppositions behind dating methods, one realizes that the "date" obtained is actually an interpretation — not a fact!

The bottom line is that it's not a matter of who has the better (or the most) "facts on their side." We need to understand that there are no such things as brute facts — *all* facts are interpreted. Thus, the next time evolutionists use what seem to be convincing facts for evolution, try to determine the *presuppositions* they have used to interpret these facts. Then, beginning with the big picture of history from the Bible, look at the same facts through these biblical glasses and interpret them differently. Then, using the real science of the present that an evolutionist also uses, see if that science, when properly understood, confirms (by being consistent with) the interpretation based on the Bible. You will find over and over again that the Bible is confirmed[6] by real science.

But remember that, like Job (Job 42:2–6), we need to understand that compared to God we know next to nothing. So we won't have all the answers. However, so many answers have come to light now, that a Christian can give a credible defense of the Book of Genesis and show it is the correct foundation for thinking about and interpreting every aspect of reality.

So let's not jump in a blind-faith way at the startling evidences we think we need to "prove" creation — trying to counter "their facts" with "our facts." (Jesus Himself rose from the dead in the most startling possible demonstration of the truth of God's Word. But still many wouldn't believe — cf. Luke 16:27–31.) Instead, let's not be intimidated by apparent "evidences" for evolution, but understand the right way to think about evidence. We can then deal with *the same evidence the evolutionists use,*[7] to show they have the wrong framework of interpretation — and that the facts of the real world really do conform to, and confirm, the Bible.

---

6. We are not talking here of the Bible being "proved" by some scientific means (science is incapable of proving or disproving past events). But faith in the Bible is confirmed (and affirmed and reinforced) whenever we find evidence to be consistent with the Bible.

7. Of course, creationists certainly may use certain evidence that an evolutionist avoids — but make sure you have the correct interpretation and that you are not just clinging to something because it "sounds good."

Chapter 28

Is the Age of the Earth a Salvation Issue?

Ken Ham and Bodie Hodge

Can a person believe in a world that is millions and billions of years old and be a Christian? First of all, let's consider a few verses that summarize an understanding of the gospel and salvation.

> Moreover, brethren, I declare to you the gospel which I preached to you, which also you received and in which you stand, by which also you are saved, if you hold fast that word which I preached to you — unless you believed in vain.

> For I delivered to you first of all that which I also received: that Christ died for our sins according to the Scriptures, and that He was buried, and that He rose again the third day according to the Scriptures (1 Corinthians 15:1–4).

> And if Christ is not risen, your faith is futile; you are still in your sins! (1 Corinthians 15:17)

> . . . if you confess with your mouth the Lord Jesus and believe in your heart that God has raised Him from the dead, you will be save. (Romans 10:9).

Jesus answered and said to him, "Most assuredly, I say to you, unless one is born again, he cannot see the kingdom of God" (John 3:3).

Of course, we could cite numerous other passages, but not one of them states in any way that one has to believe in a young earth/universe to be saved. And when one considers the list of those who "will not inherit the kingdom of God" (1 Corinthians 6:9–10), we certainly do not see "old earthers" listed in such passages.

Many great men of God who are now with the Lord have believed in an old earth. Some of these explained the millions of years by adopting the classic gap theory. Others accepted a day-age theory or positions such as theistic evolution, the framework hypothesis, or progressive creationism.

Undoubtedly, Scripture plainly teaches salvation is conditioned upon faith in Christ, with no requirement for what one believes about the age of the earth/universe. In light of this, some people assume then that for a Christian, it does not matter what one believes concerning the age of the earth and universe. However, even though it is not a salvation issue, a Christian who believes in millions of years reaps severe consequences.

The Issue of Authority

The belief in millions of years does not come *from* Scripture, but from the secularist fallible dating methods used to date the age of the earth and universe. To even attempt to fit millions of years into the Bible, one has to invent a gap of time that is not allowed by the text or reinterpret the days of creation (that are obviously ordinary-length days in the context of Genesis 1) as long periods of time.

In other words, one has to add something (millions of years) from outside the Scripture into the Word of God. This is putting man's fallible ideas *in authority* over the Word of God. Thus one unlocks a door to do this in other areas. It is opening a door that others can push open further and further — which is what tends to happen with each successive generation. Once the door of compromise is open, even just a little, subsequent generations push the door open wider. Ultimately, this is a major contributing factor to the loss of biblical authority in our Western world.

> Do not add to His words, lest He rebuke you, and you be found a liar (Proverbs 30:6).

The Issue of Contradiction

In many instances the belief in millions of years totally contradicts the clear teaching of Scripture. Here are just three:

1. Thorns — Fossil thorns are found in the fossil record, supposedly hundreds of millions of years old. So these supposedly existed millions of years before man. However, the Bible makes it clear that thorns only came into existence *after* the Curse:

> Then to Adam He said, "Because you have . . . eaten from the tree of which I commanded you, saying, 'You shall not eat of it': Cursed is the ground for your sake. . . . Both thorns and thistles it shall bring forth for you" (Genesis 3:17–18).

2. Disease — Evidence of diseases like cancer, brain tumors, and arthritis can be found in the fossil remains of animals said to be millions of years old. So these diseases supposedly existed millions of years before sin. The Scripture teaches us that after God finished creating everything, with man as the pinnacle of creation, He described the creation as "*very good*" (Genesis 1:31, emphasis added). Certainly, God calling cancer and brain tumors "very good" does not fit with the nature of God as described in Scripture.

3. Diet — Genesis 1:29–30 explains that Adam and Eve and all the animals were vegetarian before sin entered the world. However, the fossil record includes many examples of animals eating other animals — supposedly millions of years before man and thus before sin.

The Issue of Death

Romans 8:22 reveals that the whole creation groans because of the consequences of the Fall — the entrance of sin. One of the reasons it groans is because of death — death of living creatures, both animals and man. Death is described as an "enemy" (1 Corinthians 15:26), and one day death will be thrown into the lake of fire (Revelation 20:14). Romans 5:12 and other passages declare that physical death of man (and really, death in general) entered the once-perfect creation because of man's sin.

However, if one believes in millions of years, then there were millions of years of death, disease, suffering, carnivorous activity, and thorns before sin.

The first death was in the Garden of Eden when God killed an animal as the first blood sacrifice (Genesis 3:21) — a picture of what was to come in Jesus Christ, the Lamb of God, who would take away the sin of the world.

Jesus Christ stepped into history and paid the penalty required by our sin — death — by dying on the Cross. He conquered death when He rose from the dead. Although holding to an old earth is not a salvation issue per se, we believe that when a Christian insists on millions of years of death before sin it is really an attack on the work of Christ on the Cross.

> And God will wipe away every tear from their eyes; there shall be no more death, nor sorrow, nor crying. There shall be no more pain, for the former things have passed away (Revelation 21:4).

In a culture where the foundation of the gospel has come under attack by the concept of millions of years, it makes sense why the next generation is walking away from the Church. Believing in millions of years may not affect *that person's* salvation, but it can affect the next generation — particularly in their witness. It is simply a matter of putting two and two together: if the foundation of the gospel (i.e., Genesis 1–11) is not true, then why would the gospel be true? Kids in the next generation can put *and have been* putting this together (see Ken Ham's book co-authored with Britt Beemer called *Already Gone*[1]).

If people believe the opening chapters of the Bible, then why can't they trust the rest? Conversely, if people do not believe the opening chapters of the Bible, when do they think God starts to tell the truth in His Word? We, as Christians, need to start teaching the Bible — including Genesis — as the authority in every area of our lives.

When witnessing to a culture influenced by millions of years, we have found it tremendously effective to explain the "Genesis Ground" of the "Romans Road." That is, we explain the foundation of the gospel found in Genesis before explaining the gospel message of Christ's sacrificial and

---

1. Ken Ham and Britt Beemer, *Already Gone* (Green Forest, AR: Master Books, 2009).

atoning death, and subsequent burial, and Resurrection. In this way we counter the evolutionary ideas that have infiltrated the minds of the next generation. We teach the bad news in Genesis, and then we proclaim the "good news" (the gospel) that is rooted and grounded in the bad news. We call this the "Genesis-Romans Road" approach.

Genesis-Romans Road

Genesis 1:1 — God made everything.

In the beginning God created the heavens and the earth.

Genesis 1:31 — God made everything perfectly — no death or suffering.

Then God saw everything that He had made, and indeed it was very good. So the evening and the morning were the sixth day.

Genesis 3:17–19 — The punishment for sin is death; due to sin, the world is no longer perfect.

Then to Adam He said, "Because you have heeded the voice of your wife, and have eaten from the tree of which I commanded you, saying, 'You shall not eat of it': Cursed is the ground for your sake; in toil you shall eat of it all the days of your life. Both thorns and thistles it shall bring forth for you, and you shall eat the herb of the field. In the sweat of your face you shall eat bread till you return to the ground, for out of it you were taken; for dust you are, and to dust you shall return."

Romans 5:12 — Because our mutual grandfather Adam sinned, we now sin too.

Therefore, just as through one man sin entered the world, and death through sin, and thus death spread to all men, because all sinned.

Romans 3:23 — We need to realize we are all sinners, including ourselves.

For all have sinned and fall short of the glory of God.

290 • How Do We Know the Bible Is True?

Romans 6:23 – The punishment for sin is a just punishment — death — but God came to rescue us and give the free gift of salvation by sending His Son, Jesus.

> For the wages of sin is death, but the gift of God is eternal life in Christ Jesus our Lord.

Romans 10:9 — You need to believe in Jesus; salvation is not by works, but by faith (see also John 3:16 and Acts 16:30–31).

> . . . that if you confess with your mouth the Lord Jesus and believe in your heart that God has raised Him from the dead, you will be saved.

Romans 5:1 — Being saved, you are now justified and have peace with God.

> Therefore, having been justified by faith, we have peace with God through our Lord Jesus Christ.

Why I Am Committed to Teaching the Bible

John MacArthur

✤✤✤✤✤✤✤✤✤✤✤✤✤✤✤✤✤✤✤

I have never aspired to be known as a theologian, a polemicist, or an academician. My passion is teaching and preaching the Word of God.[1]

Even though I've dealt with theological questions and doctrinal controversies in some of my books, I have never done so from the perspective of a systematic theologian. It is of little concern to me whether some point of doctrine fits with this tradition or that. I want to know what is biblical. All my concerns are biblical, and my desire is to be biblical in all my teaching.

Preach the Word

That is how I have approached ministry from the beginning. My father was a pastor, and when I first told him years ago that I felt God had called me to a life of ministry, he gave me a Bible in which he had inscribed these words of encouragement: "Preach the Word!" That simple statement became the compelling stimulus in my heart. It is all I have endeavored to do in my ministry — preach the Word.

---

1. This chapter was originally published on the Grace to You website, http://www.gty.org/Resources/Articles/A349_Why-I-Am-Committed-to-Teaching-the-Bible?q=preaching+truth+season.

Pastors today face a tremendous amount of pressure to do everything but preach the Word. Church growth experts tell them they must address people's "felt needs." They are encouraged to be storytellers, comedians, psychologists, and motivational speakers. They are warned to steer clear of topics that people find unpleasant. Many have given up biblical preaching in favor of devotional homilies designed to make people feel good. Some have even replaced preaching with drama and other forms of staged entertainment.

But the pastor whose passion is biblical has only one option: "Preach the word! Be ready in season and out of season. Convince, rebuke, exhort, with all longsuffering and teaching" (2 Timothy 4:2).

When Paul wrote those words to Timothy, he added this prophetic warning: "For the time will come when they will not endure sound doctrine; but wanting to have their ears tickled, they will accumulate for themselves teachers in accordance to their own desires, and will turn away their ears from the truth" (2 Timothy 4:3–4; NASB).

Clearly, there was no room in Paul's philosophy of ministry for the give-people-what-they-want theory that is so prevalent today. He did not urge Timothy to conduct a survey to find out what his people wanted. He commanded him to preach the Word — faithfully, reprovingly, and patiently.

In fact, far from urging Timothy to devise a ministry that would garner accolades from the world, Paul warned the young pastor about suffering and hardship! Paul was not telling Timothy how to be "successful," he was encouraging him to follow the divine standard. He was not advising him to pursue prosperity, power, prominence, popularity, or any of the otherworldly notions of success. He was urging the young pastor to be biblical — regardless of the consequences.

Preaching the Word is not always easy. The message we are required to proclaim is often offensive. Christ Himself is a stone of stumbling and a rock of offense (Romans 9:33; 1 Peter 2:8). The message of the Cross is a stumbling block to some (1 Corinthians 1:23; Galatians 5:11), mere foolishness to others (1 Corinthians 1:23).

But we are never permitted to trim the message or tailor it to people's preferences. Paul made this clear to Timothy at the end of 2 Timothy 3: "*All* Scripture is given by inspiration of God, and is profitable for doctrine, for reproof, for correction, for instruction in righteousness" (2 Timothy 3:16, emphasis added). This is the Word to be preached: the whole counsel of God (cf. Acts 20:27).

Paul told Timothy, "Hold fast the pattern of sound words which you have heard from me" (2 Timothy 1:13). He was speaking of the revealed words of Scripture — all of it. He urged Timothy to "Guard . . . the treasure which has been entrusted to you" (verse 14; NASB). Then he told him to study the Word and handle it accurately (2 Timothy 2:15). Now he is telling him to proclaim it. So the entire task of the faithful minister revolves around the Word of God — guarding it, studying it, and proclaiming it.

The Apostle Paul, describing his own ministry philosophy, writes, "Of this church I was made a minister according to the stewardship from God bestowed on me for your benefit, that I might fully carry out the preaching of the word of God" (Colossians 1:25; NASB). In 1 Corinthians he goes a step further: "And I, brethren, when I came to you, did not come with excellence of speech or of wisdom declaring to you the testimony of God. For I determined not to know anything among you except Jesus Christ and Him crucified" (1 Corinthians 2:1–2). In other words, his goal as a preacher was not to entertain people with his rhetorical style, or to amuse them with cleverness, humor, novel insights, or sophisticated methodology — he simply preached Christ crucified.

Faithfully preaching and teaching the Word must be the very heart of our ministry philosophy. Any other approach replaces the voice of God with human wisdom. Philosophy, politics, humor, psychology, homespun advice, and human opinion can never accomplish what the Word of God does. Those things may be interesting, informative, and entertaining, but they are not the business of the Church. The preacher's task is not to be a conduit for human wisdom; he is God's voice to speak to the congregation. No human message comes with the stamp of divine authority — only the Word of God. How dare any preacher substitute another message?

I frankly do not understand preachers who are willing to abdicate this solemn privilege. Why should we proclaim the wisdom of men when we have the privilege of preaching the Word of God?

Be Faithful In and Out of Season

Ours is a never-ending task. Not only are we to preach the Word, we must do it regardless of the climate of opinion around us. We are commanded to be faithful when such preaching is tolerated — but also when it is not.

Let's face it — right now preaching the Word is out of season. The market-driven philosophy currently in vogue says that plainly declaring biblical truth is outmoded. Biblical exposition and theology are seen as antiquated and irrelevant. "Churchgoers don't want to be preached to anymore," this philosophy says. "The baby-boomer generation won't just sit in the pew while someone up front preaches. They are products of a media-driven generation, and they need a church experience that will satisfy them on their own terms."

But Paul says the excellent minister must be faithful to preach the Word even when it is not in fashion. The expression he uses is "be ready." The Greek term (*ephistemi*) literally means "to stand beside." It has the idea of eagerness. It was often used to describe a military guard, always at his post, prepared for duty. Paul was speaking of an explosive eagerness to preach, like that of Jeremiah, who said that the Word of God was a fire in his bones (Jeremiah 20:9. That's what he was demanding of Timothy. Not reluctance but readiness. Not hesitation but fearlessness. Not motivational talks but the Word of God.

Reprove, Rebuke, and Exhort

Paul also gives Timothy instructions about the tone of his preaching. He uses two words that carry negative connotations and one that is positive: reprove, rebuke, and exhort. All valid ministry must have a balance of positive and negative. The preacher who fails to reprove and rebuke is not fulfilling his commission.

Years ago I listened to a radio interview with a preacher known for his emphasis on positive thinking. This man had stated in print that he assiduously avoids any mention of sin in his preaching because he feels people are burdened with too much guilt anyway. The interviewer asked how he could justify such a policy. The pastor replied that he had made the decision early in his ministry to focus on meeting people's needs, not attacking their sin.

But people's deepest need is to confess and overcome their sin. So preaching that fails to confront and correct sin through the Word of God does not meet people's needs. It may make them feel good. And they may respond enthusiastically to the preacher, but that is not the same as having real needs met.

Reproving, rebuking, and exhorting are the same as preaching the Word, for those are the very same ministries Scripture accomplishes: "All Scripture is inspired by God and profitable for teaching, for reproof, for correction, for training in righteousness" (2 Timothy 3:16; NASB). Notice the same balance of positive and negative tone. Reproof and correction are negative; teaching and training are positive.

The positive tone is crucial, too. The word "exhort" is *parakaleo*, a word that means "encourage." The excellent preacher confronts sin and then encourages repentant sinners to behave righteously. He is to do this "with great patience and instruction" (2 Timothy 4:2; NASB). In 1 Thessalonians 2:11, Paul talks about "how we exhorted, and comforted, and charged every one of you, as a father *does* his own children." This often requires great patience and much instruction. But the excellent minister cannot neglect these aspects of his calling.

Don't Compromise in Difficult Times

There is an urgency in Paul's charge to young Timothy: "For the time will come when they will not endure sound doctrine; but wanting to have their ears tickled, they will accumulate for themselves teachers in accordance to their own desires" (2 Timothy. 4:3; NASB). That is a prophecy reminiscent of those found in 2 Timothy 3:1 ("Realize this, that in the last days difficult times will come"), and 1 Timothy 4:1 ("The Spirit explicitly says that in later times some will fall away from the faith"). This, then, is Paul's third prophetic warning to Timothy about the difficult times that were to come.

Note the progression: The first warning said that the time would come when people will depart from the faith. The second one warned Timothy that dangerous times were coming for the Church. Now the third one suggests that the time would come when those in the Church would not endure sound doctrine, but desire instead to have their ears tickled.

That is happening in the Church today. Evangelicalism has lost its tolerance for confrontive preaching. Churches ignore the biblical teaching on women's roles, homosexuality, and other politically charged issues. The human medium has overtaken the divine message. That's evidence of serious doctrinal compromise. If the Church does not repent, those errors and others like them will become epidemic.

Note that Paul does not suggest that the way to reach such a society is to soften the message so that its people will be comfortable with it. Just the opposite is true. Such ear-tickling is abominable. Paul urges Timothy to be willing to suffer for the truth's sake, and keep preaching the Word faithfully.

An appetite for ear-tickling preaching has a terrible end. Second Timothy 4:4 says these people will ultimately "turn away their ears from the truth, and turned aside to fables." They become the victims of their own refusal to hear the truth. "They will turn away" is in the active voice. The people willfully choose this action. "Will be turned aside to myths" is in the passive voice. It describes what happens to them. Having turned from the truth, they become victims of deception. As soon as they turn away from the truth, they become pawns of Satan.

The truth of God does not tickle our ears, it boxes them. It burns them. It reproves, rebukes, convicts — *then* it exhorts and encourages. Preachers of the Word must be careful to maintain that balance.

There have always been men in the pulpit who gathered crowds because they were gifted orators, interesting storytellers, entertaining speakers, dynamic personalities, shrewd crowd-manipulators, rousing speech-makers, popular politicians, or erudite scholars. Such preaching may be popular, but it is not necessarily powerful. No one can preach with power who does not preach the Word. And no faithful preacher will water down or neglect the whole counsel of God. Proclaiming the Word — *all of it* — is the pastor's calling.

Author Biographies

Mr. Tim Chaffey earned a M. Div., specializing in Apologetics and Theology, and a Th. M. in Church History and Theology from *Liberty Baptist Theological Seminary*. He also holds a B. S. and M. A. in Biblical and Theological Studies. He works at *Answers in Genesis* as a writer and editor in the Web Department. Tim is also a cancer survivor and has authored several books, including *Old-Earth Creationism on Trial, God and Cancer,* and *The Truth Chronicles* series.

Pastor Brian Edwards was pastor of an evangelical church in a southwest London suburb for 29 years, and then president of the Fellowship of Independent Evangelical Churches from 1995–1998. He is the author of 16 books, and continues a ministry of writing and itinerant preaching and lecturing. His wife, Barbara, died in 1998; he has two sons and three granddaughters.

Mr. Steve Fazekas helps schedule ministry engagements for the Answers in Genesis speakers. He has earned a B.R.E. and an M. Div. from Temple Baptist Theological Seminary in Church History and has been a valuable reviewer over the years for theological and historical material at Answers in Genesis.

Mr. James Gardner is the founder and CEO of Canopy Ministries and a lecturer and adjunct speaker for Answers in Genesis. He has taught extensively on the subject of creation vs. evolution in the U.S. and internationally in churches, schools, and colleges since 1993. Mr. Gardner has been involved in numerous archaeology and geology research trips to sites in the U.S., including the Grand Canyon, Yellowstone, and Glacier National Park.

Mr. Ken Ham is CEO/president of Answers in Genesis, and is one of the most in-demand Christian speakers in North America. A native Australian now residing near Cincinnati, Ham has the unique ability to communicate deep biblical truths and historical facts through apologetics. He is the author of numerous books on evangelism, dinosaurs, and the negative fruits of evolutionary thinking, including *The Lie: Evolution* and *Already Gone*.

Mr. Steve Ham oversees all outreach and operations of the Answers in Genesis ministry. He has been a regular speaker on the authority of Scripture and authored many materials including the biblical authority book *In God We Trust*, co-authored *Raising Godly Children in an Ungodly World*, and the popular curriculum on creation evangelism entitled *Answers for Life*. He has a passion for the encompassing authority of Jesus Christ in all aspects of ministry.

Mr. Bodie Hodge attended Southern Illinois University at Carbondale and received a B.S. and M.S. in mechanical engineering. His specialty was a subset of mechanical engineering based in advanced materials processing, particularly starting powders. Currently, Bodie is a speaker, writer, and researcher for Answers in Genesis–USA. He is the author of *The Fall of Satan* and co-author of *Dragons: Legends & Lore of Dinosaurs*.

Dr. Jason Lisle received his Ph.D. in astrophysics from the University of Colorado at Boulder. He specializes in solar astrophysics and has interests in the physics of relativity and biblical models of cosmology. Dr. Lisle has published a number of books, including *Taking Back Astronomy* and *The Ultimate Proof of Creation*, plus articles in both secular and creationist literature. He is a speaker, researcher, and writer for Answers in Genesis–USA.

Dr. John MacArthur holds a M. Div. and D.D. from Talbot Theological Seminary, as well as a Litt.D. from Grace Graduate School. He is the pastor-teacher of Grace Community Church in Sun Valley, California, as well as an author, conference speaker, president of The Master's College and Seminary. He is also president and featured teacher on the Grace to You radio and television programs which air more than 1,000 times daily throughout the English-speaking world and reach major population centers on every continent. Dr. MacArthur has written nearly 400 books and study guides, including *Ashamed of the Gospel*, *The MacArthur New Testament Commentary* series, and *The MacArthur Study Bible*.

Dr. Jobe Martin graduated from the University of Pittsburgh Dental School in 1966. Dr. Martin rejected evolution after being challenged by some of his Christian students at Baylor College of Dentistry and studying the issue in detail. He is the author of *The Evolution of a Creationist* and is featured on several videos discussing the incredible design features of living creatures. As president of Biblical Discipleship Ministries, he is a frequent speaker on the topic of creation v. evolution.

Dr. Robert McCabe is professor of Old Testament and Registrar at Detroit Baptist Theological Seminary. He earned the M.Div degree at Temple Baptist Theological Seminary in 1974, and the Th.M. and Th.D. degrees at Grace Theological Seminary, in 1980 and 1985 respectively. He is the author of "A Critique of the Framework Interpretation of the Creation Account" which originally appeared in the *Detroit Baptist Seminary Journal*. Dr. McCabe has conducted seminars on biblical creationism in local churches in the Detroit area.

Dr. Tommy Mitchell is a graduate of Vanderbilt University School of Medicine. He received his M.D. in 1984 and completed his residency in internal medicine in 1987. For 20 years Tommy practiced medicine in his hometown of Gallatin, Tennessee. In 1991, he was elected a Fellow of the American College of Physicians. Dr. Mitchell has been active in creation ministry for many years. He felt the Lord's call to full time service, and in 2007 he withdrew from the active practice of medicine to join Answers in Genesis–USA as a full-time speaker and writer.

Dr. Terry Mortenson earned a Ph.D. in the history of geology from Coventry University in England. His thesis focused on the "scriptural geologists," a group of men in the early 19th century who fought the rise of old-earth geological theories. A former missionary (mostly in Eastern Europe), Dr. Mortenson has researched and spoken on creation and evolution for many years. He is now a speaker, writer, and researcher with Answers in Genesis–USA.

Mr. Roger Patterson earned his B.S. Ed. degree in biology from Montana State University. Before coming to work at Answers in Genesis, he taught for eight years in Wyoming's public school system and assisted the Wyoming Department of Education in developing assessments and standards for children in public schools. Roger now serves on the Educational Resources team at Answers in Genesis–USA. He is the author of *Evolution Exposed 1 and 2*.

Dr. Georgia Purdom received her Ph.D. in molecular genetics from Ohio State University. Her professional accomplishments include winning a variety of honors, serving as professor of biology at Mt. Vernon Nazarene University (Ohio), and the publication of papers in the *Journal of Neuroscience*, the *Journal of Bone and Mineral Research*, and the *Journal of Leukocyte Biology*. Dr. Purdom is also a member of the Creation Research Society, American Society for Microbiology, and American Society for Cell Biology.

Dr. Herb Samworth is Instructor of Biblical Research and Education at Sola Scriptura in Orlando, Florida. He earned his doctorate in Reformation and Post-Reformation Studies from Westminster Theological Seminary in Philadelphia. Samworth is a prolific author who writes for lay readers. His articles include "The Work of John Wycliffe and its Impact," "The Council of Trent," and "From the King James to Modern Translations."

Mr. Paul Taylor was the senior speaker for Answers in Genesis (UK/Europe). He holds a B.S. in chemistry from Nottingham University and a masters in science education from Cardiff University. He is the author of several books, including *Cain and Abel, In the Beginning*, and *The Six Days of Genesis*. Paul and his wife, Geri, have five children between them.

Too Many Questions for Just One Book

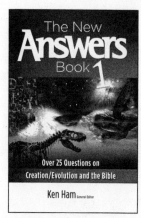
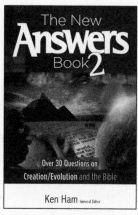
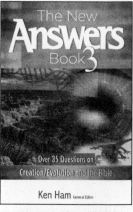

ISBN: 978-0-89051-509-9   ISBN: 978-0-89051-537-2   ISBN: 978-0-89051-579-2

Christians live in a culture with more questions than ever — questions that affect one's acceptance of the Bible as authoritative and trustworthy. Now, discover easy-to-understand answers that teach core truths of the Christian faith and apply the biblical worldview to subjects like evolution, the fall of Lucifer, Noah and the Flood, the star of Bethlehem, dinosaurs, death and suffering, and much more.

Explore these and other topics, answered biblically and logically in these three books from the world's largest apologetics ministry, Answers in Genesis.

Timely and scientifically solid, *The New Answers Books 1, 2,* and *3* offer concise answers from leading creationist Ken Ham and scientists such as Dr. David Menton, Dr. Georgia Purdom, Dr. Andrew Snelling, Dr. Jason Lisle, Dr. Elizabeth Mitchell, and many more.

6 x 9 • Paperback • 384 pages • $14.99 each

Available at your local Christian bookstore or at www.nlpg.com

Connect with Master Books®

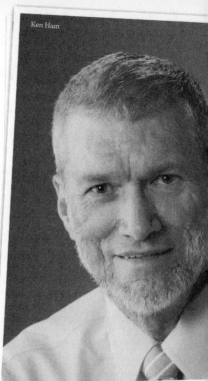
Ken Ham

nlpgblogs.com

facebook.com/masterbooks

@masterbooks4u

youtube.com/nlpgvideo

Connect with Ken Ham

blogs.answersingenesis.org

facebook.com/aigkenham

@aigkenham

Connect with Creation Museum

Bodie Hodge

creationmuseum.org

facebook.com/creationmuseum

@creationmuseum

Connect with Answers in Genesis

answersingenesis.org

facebook.com/answersingenesis

@aig

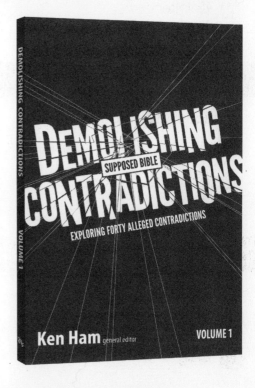